D0820306

NATIONAL UNIVERSITY LIBRARY

CONSERVATION
IN THE LIBRARY

CONSERVATION IN THE LIBRARY

A HANDBOOK OF USE AND CARE OF TRADITIONAL AND NONTRADITIONAL MATERIALS

Edited by Susan Garretson Swartzburg

GREENWOOD PRESS
Westport, Connecticut

Library of Congress Cataloging in Publication Data
Main entry under title:

Conservation in the library.

  Bibliography: p.
  Includes index.
  1. Library materials—Conservation and restoration—
Handbooks, manuals, etc. I. Swartzburg, Susan G.,
1938–
Z701.C586 1983   025.8'4   82-15582
ISBN 0-313-23267-9 (lib. bdg.)

Copyright © 1983 by Susan Garretson Swartzburg

All rights reserved. No portion of this book may be
reproduced, by any process or technique, without the
express written consent of the publisher.

Library of Congress Catalog Card Number: 82-15582
ISBN: 0-313-23267-9

First published in 1983

Greenwood Press
A division of Congressional Information Service, Inc.
88 Post Road West
Westport, Connecticut 06881

Printed in the United States of America

10 9 8 7 6 5 4 3 2 1

Contents

Preface   vii

About the Contributors   ix

1. General Care
   Susan G. Swartzburg   3

2. Paper: Manuscripts, Documents, Printed Sheets,
   and Works of Art
   Karl Buchberg   31

3. Books and Bindings
   Angela Fitzgerald   55

4. Photographs
   Gary Albright   79

5. Slides
   Nancy Carlson Schrock and Christine L. Sundt   103

6. Microforms
   Helga Borck   129

7. Motion Picture Film
   Eileen Bowser   139

8. Videotape
   Susan G. Swartzburg and Deirdre Boyle   155

9. Sound Recordings
   Jerry McWilliams   163

10. Videodiscs
    Judith Paris and Richard W. Boss   185

11.   The Computer: When Tomorrow Becomes Yesterday
      Susan B. White and Allan E. White   205

      Appendix 1:   Suppliers and Supplies   221

      Appendix 2:   Sources of Advice and Assistance   225

      Index   227

Preface

This volume has been compiled to assist the librarian, archivist, and curator in all aspects of the care of materials to be found within a library. While chapters are devoted to books and documents, we have tried to move beyond the "traditional" library materials to discuss the care and handling of the nonprint materials that are found in today's library. A list of suggested reading is appended to each chapter as a guide to further research. Sources mentioned in the text without full citations may be found in these bibliographies. Appendix 1 provides a list of suppliers and supplies and Appendix 2 provides a list of sources of advice and assistance. These are helpful points of departure in seeking items mentioned in the text.

The editor's contribution has been to assemble a group of talented and dedicated conservators and preservation specialists. The contributors worked closely together, despite geographic distance, to provide complete and up-to-date coverage in their fields.

The Rutgers University Research Council and the Rutgers University Libraries provided the support to make this book possible. We are grateful for their help.

The editor and the contributors owe a debt of gratitude to the readers and technical reviewers who read sections of the manuscript and took the time to add a considerable amount of information. They are: Hubbard Ballou, Dennis Benson, Ilona Caparros, Barbara Cerny, Randall Couch, Benjamin DeWhitt, Marianne Gaunt, Mary Todd Glaser, Thomas T. Hill, David Ignat, David Kolody, Nancy and Duncan MacArthur, Ellen McCrady, Melissa Menthe, Lynn Miller, Martha Morales, Thomas H. Mott, Jr., Sherelyn Ogden, Jill and Robert Parliament, Judith Soncrant, William Storm, Marilyn Kemp Weidner, and Henry Wilhelm.

The editor would like to thank those who assisted in the production of the book: Susan Danielsen, Jennifer Hamm, Lorraine Perrotta, and especially Amy Underhill, who typed letters, photocopied, and tracked down many an elusive reference; Roberta Hirshman, who typed the manuscript; Henry Cioch, who produced the drawings that were needed; Frank and Helen Garretson, Eleanor Ignat, and my father, Edwin P. Garretson, who proofread the manuscript; Mark Lieberman, for his wise council; and editors Marilyn Brownstein and Pamela Jeffcott Parry, who have been both patient and helpful. Both the editor and the contributors owe a great deal to technical editor Neha Weinstein, who can transform technical jargon into English and spot a gremlin at twenty paces.

We hope that the reader will find this volume a continually helpful addition to the library.

About the Contributors

Gary E. Albright, photographic conservator at the Northeast Document Conservation Center, Andover, Mass., is a graduate of the Winterthur/University of Delaware Graduate Program in the Conservation of Artistic and Historic Objects. He is an Associate of the American Institute for the Conservation of Historic and Artistic Works.

Helga Borck, formerly Head of the Preservation Microfilming Office at the New York Public Library (Research Libraries), was in charge of an in-house filming program which produces about 1.5 million exposures per year. She has published several articles on microforms and is a reviewer for *Microform Review.*

Richard W. Boss, Senior Management Consultant with Information Systems, Inc., Bethesda, Md., is a specialist in information technologies including micrographics, telefacsimile, and videodisc systems. He has published extensively in the field of information science and was formerly director of Libraries at the University of Tennessee and at Princeton University.

Eileen Bowser is Curator of the film archive, Department of Film, The Museum of Modern Art, New York, and Vice President of La Federation Internationale des Archives du Film. She is known as a film historian and film archivist. Her publications include *A Handbook for Film Archives* (1980, coeditor and author); *The Movies* (3rd edition, 1981, coauthor); *D. W. Griffith* (2nd edition, 1965, coauthor); *Film Notes* (1969); *Biograph Bulletins 1908-1912* (1973, preface); and *The Films of Carl Dreyer* (1964).

Deirdre Boyle, Writer, Critic, and Media Consultant, is on the faculties of the New School for Social Research and Fordham University College at Lincoln Center. She is the editor of *Expanding Media* (1977) and *Children's*

Media Market Place (1978) and video editor of *Sightlines*. Boyle has a master's degree in media from Antioch College/The Center for Understanding Media.

Karl D. Buchberg, Rare Books and Manuscripts Conservator, Princeton University, is a specialist in the conservation of manuscripts, documents, and works of art on paper. He received his training at the New York University Institute of Fine Arts Conservation Program and the Library of Congress. He is an Associate Member of the American Institute for Conservation.

Angela Fitzgerald, Binder/Conservator, served her apprenticeship with Kasper Reder at the Library Company of Philadelphia, and has also studied at the French National Library, Paris, and at the State Institute of Book Pathology, Rome. She is a member of the Guild of Book Workers and an Associate Member of the American Institute for Conservation.

Jerry McWilliams, author of *Preservation and Restoration of Sound Recordings* (1979), is a frequent contributor to professional journals and magazines. He received his undergraduate degree from Harvard and continued his studies at Stanford and Columbia, where he earned a graduate degree in librarianship. He is presently Librarian and Archivist at Utah International, Inc.

Judith Paris, President of Advanced Information Management Technology, Inc., in McLean, Va., is Editor-in-Chief of *Videodisc/Videotex*. She is Associate Producer of an office management videodisc and of a series of videodiscs on basic skills education for the Department of the Army.

Nancy Carlson Schrock, Bookbinder and Consultant on library conservation, is the author of a number of articles on preservation and graphic art. She was formerly Visual Collections Librarian of the Rotch Library of Architecture and Planning, Massachusetts Institute of Technology. She holds a bachelor's degree in art from Brown University, and master's degrees in art history from the University of Delaware, and in librarianship from Simmons College.

Christine Sundt, Curator of Slides and Photographs, Department of Art History, University of Wisconsin-Madison, is a specialist in the care, storage, and stability of colored slides. She is conservation columnist for *The International Bulletin for Photographic Documentation in the Visual Arts*, and serves as a consultant to other institutions.

Susan Garretson Swartzburg, Preservation Specialist at Rutgers University Library, is a recognized authority in the field of the preservation of library materials. She is the author of *Preserving Library Materials* (1980) and writes on preservation topics for several journals. She holds graduate degrees in English and librarianship. Swartzburg is an Associate Member of the International and American Institutes for Conservation and is active in a number of other organizations concerned with preservation.

Allan E. White, an Associate Member of the Technical Staff at the David Sarnoff Research Center, RCA Corporation, is a specialist in the areas of digital logic and control circuitry. He is a member of the Institute of Electrical and Electronics Engineers (IEEE).

Susan B. White, formerly Annex Librarian at Princeton University, has also served as a systems trainer for the RLIN and OCLC bibliographic utilities for the Princeton University Library. She attended the Columbia University Preservation Institute in 1978 and was active in the formation of the Preservation of Library Materials Section of the American Library Association. White is an Associate Member of the American Institute for Conservation.

CONSERVATION
IN THE LIBRARY

1

General Care

SUSAN G. SWARTZBURG

The 1980s is a decade of consolidation rather than expansion for libraries. Librarians are turning their attention to the collections that they have rather than to collections that they would like to have. As budgets shrink and the cost of books and other library materials escalates, librarians are obliged to see that their existing collections last as long as possible. Thus the conservation and preservation of library materials have become primary concerns of the library administrator and should be a part of the job of every staff member.

Libraries contain books, but they also contain many other materials, such as maps, prints, photographs, microforms, slides, films, sound recordings, and videotapes. They frequently contain other objects of value, such as paintings, furniture, or sculpture. Many libraries now have videodiscs and computers. Each of these library materials is subject to a number of hazards and each requires special care if it is to last as long as possible in the environment of the circulating library, open to the public. The authors of the chapters that follow offer much practical advice for librarians who are responsible for the care and management of their collections. Each chapter discusses the causes of deterioration and how the library can provide the conditions that will retard that deterioration.

HISTORY OF THE PRESERVATION MOVEMENT

While over the centuries astute bibliophiles have observed that paper and books are subject to deterioration, it was only a little over a hundred years ago, as the public library movement was gaining impetus and the manufacture of both paper and books became mechanized, that book collectors and librarians became seriously concerned at the rate of decay. William Blades's *The Enemies of Books* appeared first in 1880 and went through several editions.

The enemies that Blades cites—dirt, climate, air pollution, fungi, and people—are the same that we must cope with today. By the beginning of the

Figure 1.1. The Death of a Book. Peter Waters, Chief of the Restoration Department, Library of Congress. Photograph courtesy of Yoichi Okamoto.

twentieth century library associations in Great Britain and America turned their attention to book construction and library binding, but the impetus of the effort to produce sturdy and well-designed books was curtailed by the Great Depression and the Second World War.

It took a disaster with international impact, the Florence flood of 1966, which damaged some of the greatest monuments of Western culture, to direct the librarian's attention once again to the book, its significance in our cultural history, and its impermanence. This impact is well documented in an article by Sherelyn Ogden, "The Impact of the Florence Flood on Library Conservation in the United States of America," (*Restaurator*, 3:1–2 (1979), pp. 1–36). Prior to the flood, librarians and conservators such as Verner Clapp of the Council on Library Resources; William Barrow of the Virginia Historical Society and later of the Barrow Laboratory; Frazer Poole of the Library of Congress; and George Cunha of the Boston Athenaeum, who founded the Northeast Document Conservation Center, the first publicly funded and supported conservation facility for library and archival materials, were concerned about the preservation of library materials. These men did the ground work in investigation and analysis that has led to the activity of the preservation movement today. In his chapter on paper, conservator Karl Buchberg details the causes of the problems we face in preserving our printed heritage. Once worldwide attention focused upon the massive operation in Florence to restore that city's patrimony, more attention was paid to the preservation of our American cultural heritage. Peter Waters, a young English bookbinder and conservator who directed the salvage operation at the National Library in Florence, came to the United States to join the staff of the Preservation Office at the Library of Congress, working with its chief, Frazer Poole. He brought his assistant, Christopher Clarkson, with him to establish a restoration center at the library.

Within a few years, preservation or conservation programs and departments were established at Harvard, Yale, and New York Public Library. Under the direction of the capable American conservator Paul Banks, the Conservation Section at the Newberry Library, a rare book repository in Chicago, expanded to encompass the entire gamut of preservation problems facing that library, which has resulted in a major program of construction as well as scientific investigation which will benefit the entire library community.

The first graduate program to train American conservators began in 1960 at New York University's Institute of Fine Arts. Its first graduate, Mary Todd Glaser, is now the Senior Conservator at the Northeast Document Conservation Center. In the early 1970s graduate programs were also established at the State University of New York—Oneonta (the Cooperstown Program) and the University of Delaware (the Winterthur Program). While these programs do not specifically train book conservators, a number of capable people, including Glaser, Gary Albright, and Karl Buchberg, have emerged from them. In the fall of 1981 a program to train book conservstors was established at the New York University Institute of Fine Arts in conjunction with Columbia University. Its first students will complete the program in 1984 and will be trained to work with library materials. Columbia's School of Library Service has also begun a two year postgraduate program to train librarians to become preservation specialists. Paul Banks left the Newberry Library to become the director of the program.

Prior to 1981, librarians had gravitated toward the specialty of preservation from the art or the rare book world, and were self-educated. For this reason, many of the basic principles that guide the library preservationist are the same as, or similar to, those of the museum curator. Until recently a great deal of attention has been paid to saving the old and the rare—the objects that document our cultural heritage. Banks, at the Newberry, was the first conservator to pay attention to the building and the environment where rare materials are housed.

Although the library profession at large has been slow to recognize the problems inherent in the custodial aspects of librarianship, by 1970 the American Library Association's Resources and Technical Services Division's Bookbinding Committee became a division-level Committee on Preservation of Library Materials. Largely due to the effort of Esther Percy award-winner Pamela W. Darling, the committee expanded and sub-committees were formed. By 1980 the Preservation of Library Materials Section (PLMS) was established with over one thousand three hundred members and a number of active committees investigating preservation issues ranging from library binding to education. Thirteen western states, working together to analyze their preservation needs, established the Western Conservation Congress in 1980. On a smaller regional level, the Book Conservation Center at the New York (City) Botanical Garden, with funds from the National Endowment for the Humanities serves as a regional center for the New York metropolitan area, meeting a need for education and training. The Research Libraries Group (RLG), a corporation of the larger research libraries, began the decade with an active preservation committee, concerned with the long-term preservation of basic library materials. Courses on the preservation of library materials are now given in a number of library schools.[1] Today's preservation specialists are concerned with the library building, its environment, and its contents. This volume reflects that professional concern.

HOUSEKEEPING

In a pamphlet, *Caring for Books and Documents*, the conservator A. D. Baynes-Cope of the British Museum writes in his acknowledgment, "From my mother I learned the importance of proper ventilation and building maintenance."[2] Baynes-Cope has hit upon the essential ingredient of good library management: housekeeping. In America, librarians and conservators such as Paul Banks and Pamela W. Darling have repeatedly stressed this aspect of preservation in the library literature. If the physical plant housing library materials is not cared for, the materials within it will wither and die.

Dirt and air pollutants hasten deterioration. Insects and mold will feed and breed if they are not quickly discovered. The library building requires periodic cleaning, which should be undertaken in a systematic way. While cleaning is a function of the maintenance staff, the librarian is responsible for seeing that the staff performs its job correctly. The maintenance staff should consist of careful, responsible individuals who are thoroughly trained in cleaning procedures and who are made to feel responsible for the building and the objects in their care.

In the *Manual for Museums* by Ralph H. Lewis, an excellent and inexpensive publication prepared for the museums in the National Park Service, it is suggested that the director should survey the building and record each task that is to be done. Then a lengthy list can be grouped and consolidated to assure maximum efficiency. The librarian can estimate the amount of time it should take to perform each task, and then multiply the labor-hours for each by the number of times that it will be done each year. This will indicate the hours needed for proper housekeeping and will allow tasks to be scheduled on a daily, weekly, monthly, or annual basis.

Each chapter in this volume will discuss the effects of dirt and air pollution on a given medium and will provide careful instructions for storage and care. Overzealous and unthinking cleaning of library materials can cause far more damage than dirt and grime, and instructions for cleaning should be carefully followed. Some objects, like old photographs or film, should probably not be cleaned in-house, but rather given to a conservator or laboratory for treatment. Even surface cleaning of books and prints should be undertaken with great care, for this simple task can easily go awry in unskilled hands.

In addition to preserving library collections by curtailing their exposure to dirt and air pollutants, a neat and tidy library tells the public that the staff cares about its collections, and the public will be more inclined to care for them as well. A neat and tidy library where good housekeeping is scrupulously practiced suffers less from theft and mutilation of materials than does an untidy library. The library administrator should reflect upon this fact very carefully, for good housekeeping does pay for itself. An additional custodian may well cost less than the replacement of mutilated or stolen library materials.

ENEMIES OF LIBRARY MATERIALS

There are a number of enemies of library materials that, working alone or in conjunction with one another, will hasten the deterioration of a library's collections. In the chapters that follow, each author will discuss how these enemies will particularly affect each medium. A list of these enemies, and a few general remarks about the harm that they can cause, precedes more specific discussion in each chapter.

DIRT AND AIR POLLUTION

The effects of dirt and air pollution have been discussed in the previous section and it is obvious that scrupulous housekeeping practices will retard their effects. Air filtration systems, which are coupled with air conditioning systems, are a highly effective protection against dirt and chemicals in the air. The installation of such a system should be a priority for libraries that are located in industrial areas subject to a high level of air pollution. The effect of such a system can be quite dramatic, as I observed when comparing books housed in the main libraries at Yale and Rutgers. Both institutions are located in industrial regions with significant air pollution and are also subject to fluctuations in temperature and humidity. However, the library that houses the research collections at Rutgers was constructed in 1956 with temperature and humidity controls and an air filtration system. Only now is the Sterling stack tower at Yale, constructed in 1931, installing such a system. In 1972, when the survey was made, titles that were nearly beyond repair at Yale were found to be in fine condition at Rutgers. In the industrial world of the later twentieth century, even a few years can make a significant difference, although William Blades first observed the effect of air pollution on books in industrial London a hundred years ago.[3]

TEMPERATURE AND HUMIDITY

Temperature and humidity, working alone, together, and in conjunction with air pollution, can cause great harm to library materials. The notion that what is good for people is good for books is simplistic and not entirely true, as the careful reader will learn as he studies this volume, but it is a concept that is useful for the custodians of circulating library collections to remember.

The cooler the temperature the better, it appears, for all library materials. However, people are usually uncomfortable in cooler temperatures, so it is best to maintain a *constant* temperature of 65 °F (18 °C) in the library. The word *constant* is the key to the protection of collections, for fluctuations of temperature and humidity will cause the greatest harm to library materials. These fluctuations cause objects, such as books, to expand and contract, and hasten the disintegration of the object. Relative humidity (RH) should be kept within the 35–55 percent range. Humidity levels that exceed 60 percent, especially when coupled with a temperature that exceeds 70 °F (24 °C), will cause the growth of mold and fungi and can cause even more severe damage. High temperature and high levels of relative humidity must be cur-

Figure 1.2. Sling Psychrometer. Photograph courtesy of Science Associates, Inc., Princeton, N.J.

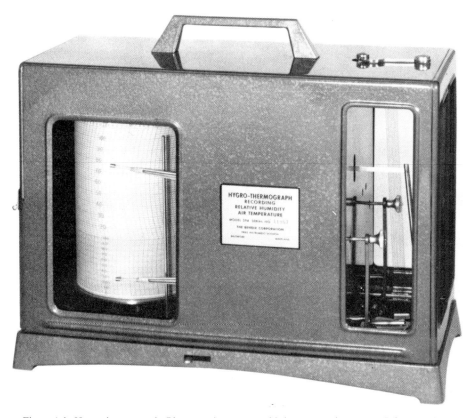

Figure 1.3. Hygrothermograph. Photograph courtesy of Science Associates, Inc., Princeton, N.J.

tailed in libraries; libraries, like museums, were exempted from federal guidelines on temperature and humidity controls during the energy crisis in the late 1970s because of the sensitivity of their collections to temperature and humidity changes. While a low temperature per se is ideal for library and archival materials, a relative humidity level below 35 percent, because of its dryness, can prove as destructive to many objects as a high RH level, because materials such as books and films will dry out and disintegrate. In the temperate zone of North America, RH will fluctuate somewhat with the seasons, with a high of 55 percent in the summer and a low of 35 percent in the winter. Trying to maintain a building at a constant RH of 55 percent is costly and will cause problems with condensation within the building that can be more harmful than a gradual seasonal fluctuation in RH. Temperature and humidity are discussed in detail by conservator Karl Buchberg in his chapter on paper.

If a library discovers problems, measurements of temperature and humidity should be made to document the fluctuations. A sling psychrometer, used to measure relative humidity, is small, inexpensive, and fairly simple to use, although its measurements are not entirely accurate. A variety of equipment to measure temperature and relative humidity is available. Libraries lacking air conditioning, and even those with temperature controls, would do well to invest in the best equipment they can afford. Humidifiers, dehumidifiers, and fans are available at reasonable cost and will help to control the environment in a library if a temperature control system cannot be installed.

LIGHT

The radiant energy of light absorbed by the molecules in an object can cause chemical changes that will damage an object; in short, light is harmful to library materials. The ultraviolet rays, the shorter ranges of light, are the most damaging. Sunlight and fluorescent lighting are the primary sources of ultraviolet radiation in libraries. While large windows, even skylights, make a library a warm and welcoming place, the light that they allow to enter is very destructive to the materials in the vicinity, as librarians are discovering. Skylights should be covered or whitewashed. While windows cannot usually be covered with whitewash, they can be curtained, and the curtains should be drawn when the light (and heat) from the sun is intense. While ultraviolet (UV) absorbing films are expensive, they can be applied directly to glass to cut off ultraviolet rays. They will also serve as insulation and cut heating costs, so the administrator may be able to justify their expense. These films are effective for about two years. Ultraviolet blinds are also available. Library materials of any permanence should not be kept in areas with many windows.

Fluorescent light is far more harmful to library materials than incandescent light, but unfortunately fluorescent lighting is still used in many libraries today. If it cannot be replaced, it can be covered with special filters—plastic sleeves that will cover the tube and greatly curtail the ultraviolet rays. The manufacturers claim that the shields are effective for up to ten years, but their effectiveness should be monitored. Sources of these shields can be found in the list of suppliers in the appendix.

Stack areas should be kept dark when library attendants or patrons are not there. A simple sign, Conserve, placed next to each light switch will suffice in this era of energy-consciousness; the public is more aware of the library's utilities budget than of its need to protect materials from the physical damage caused by light.

MOLD AND FUNGI

Fungi and molds are numerous and they subsist on organic matter. The materials discussed in this book are made wholly or in part of organic matter and the chapters that follow will discuss precisely how mold and fungus destroy each object. As mentioned previously, if the temperature and the relative humidity exceed 70 °F (24 °C) and 70 percent RH, molds and fungi will flourish. Fungi spores are everywhere and they thrive in a warm atmosphere where there is poor ventilation (as Mrs. Baynes-Cope and her son observed). Infected materials must be removed from the collection. In the short term they can be placed in a well-ventilated dry area, preferably out of doors. Active mold spores can sometimes be brushed off an object with a small sable-tipped brush. Further action should be taken carefully, according to the needs of the medium.

Badly affected materials should be fumigated. This can be done through a commercial fumigating company that is able to treat books, paper, and other library materials, or through a regional center. The Northeast Document Conservation Center, in Andover, Mass., has a large fumigation chamber where affected books can be shipped for treatment. In the early 1970s the Vacudyne Company designed small fumigation chambers that can be installed in libraries and museums, although ventilation can provide problems in installation and use. More and more institutions are purchasing the Vacudyne fumigator and many will treat materials from neighboring institutions at a nominal fee. The state of New Jersey recently installed a fumigator with 100 cubic foot capacity which will be available to New Jersey institutions. Fumigation of infected material is the surest way of preventing reinfestation and further damage.

PESTS AND PEOPLE

As preservation librarian R. Gay Walker has written in an article, "The Quiet Disaster II: Pests and People": "Pests are not just an annoying nuisance. They can seriously damage or destroy whole collections if they once infest an area are left unchecked. Many are attracted by the same conditions which encourage the growth of mold and other fungi.''[4] Pests are attracted to library media itself: starch in book bindings, glues, sizing on paper, emulsions. And they are capable of eating their way through library collections very quickly, as has been recorded throughout history. The most voracious insects to be found in North American libraries are the ubiquitous cockroach in all its many strains, silverfish, termites, and a variety of "bookworms," which are the larvae of over 160 species of beetle. The book louse is a minuscule creature that also eats animal and vegetable matter. Book lice are usually found in older books that have been stored in musty conditions. Even if the library has an ongoing program of fumigation, further fumigation is necessary at the first sign of infestation. The extermination of insects should be carried out by a professional exterminator; ad hoc methods by the library staff are ineffective. Good housekeeping procedures will greatly curtail infestation, but as we cannot guarantee the housekeeping practices of the patrons who use the circulating library, the library staff will have to maintain constant vigilance for the first signs of infestation.

Older libraries that are located in cities are subject to infestation by rodents. The conservator Yash Pal Kathpalia, who has served as a consultant for UNESCO, has estimated that as much as 20 percent of the world's books have been destroyed by rodents.[5] Once they have invaded a building, they are difficult to dislodge. Fortunately newer library buildings are not as vulnerable, due to care in construction. Older buildings can be protected against rodent infestation by plugging all holes in foundation walls, especially around water and sewer pipes and gas mains, and by using screens over other openings. Routine servicing of the building will further curtail infestation.

People are injurious to library materials because they may handle the materials carelessly and because of the bacteria that they carry. But libraries are for people and it is the librarian's responsibility to instill a sense of respect for library materials in the patron. The greatest enemy of library materials is the librarian who neglects collections in the quest for ever more efficient management systems, as Randolph G. Adams wisely pointed out in his 1937 essay, "Librarians as Enemies of Books."[6]

CARING FOR ART AND ARTIFACTS

In addition to books, films, and other media, libraries frequently own paintings, furnishings, and other objects that document our cultural heritage. These objects require the same environmental conditions as other library materials: stability of temperature and humidity; an atmosphere free of air pollutants; minimal exposure to light; careful and frequent cleaning;

and protection from living things, including people. A few tips on basic care for some of these objects follow. However, if a library has a considerable collection of artifacts, the staff will need to become familiar with museum literature. The publications of the American Association for State and Local History (AASLH), Nashville, Tenn., are especially helpful. Their monthly magazine, *History News*, contains a "Technical Leaflet," a four page pamphlet on one aspect of the care of collections. These leaflets are also available separately at a nominal cost.

If an object shows obvious signs of deterioration, a reputable conservator should be contacted. The American Institute for the Conservation of Artistic and Historic Works (AIC), 3545 Williamsburg Lane, Washington, D.C. 20008, is the professional organization for conservators in the United States, and a list of AIC members is available. More and more able conservators are being trained in the United States today and regional centers specializing in the restoration of art and artifacts are located throughout the country. Unskilled hands should not attempt to repair damaged artifacts.

PAINTINGS

Paintings in the library may be pictures of local sites or personages, or works by local artists. All too frequently they are neglected because of the feeling that if they were really good they would be in museums. While these paintings may not be important for artistic reasons, they are artifacts that document our history and are deserving of care and repair. A number of libraries also collect the works of local and regional artists, both to be exhibited and to be circulated to the library's patrons.

Paintings may be done on any surface, but most are on wood panels or on canvas. Both of these materials respond to their environment as does paper and they require the same environmental controls to prevent irreparable damage. Some paints are especially fragile and fall away from their backing after only a short period of time when paintings are placed in an inhospitable environment.

A painting should be placed in a frame that provides sufficient support for its weight. Many of the suggestions for framing works of art on paper, which are found in chapter 2, hold true for paintings as well. It is best to cover paintings that are displayed in public areas with glass or Plexiglas to protect them. Paintings should be stored carefully in an environmentally controlled area when they are not on display or on loan.

Paintings should be examined periodically for signs of deterioration. Cracked and peeling pigment is an obvious sign of decay, but if a painting has a yellow-brown tonal quality and the image appears slightly blurred, it is a sign that the painting is in need of cleaning. The varnish applied fifty or a hundred years ago also yellows with age. Cracked or warped frames are another sign of deterioration. If deterioration is obvious, a reputable conservator of paintings should be contacted. The conservator will examine the painting carefully and make a full report on the extent of the damage and the cost of repair. Often the documentation can be presented to the trustees of the library or a local benefactor to obtain the necessary funds for the repair.

FURNITURE[7]

Historic furniture may also be used for a functional purpose; certainly the library's newer furniture is. Wood is particularly sensitive to the climate around it. A poor environment can lead to cracked, loosened, or broken joints; nails, screws, wooden pins and pegs can loosen; veneers can crack. A number of insects are partial to wood. A good environment in the library prolongs the life of its furnishings as well as its collections.

Furniture should be moved with dollys and padded blankets. If an extensive move is to be undertaken, it is best, and may well prove least expensive in the long run, to hire professional movers. The repair of antiques should only be undertaken by skilled craftspeople or conservators.

SCULPTURE

Many libraries enjoy outdoor sculpture and some have collections within. Sculpture can be made from a number of media: stone, bronze, marble, wood, clay—whatever medium lends itself to being modeled into an object that might be considered a work of art. Outdoor sculpture, no matter what its medium, is subject to the hazards of our contemporary environment, and air pollution has proven particularly destructive to public sculpture. Degradation of image can become visible quickly. Monuments that have lasted for centuries, such as the Parthenon in Athens and Notre Dame cathedral in Paris, have deteriorated at a rapid rate in this century. Birds also seem to enjoy public sculpture and the chemicals in their droppings can cause considerable damage over a short period of time. Another enemy of public sculpture is the vandal, who gets perverse pleasure from the mutilation or destruction of a work of art. While conservators can provide few suggestions for protecting public sculpture from vandalism, their advice should be sought on the best means for caring for and protecting it from the elements.

Sculpture in the library should be treated like any other prized possession. Most materials used to create sculpture are susceptible to grime and bacteria from the hands and should not be handled. When they must be moved or cleaned, the curator or custodian should wear inexpensive white cotton gloves, available from several of the suppliers listed in the appendix. These gloves are recommended throughout this book for the handling of library materials. Most sculptures can be cleaned by dusting them lightly with a soft cloth, but specific instructions should be obtained from a conservator.

FABRIC

Textiles, like paper, are particularly susceptible to damage from light. It is unlikely that draperies covering the library's windows to protect its contents from the effect of light will survive more than a few years; sunlight causes fabric to disintegrate.

If a library houses a historic collection of textiles or costumes, the advice of a conservator should be sought on storage and display. A helpful booklet, *Considerations for the Care of Textiles and Costumes; A Handbook for the Nonspecialist*, by Harold F. Mailand (3rd ed., 1980), is available from the Indianapolis Museum of Art.

The above list of artifacts that are found in libraries is by no means complete. Almost anything can be found in the library: coins, rocks, matchbooks, dolls, stuffed birds and other animals, etc. The primary factor affecting their care and maintenance is good housekeeping. If these objects are a valued part of the library's collections, appropriate specialists should be consulted so that the staff can provide the best care for them. If a library cannot afford to care for such artifacts properly, they should be sold or deposited in an institution that can do so.

EXHIBITION

A part of the educational and cultural function of the library is the exhibition of its resources, yet exhibition will hasten the deterioration of an object, even if it is imperceptible to the eye. Library materials such as books, prints, maps, and photographs are especially susceptible to damage during exhibition. Such objects should not be exhibited for more than three months.

Before it is placed on display, an item should be carefully examined to determine its condition. Some objects are too fragile for display; a facsimile (so marked) can often be substituted for the original artifact in an exhibition. Objects that are loaned to other institutions will be subject to a wide variety of hazards, both in shipping and during exhibition. No matter what restrictions the lending institution places on the display of an object, in the final analysis it has no real control over the conditions under which the borrowing institution exhibits. Fragile items should never be loaned.

A poor environment takes a heavy toll on the life of a book or manuscript. Exhibition areas should have temperature and humidity controls and should provide a stable environment for the objects on display. Electrical wiring in exhibition areas should be checked periodically. Fire extinguishers should be kept nearby. An exhibition area should have adequate security and the objects on display should be insured. Smoking, eating, and drinking should not be permitted in exhibition areas. The opening is definitely a risk to the objects on display if the festivities take place in the exhibition hall.

Light is the greatest threat to objects on display, due to the photochemical changes that will take place because of their exposure to light. The amount of damage produced by light is directly proportional to the level of illumination and the length of exposure time. Thus, the same damage will be produced by a strong light over a short span as by a weak light over a lengthy span. Illumination should be kept as dim as possible; the eye can accommodate itself to various levels of light and an item can be examined under a low level of illumination if the light in the room is dimmer. Light meters should be used to measure illumination levels. Ultraviolet filters can be purchased for lights in exhibition areas, cases, and windows, and for the cases themselves.

Objects on display should never be held in place by pins or thumbtacks. Opened books should be supported so that no strain is placed upon the hinges or the text block. Polyester strips can be used to hold pages down; glass or polyester weights should be used with care. Under no circumstances should elastic bands be used. If possible, the pages of books on display should be turned every few days to prevent undue strain and to curtail the amount of time that a particular page is exposed to light. Cradles can be constructed out of cardboard and covered with felt or buckram to support and protect books on display. Institutions that frequently exhibit books may want to invest in Plexiglas cradles which are designed to be assembled to accommodate several sizes of books.

Over the past decade great advances have been made in the design of exhibition areas, from the development of Plexiglas cradles to the design of exhibition cases. There is no excuse for any institution to mount exhibitions under conditions that are harmful to the objects on display. Several of the references at the end of this chapter discuss the exhibition of library materials in some detail and the librarian should read them carefully before embarking upon an exhibition program.

LIBRARY CONSTRUCTION AND RENOVATION

Many librarians have to make the best of buildings that were constructed with little or no attention to overall design of facilities for the care of the collections that they were to house. Furthermore, libraries have expanded so that their collections range far beyond the books that many buildings were originally constructed to house. Slides, films, microforms, sound recordings, videotapes, videodiscs, and computers all require appropriate facilities, including electrical outlets, which the designer of the original building probably never dreamed of.

Funds for new library construction are no longer readily available. Today librarians are analyzing their physical plant to determine how it can best be used to house the library's collections over the next two decades. Renovations will have to be made to better house and protect existing collections and to provide for new modes of library service brought about by the technological developments of the past decades.

Keyes Metcalf discusses the considerations when building or renovating libraries in his book, *Planning Academic and Research Library Buildings* (New York: McGraw-Hill, 1965). This volume remains as timely today as when it was first published, and serves to summarize the preceding part of this chapter.

1. Air conditioning equipment, humidifiers, and filtering systems should be installed to inhibit atmospheric damage to libraries.
2. The building should be designed so that incandescent light with minimal illumination is installed in all areas where library materials are to be housed.
3. Construction should prevent infestation from rodents and insects.
4. Construction should reduce the hazard of fire and water damage.

Effective stabilization of collections can be accomplished at a low unit cost in the long run through the installation and use of comprehensive environmental controls.

Librarians engaged in building and renovation programs should be thoroughly familiar with the standards and specifications issued by the National Bureau of Standards, the National Fire Protection Association, and the American Association of Museums, and they must be able to communicate the library's needs to the architect, engineer, and contractors.

DISASTER PLANNING

Planning for disaster is a primary responsibility of library management, yet it is a task that is rarely done prior to an emergency. It is human nature to think that "it can't happen here" and to put off the task of planning in order to meet the more immediate needs of the day-to-day operation of the library. However, disaster can strike, suddenly and with devastating impact. The four elements, earth, air, fire, and water, separately or in combi-

Figure 1.4. After the Water Comes. Photograph courtesy of The Corning Museum of Glass.

nation, can wreak havoc upon a library and its collections. Fire, flood, tornado, hurricane, earthquake—no matter where we live in North America, our libraries are subject to several of these hazards. And, as preservationist George Cunha reminds us, disaster has a way of striking on nights and weekends. Prompt action is necessary to prevent irreparable damage to collections, yet it is difficult to take prompt action in a general emergency that will frequently accompany a library disaster.

The best protection against disaster, be it natural or man-made, is prevention. This involves good housekeeping, regular building maintenance, adequate library construction, and a well-trained staff. These four factors are the key to the preservation of library materials. They have been discussed earlier in this chapter and will be mentioned again throughout this volume.

The library staff should conduct a thorough inspection of the physical plant and classify all fire hazards that are discovered. The National Fire Protection Association (NFPA), 470 Atlantic Avenue, Boston, Mass. 02210, publishes *Protection of Library Collections*, NFPA publication no. 910, which is updated frequently. Its recommendations are essential for a good protective program. It includes "Self-Inspection Form for Libraries," which is the basic checklist that can be followed when an inspection of the building is made. The library may also wish to call in a specialist from the local fire department to assist in the inspection, for a trained eye will catch hazards that the untrained will miss. A thorough survey of the building will expose problems many of which can be easily remedied.

The following factors should be considered during the inspection of the library:

1. *History.* How old is the building? Has it ever had fire or water damage? If so, were the causes eliminated or only patched up?

2. *Design of the building.* Is there an up-to-date set of plans for the building that shows both the design of the structure and the placement of plumbing, heating, air conditioning, and electrical systems?

3. *Heating plant.* Does it have the capacity to heat the building without forcing? Is it adequately cut off from the rest of the building by walls, floor, and ceiling, all of which have the appropriate fire-resistance rating? Are all openings connecting the building to the heating plant properly protected with fire doors? If the heating plant is to be replaced, will the heating capacity of a new plant provide for further library expansion? Are ducts and pipes which pass through the floors and walls properly protected? Is fuel storage safe?

4. *Electricity.* Where is the fuse box or master panel; and, if it is kept locked, where is the key? Do fuses and circuit breakers provide protection? Have circuits become overloaded because of additions to the library or from the use of more electrical equipment, such as film or slide projectors? Has insulation on wiring become worn or deteriorated? Has temporary wiring been eliminated?

5. *Concealed spaces.* Are all pipe-chases fire-stopped? Are walls fire-stopped between floors? Can such defects be remedied by the use of noncombustible material? Do fire walls and fire partitions extend through the floors and the roof? Is the attic undivided? Can other hidden spaces, such as those formed by furred walls and hanging ceilings where fire may breed and travel, be made safe?

6. *The roof.* When was it constructed? Are there signs of old or new leaks? (Even the best of roofs cannot be expected to remain free of problems beyond a decade.) Is there a skylight that might leak? Are drains and downspouts regularly checked for clogging or breaks?

7. *Windows.* Are they tight? Are they ever left open for ventilation, which could allow driving rain to blow in and damage nearby material?

8. *Plumbing.* Do pipes pass above or near the book stacks? Where can the water supply be cut off?

9. *Furnishings.* What are curtains, drapes, and furniture made of? Are they flammable?

10. *Lighting protection.* Is it in good repair and properly grounded? Are storage areas adequately lighted? Are there emergency lights on separate circuits?

11. *Exits.* Are exit points clearly marked and unimpeded by security measures? This will take careful planning on the part of an administrator faced with the increasing problem of book theft, but it can be overcome by a review of existing standards and common sense.

12. *Fire protection equipment.* Are automatic sprinklers or fire detection devices installed and are they maintained to be sure that they are working properly? Are fire extinguishers located conveniently throughout the library? Do they function properly? Are members of the staff familiar with this equipment? Have they been trained to use fire extinguishers?

The library can easily develop a good in-house program of fire prevention based upon sensible housekeeping practices. Common sense dictates that the following practices should be routinely followed:

1. Safe containers should be provided for the collection of waste paper, smoking materials, and other refuse. Waste and rubbish should be removed from the premises at regular intervals.

2. Paint rags and custodian's oily cloths should be disposed of immediately as they are subject to spontaneous combustion.

3. When exhibits made of combustible material cannot be avoided, they should be located in an area that will minimize the hazard if they ignite. Portable extinguishers should always be located nearby.

4. Holiday decorations should always be of fire-retardant material and should be placed well away from sources of heat, such as light fixtures.

5. Frequent inspections should be made by a designated staff member to detect unsafe conditions and to impress upon the staff the importance of good housekeeping.

6. Smoking should be prohibited in book stacks and, if permitted at all, restricted to designated safe areas. Suitable ashtrays should be provided for the disposal of smoking materials.

7. Heating and air conditioning equipment should be maintained, inspected, and tested in accordance with recognized safe practices. Heaters and ductwork should be kept free of combustible deposits.

8. Portable heaters and small appliances should not be permitted in the library.

It is a good practice to have a responsible staff member appointed the fire inspection officer. This person will be responsible for the library's program of prevention, insurance coverage, the maintenance of fire protection equipment and services, the maintenance of the physical plant, and public relations regarding fire safety. He or she should assume the responsibility for the library's entire disaster preparedness program.

As the disaster plan is prepared, the librarian should take advantage of the library's counsel and technical consultants. The general objectives of a disaster plan are as follows:

1. To lessen the potential for loss by anticipating the possibilities and appropriately reducing them whenever possible.

2. To assure that agencies, both public and private, who will be called in during an emergency understand the nature of the library's collections and its priorities.

3. To establish normal conditions after a disaster promptly and efficiently.

4. To lessen the chances of recurrence by taking advantage of experience gained.

5. To assure that adequate orientation and training have been given to the staff and that this training is updated on a continuing basis.

6. To assure frequent inspection by appropriate agencies in order to prevent changed conditions from having a deleterious effect upon the safety of the building.

In the pamphlet, *Disaster Protection and Disaster Preparedness*, prepared by Hilda Bohem of UCLA for the University of California library system, it is recommended that the library form a Disaster Action Team (DAT) made up of cool and quick-witted staff members, with the coolest and quickest appointed director, for he/she will have to make a number of decisions under a great deal of pressure during a disaster. It will be the leader's responsibility to keep thoroughly informed and up-to-date in disaster recovery techniques and to make periodic reports to his/her colleagues so that they will also be familiar with the latest procedures. Bohem further recommends that a reference library of disaster literature be assembled. The Northeast Document Conservation Center and other disaster specialists have issued excellent bibliographies, and a list of key references is a part of the suggested reading at the end of this chapter.

In addition, notebooks should be prepared that include the following information:

1. A telephone list of the library's Disaster Action Team, or its equivalent, designating the functions assigned to each member.

2. A list of staff members who will be responsible for telephoning a given number of library employees, with all staff telephone numbers, so that all employees can be alerted to the emergency within a relatively short period of time.

3. Floor plans for all areas of the library, indicating not only what collections are housed there, but also the location of wiring, ducts, false ceilings, etc.

4. A list of names and telephone numbers of resource people

and agencies including police and fire officials who can
authorize emergency parking, pumping, etc., and possible
volunteer helpers from community groups, library organizations, etc.

5. A list of suppliers of necessities such as newsprint, plastic
   crates, plastic garbage bags, polyethylene sheeting and bags,
   portable pumps, generators, and fans.

6. A list of commercial freezers where water-damaged materials
   can be stored and of truckers to transport the materials.

7. The telephone numbers of disaster recovery specialists in the
   area, as well as the numbers of the Library of Congress Preservation Office and the Northeast Document Conservation
   Center, both of which will provide telephone assistance free
   of charge and on-site assistance if necessary.

8. A list of chemical supply companies who can provide chemicals that will be used under the supervision of a conservator
   who will supervise the clean-up operation.

9. An arrangement for paying for emergency needs that will by-
   pass customary procedures. Such an arrangement can be vital
   when quick decisions are necessary and, as disaster recovery
   expert Willman Spawn has pointed out, can spell the success
   or failure of a salvage operation.[8]

Copies of the notebook should be kept in the homes of the librarian, the
disaster recovery director, and other key library personnel, as well as in the
library. Needless to say, the notebook should be reviewed and updated
frequently.

The primary record of the holdings of a library today is its card catalogue, which is to be found within the library. However, as more libraries
computerize cataloguing operations and records, this information will be
stored outside the library, with less chance of destruction in an emergency
situation. If the library's catalogue and shelf-list are destroyed, the job of
assessing loss is almost impossible. The library's card catalogue should be
microfilmed and kept in a safe place away from the library, such as a bank
vault or the home of a trustee. In addition, it is wise to keep blueprint maps
of the library, giving location of all collections, with a copy of the
catalogue.

The librarian or the appropriate specialists within the library should
review all collections and determine which will receive primary attention in
the event of a disaster. Material that should be salvaged, if possible, should
be clearly identified. Estimates of the cost of each collection should be prepared, as they are an aid at the moment of disaster and will serve as a guide
in the weeks to follow. A general knowledge of the cost of each collection

will aid in determining what is to be discarded, replaced, or restored, and is a necessity for insurance purposes.

When disaster strikes, as it surely will at least once in the course of a librarian's career, the cool and quick-witted recovery director should be given command of the situation. Both Spawn and Cunha, experienced hands in an emergency, remind us that nothing will be gained by acting hastily or by ignoring the feelings of staff members who may well be in a state of shock. The better prepared the library is beforehand, the less chance there will be of making foolish and costly decisions on the spur of the moment.

The water that comes with flooding or in the wake of a fire or a natural disaster wreaks the greatest havoc upon library materials. Weather is the critical factor in determining what action is to be taken. If the weather is hot and humid, salvage must begin as soon as possible to prevent or control the growth of mold, which will begin to grow within thirty-six hours. If the weather is cold, more time can be taken to plan the salvage operation and to experiment with various drying procedures. It can often be a week or more before areas affected by fire can be approached, but if certain areas are identified as containing material of great value or as being particularly susceptible to destruction, the fire marshall may be able to provide access to the area.

The accepted method of stabilizing damaged materials, including paper, leather, fabric, and film, is by freezing and storing them at low temperatures ($-20\,°F$ / $-30\,°C$). This procedure allows for time to plan and coordinate drying operations and to identify what will be restored and what can be discarded. Interlocking plastic milk crates make excellent containers for packing wet materials, although strong cardboard boxes can also be used.

A pamphlet that is of invaluable help at the moment of disaster as well as for disaster planning is *Procedures for Salvage of Water-Damaged Library Materials*, written by Peter Waters, Chief of the Conservation Division, Library of Congress, the person who directed the salvage operations at the National Library in Florence following the devastating flood in 1966. It includes a great deal of practical advice on salvaging operations. Waters advises librarians that it is imperative that the advice of trained conservators with expertise in salvaging water-damaged materials be sought as soon as possible.

The more thoroughly the library has prepared, the more capably its staff will be able to cope efficiently and effectively in an emergency and the better the chance of salvaging valued materials and holding the cost of the operation within reasonable bounds. The Office of Management Studies, Association of Research Libraries, has published a collection of disaster plans and reports from its member libraries. While most libraries are not research libraries, a review of this material will be of great use when a library, no matter what its scope or size, plans for disaster in its own institution.

THE FUTURE

As we approach the second millennium, libraries have changed dramatically from those of the first. Repositories for carefully hand-written and illuminated volumes, chained to their shelves to prevent their loss, which quite literally meant the loss of the cultural heritage of the Western world, have developed into institutions containing a multitude of media and providing a wide variety of services to a large body of constituents. By the twelfth century, paper, a writing material more easily produced and used than vellum or parchment skins, was manufactured in Europe. The fifteenth century saw the advent of printing, an innovation that revolutionized the Western world as drastically as the computer and satellite transmission have done today, half a millennium later. By the nineteenth century the industrial revolution was under way. Paper and books were mass-produced; photography was invented and led the way to microfilm. By the beginning of the twentieth century the first sound recordings were made, which led to the tape and digital recordings of today. Sight and sound merged to produce motion pictures, videotape, and videodiscs. Computer and video technology have linked together so that by the late 1960s people were able to turn on the television and instantaneously watch the events of the world. And today the laser has joined with the computer, the moving image, and the sound recording to create wholly new communication media with the potential to revolutionize society as profoundly as did the Gutenberg revolution.

Librarians and curators, custodians of our cultural heritage, are on the cutting edge of a new society and bear the responsibility, as they have since the days of Nineveh, for the preservation of civilization's heritage. Like Aldus Manutius, that early publisher of the Greek and Latin classics, librarians will use the new technological innovations to preserve and to make available the older works, as well as the new.

What shall we preserve and how shall we preserve it? These are the questions that librarians will ask at the close of this millennium, just as they did at the end of the tenth century and certainly at the end of the fifteenth. How long is the life of the medium of preservation? Will the metal optical disc, with its capacity to make a virtual facsimile of an Aldine imprint, survive as long as the Aldine edition itself?

In the chapters that follow, Buchberg and Fitzgerald discuss massdeacidification, a developing technology that will enable us to save in its original form much of the written material of the nineteenth and twentieth centuries. Without such treatment, 90 percent of this material will turn to dust within a century. Microfilm and optical disc technology enable us to preserve the content of books and other visual material. As this chapter is written, research continues on film and microform technology, and this will be discussed in the chapters to follow. The videodisc will be tested for its permanence as its uses are explored, much as was the printing press five hundred years ago. The contributors hope that not only will readers find information of immediate and practical value in this volume, but also that they will be stimulated to consider the new to preserve what has come before.

NOTES

1. Susan G. Swartzburg and Susan B. White, eds., *Preservation Education Directory*, 4th ed. (Chicago: Education Committee, Preservation of Library Materials Section, Resources and Technical Services Division, American Library Association, 1981).

2. London: Trustees of the British Museum, 1981.

3. William Blades, *The Enemies of Books* (London: Eliot Stock, 1888).

4. R. Gay Walker, "The Quiet Disaster II: Pests and People," in *Disaster Prevention and Coping*, Proceedings of the Conference at Stanford University Libraries, May 21–22, 1980 (Stanford, Calif.: 1981), p. 24.

5. Yash Pal Kathpalia, *Conservation of Library Materials* (Paris: UNESCO, 1963), p. 64.

6. Randolph G. Adams, "Librarians as Enemies of Books," *Library Quarterly* 7 (1937): 317–31.

7. Much of the information for this section has come from the pamphlet *Basic Furniture Care*, by Robert F. Griffin, furniture conservator, New York State Office of Parks & Recreation, Conservation Collections Care Center, Peebles Island, Waterford, N.Y. 12188.

8. Willman Spawn, "Disasters: Can We Plan for Them? If Not, How Can We Proceed?" *Preservation of Library Materials*, ed. Joyce R. Russell. New York: Special Libraries Association, 1980, pp. 24–29.

SUGGESTED READINGS

Baker, John P., and Marguerite C. Soroka. *Library Conservation: Preservation in Perspective*. Stroudsburg, Pa.: Dowden, Hutchinson, Ross, Inc., 1978.

A key selection of readings on the nature of library materials, causes of deterioration, binding, microforms, disaster planning, and salvage.

Banks, Paul N. *Preservation of Library Materials*. Chicago: The Newberry Library, 1978. Reprinted from *Encyclopedia of Library and Information Science*, Vol. 23, 1978, pp. 180–82.

A discussion of the causes of deterioration and conservation methods.

Casterline, Gail F. *Archives and Manuscripts: Exhibits*. Chicago: Society of American Archivists, 1980.

This manual covers all aspects of exhibition.

Cunha, George M., and Dorothy G. *Conservation of Library Materials.* 2 vols. Metuchen, N.J.: Scarecrow Press, 1971–1972.

Vol. 1 contains historical background and information on preventive care, repair and restoration, and disaster planning. Vol. 2 is a comprehensive bibliography.

Cunha, George Martin, and Dorothy Grant. *Library and Archives Conservation: 1980s and Beyond.* 2 vols. Metuchen, N.J.: Scarecrow Press, 1983.

Volume 1 approaches conservation from a management perspective; volume 2, the bibliography, updates the bibliography cited above.

Guldbeck, Per E. *The Care of Historical Collections: A Conservation Handbook for the Non-Specialist.* Nashville: American Association for State and Local History, 1972.

A basic handbook covering security, fire protection, environment, packing and shipping, paper, and treatment of museum objects.

Gwinn, Nancy E. "CLR and Preservation," *College and Research Libraries,* 42:2 (March 1981): 104–26.

A history of the contribution of the Council on Library Resources, Inc., to the advances in the field of preservation over the past twenty-five years.

Lewis, Ralph H. *Manual for Museums.* Washington, D.C.: National Park Service, 1976.

A handbook covering all aspects of museum care.

Metcalf, Keyes D. *Planning Academic and Research Library Buildings.* New York: McGraw Hill, 1965.

The basic study on building needs for libraries; a new edition is in preparation.

Swartzburg, Susan Garretson. *Preserving Library Materials: A Manual.* Metuchen, N.J.: Scarecrow Press, 1980.

A basic guide for preservation.

DISASTER PLANNING

Association of Research Libraries. Office of Management Studies. *Preparing for Emergencies.* Washington, D.C.: ARL, November–December 1980 (SPEC Kit, 69).

A collection of policies and procedures from the ARL membership.

Bohem, Hilda. *Disaster Prevention and Disaster Preparedness.* Berkeley: University of California, 1978.

An outline for a disaster preparedness plan with a disaster prevention checklist and sources of assistance.

Corning Museum of Glass. *The Corning Flood: Museum Under Water.* Corning, New York: Corning Museum of Glass, 1977.

A case history of the flood and its aftermath with analysis of successes and failures.

Morris, John, and Irvin D. Nichols. *Managing the Library Fire Risk.* 2nd ed. Berkeley: University of California Press, 1979.

Information on fire risk in libraries and on the means of protecting collections.

Myers, Gerald E. *Insurance Manual for Libraries.* Chicago: American Library Association, 1977.

A concise but thorough discussion on insurance for libraries.

National Fire Protection Association. *Protection of Library Collections.* Boston: NFPA (NFPA Pamphlet, 910) Updated frequently.

Recommended practices for the protection of library collections from fire. Included is their "Self-Inspection Form for Libraries."

Spawn, Willman, "Disasters: Can We Plan for Them? If Not, How Can We Proceed?" *Preservation of Library Materials*, ed. Joyce R. Russell. New York: Special Libraries Association, 1980, 24–29.

Basic information on planning and coping.

Stanford University Libraries. *Disasters, Prevention and Coping*, Proceedings of a Conference, May 21–22, 1981. Stanford: Stanford University Library, 1981.

Waters, Peter. *Procedures for Salvage of Water-Damaged Library Materials.* 2nd ed. Washington, D.C.: Library of Congress, 1978.

The basic instruction book. This belongs in the library and should be an integral part of the library's disaster plan.

2

Paper: Manuscripts, Documents, Printed Sheets, and Works of Art

KARL BUCHBERG

The class of material known as paper and parchment artifacts which are found in libraries, archives, and historical societies comprises one of the two largest bodies of items to be housed in these repositories, surpassed perhaps only by books.

Paper items, sometimes referred to as *flat paper* to differentiate them from bound books, are usually understood to include parchment and vellum, and are most often classified by their method of production. The largest group for the majority of institutions would be printed items: broadsides, single leaves of printed books, maps, posters, newspapers, stamps, and ephemera. The second group consists of manuscripts and documents. The third group is works of art on paper: prints (woodblock, etching, engraving, lithography, and photomechanical reproduction), watercolors, charcoals, pastels, and chalk and pencil drawings.

All these items are composed of two basic constituents: the support layer, which is either paper or parchment, and the media layer, which includes the inks and colors applied to the paper or parchment.

An understanding of the properties of the support and media layers will help the curator understand what materials make up an artifact he or she is dealing with, what problems can be expected of any particular item, and how a problem might best be solved.

HISTORY OF PAPERMAKING

The invention of paper is ascribed to Ts'ai Lun, a Chinese court official, in 105 A.D. Recent archaeological finds in China suggest that papermaking might indeed be even two hundred years older, but dating of newly excavated tombs containing fragments of paper is not conclusive. The earliest paper was meant as a substitute for silk cloth, and may have been made from scraps of silk. However, early paper remains contain fibers of vegetable material other than silk.

The art of papermaking spread eastward from China to Korea and

Japan. The earliest known Korean paper samples date from the eighth century although Japanese tradition places the introduction of papermaking in the year 610 A.D.

Trade along the silk route was responsible for the spread of paper to the West. Paper was introduced to the Arab world in the eighth century. The first European paper mills were built in Spain by the Moors in the twelfth century. Italian mills were established at Fabriano at the end of the thirteenth century. The earliest French papers date from the beginning of the fourteenth century; German papers date from the middle of the century; and paper from the Netherlands, although introduced in the beginning of the fifteenth century, did not become fully established until the end of the sixteenth century. The first English mill was begun in 1495 by John Tate but the second was not established until 1557.

Although European papermaking techniques were introduced into Mexico in 1580, the Mayas and Aztecs had long made their own version of paper from the bark of fig and mulberry trees. The first mill in the United States was built by William Rittenhouse in Pennsylvania in 1690.

TECHNIQUES OF PAPERMAKING

In the West paper was preceded by parchment as the major writing base. Its invention is traditionally ascribed to Eumenes II of Pergamum (179–158 B. C.) who wanted to enlarge his royal library but was denied papyrus by his political rivals in Egypt. He was therefore forced to use animal skins.

Parchment is made from the ordinary skin of sheep or goat while vellum, a thinner, more delicate variety, is made from the finer skin of calf or kid and sometimes from the skin of stillborn or newborn calf or lamb.

The process of making a usable sheet of parchment or vellum consists of washing the skin, liming, unhairing, scraping, washing a second time, stretching on a frame, scraping a second time, paring down the inequalities in the skin, dusting with a sifted chalk, and rubbing with pumice.

All parchment retains a hair side and a flesh side. To make this difference as unnoticeable as possible, parchment manuscripts are usually bound with hair side facing hair side, flesh side facing flesh.

Parchment is a material of great strength and malleability. Its greatest structural drawback is that it is flattened by extensive stretching and tends to revert to its original "animal" shape if not stored in a stable environment. Consequently, many parchment documents and bound manuscripts have cockled badly over the years.

Paper is essentially a sheet of felted fibers. The sheet is held together by the overlap of one fiber with its many neighbors as well as by some chemical bonding from fiber to fiber. The strength of the sheet of paper is related to fiber length; the longer the fibers the more possibility for felting.

A second major constituent of the paper sheet is size. Size is a water soluble substance added to the paper sheet, either before the sheet is formed or after, in order to make the paper less absorbent. Paper with no size is essentially like a blotter and will absorb liquid at a rapid rate. Writing ink and printing ink would not remain distinct without the addition of size to harden the paper. Papers for different purposes, such as writing, printing, or watercolor, have different amounts of size depending on the desired working characteristics of the sheet.

The raw material for the vast majority of Western papers prior to the middle of the nineteenth century was cotton and linen rags. Old rags were collected and sorted according to quality. Rags were sometimes left in large piles to putrify in order to break them down into their constituent fibers, but the putrification process led to a great deal of waste. More often rags were immediately wet and beaten. Initially they were handbeaten with large wooden mallets but as technology progressed to meet the demand, the rags were beaten with sets of water-powered mallets. The action of the mallets against the wet rags served to pull the fibers apart instead of cutting them, producing the long-fibered papers which have proven to be so durable.

When the pulp was of a desired consistency, it was transferred to the vat where it was kept from settling by constant stirring. The paper mold, a rigid wooden frame with a lattice of wooden ribs and brass wires, was dipped into the vat, picking up paper fibers suspended in water. It was then removed from the vat and shaken in all four directions to remove excess paper pulp and water, thus producing an even sheet of paper. The quality of fine handmade paper was due in great measure to the skill of the vatman, the worker who formed the sheet knowing exactly how much pulp to scoop out for a single sheet and maneuvered the pulp in the mold to make an even sheet of a desired thickness. The still-wet sheet was then transferred to a felt or woolen cloth, in a process called couching. After a stack of paper was made, it was pressed to remove excess water. The stack of paper was removed from the felts with which it was interleaved and given a series of pressings until a specific finish and smoothness were achieved. Then groups of four or five sheets were pulled off the stack and hung up to dry.

The first major technological improvement in the papermaking process was the Hollander beater, perfected in Holland during the middle of the seventeenth century. The Hollander beater, an oblong metal tub equipped with a set of thirty or so blades which rotated constantly against the floor of the tub, macerated fibers far more quickly and uniformly than hand or water driven mallets, which were replaced over a period of time by this superior machine, which could be driven by water or wind. One drawback of the Hollander beater was the quality of paper which it produced. It produced shorter fibers than the stampers because it cut the fibers instead of drawing them out, making an inherently weaker sheet of paper.

The discovery of chlorine in 1774 by Karl Wilhelm Scheele, a Swedish chemist, led to a practical way of bleaching rags prior to the sheet formation stage. This was of major importance to papermakers since white paper was considered to be the highest quality paper, and sun bleaching was only moderately effective on colored rags. Chlorine bleaching, a boon to papermakers, left a disastrous legacy in the form of chlorine residues which formed acidic compounds in the papers bleached in this way. Acidic chlorine compounds hastened the chemical breakdown of paper fibers.

In 1798, Nicholas-Louis Robert patented a machine which made paper on a continuous wire mesh, the first automated papermaking machine. It became known as the Fourdrinier machine, named after its financial backers. Improvements upon the machine design by Bryan Dinken, an English engineer, and a new design by John Dickinson led to commercially viable papermaking machines by the early 1800s.

During the second half of the seventeenth century, papermaker's alum, potassium aluminum sulfate, was introduced into the papermaking process. Alum, still used today, helps to precipitate size onto the fibers of the paper sheet. Gelatin and animal size were the two traditional sizes until the middle of the nineteenth century, when rosin size was introduced. The alum-rosin combination, an efficient and cost-effective product, produced sulfuric acid as a by-product, which has proven to deteriorate rag papers as well as proving fatal to the newly discovered wood pulp papers.

The search for new raw materials to substitute for a woefully inadequate supply of cotton and linen rags started as early as the seventeenth century. During the eighteenth and early nineteenth centuries a variety of new materials was employed to make papers which unfortunately lacked the whiteness of fine papers or their durability and strength.

In 1840 a patent for a wood-grinding machine awarded to Friedrich Gottlieb Keller produced the impetus to make papers from wood. By 1866, paper made with wood pulp boiled in caustic alkali made wood pulp papers a reality. In 1867, groundwood pulp, a totally mechanical noncooked pulp, was introduced. In 1884 sulfite pulp, a longer-fibered, stronger pulp, was invented. In 1910, sulfate or kraft pulp, familiar as brown wrapping paper and bags, was introduced. More recently, alpha pulp, the purest chemically produced wood pulp, has been put on the market.   .

Groundwood pulp, which is produced without removing any chemical impurities found in wood, and also has the shortest fiber length, is the poorest of all wood pulps. The four chemically separated pulps—soda, sulfite, sulfate, and alpha—have longer fibers and fewer impurities. Of these, sulfate pulp—bleached for use in white papers—and alpha pulp are the highest quality. The addition of wood pulp in some proportion in almost all post-1866 papers has produced a legacy of seriously deteriorated paper artifacts dating from this period.

Recent interest in producing permanent and durable papers as well as new technological developments have led to commercially available high quality non-rag papers. High quality pulp such as alpha pulp, non-acidic size, and alkaline buffers such as calcium carbonate to protect against acid build-up in paper have produced papers which will last for many hundreds of years.

Many small European and American papermakers continue to make fine all-rag papers following traditional techniques. However, the percentage of items made with these papers is very small when compared with those using lesser quality paper.

Handmade Japanese papers, used in Japan for centuries for writing, painting, printing, and more recently used in the West for restoration treatments, have been recognized as having outstanding characteristics. Japanese papers have extremely long fiber length, non-acidic size, and a naturally alkaline character. It is for these reasons that conservators use traditional Japanese papers in numerous procedures.

CARE OF LIBRARY, ARCHIVE, AND HISTORICAL SOCIETY COLLECTIONS

ENVIRONMENT

The most important method of protecting library and archive materials, especially organic materials, is by providing a beneficial and stable environment.

Air quality. Air quality is an important factor in the preservation of library materials. Institutions in rural areas run a lesser risk than urban institutions where high levels of ozone and sulfur dioxide, among other gases, cause cellulosic materials to deteriorate. The most effective way to provide satisfactory air quality is to create a completely climate-controlled environment, where air intake is regulated and adjusted and harmful pollutants are removed. For many institutions this is not financially possible.

A less thorough but less costly alternative is a climate-controlled storage area, providing acceptable air quality where the majority of the collection is kept for the longest periods of time.

Light. Light is one of the great enemies of library and archive materials. All levels of light, no matter how low, contribute to cellulose degradation and the fading of certain pigments and dyes. Certain portions of the light spectrum are more harmful than others. The blue-violet range of the visible light spectrum and ultraviolet light are the most deleterious.

Overhead lighting should be incandescent, not fluorescent. If fluorescent lights cannot be replaced, filters in the shape of tubes can be purchased to filter out the harmful ultraviolet portion of the light. Check manufacturers' warranties to see how long each product will last and test periodically to make sure that filters have not worn out. Light levels in public spaces such as reading rooms and corridors must be bright enough to insure patron comfort. These light levels are too high for proper storage and exhibition, so these two functions should be separate from general reader access.

Manuscript material, works of art on paper, and printed items should be stored in the dark. This is usually accomplished by placing items in folders or mats and then in boxes or cases. Therefore, no light can harm the item. If an item must be stored without any protection, lights should only be turned on when necessary.

Exhibition areas should have low levels of illumination. For very valuable and rare materials, five footcandles of light are sufficient. This level will seem dim in comparison to a normally lit room, but the eyes will adjust to the lower level. Maximum exhibition time should not exceed three months. If longer exposure is necessary, the curator must understand that some damage, even if it is not evident to the eye, will occur. Glass exhibition cases will filter some of the harmful ultraviolet rays but not all. An additional sheet of ultraviolet filtering plastic placed in cases will help. This can be done by placing a piece of ultraviolet filtering plastic between the lights in the upper part of the case and the exhibited items, or by coating all the glass in the case with ultraviolet filtering plastic which is designed to adhere to glass. Pieces of ultraviolet filtering plastic can be placed over matted items in a case to provide extra protection. UF 4, a virtually clear Plexiglas, filters most ultraviolet rays. UF 3, a very slightly yellow tinted plastic, filters even more and is recommended for very fragile or degraded pieces, objects with inks or colors subject to fading or papers containing poor materials such as groundwood pulp or alum size.

Blinds or drapes should cover all windows which allow light to fall on important material. Open blinds only when the public needs to see the collection. Before opening hours and especially during the summer keep rooms dark as much as possible. Ultraviolet filtering mylar roller blinds are available.

An ordinary light meter used in photography can be used to measure light levels although more sophisticated devices do exist.

Temperature and relative humidity. Controlled temperature and relative humidity are vital for proper protection of cellulosic materials. Cellulose deteriorates twice as rapidly for every increase in temperature of 10 °F. This means that cold storage will prolong the life of paper. However, this is not usually feasible for a collection of any size because material stored in the cold must be brought up to room temperature slowly to avoid condensation. For a collection where storage areas and reader services are to be kept at the same temperature, a maximum of 70 °F (21 °C) and a minimum dictated by reader comfort would be practical. It is essential that the fluctuation between high and low temperature remain as small as possible. A goal of 3 °F–5 °F of fluctuation is good. Heating and cooling units should not be shut off at night, but allowed to run in a way which will maintain constant temperature levels.

Relative humidity, the amount of moisture contained in the air as compared to total saturation for a given temperature (expressed in percent RH), is another vital indicator of storage acceptability. Mold begins to grow at about 68 percent RH, so an upper limit of 60 percent RH, with a range of 50-60 percent RH is good. As with temperature, it is important that RH fluctuate as little as possible. A seasonal RH fluctuation of 40-60 percent is acceptable in colder climates if the change from season to season is achieved gradually. Paper is a hydroscopic material, which means that it absorbs water when the atmosphere is wet and gives off water when it is dry. This creates a pattern of expansion and contraction of the paper which causes buckling and pigment loss due to unstable support. RH fluctuation is very bad for parchment, which buckles easily and is flattened only with extreme difficulty.

Even when a proper RH level is maintained, isolated areas in a collection can have dangerously high levels. Such danger spots are corners, basements floors, outside walls, closed drawers and cases, and boxes without any air vents. A good precaution against unexpected mold growth is good air circulation, created by air conditioners, blowers, or even small fans.

A thermometer will register temperature and a dial RH meter will do the same for relative humidity. However, neither gives a record which can be examined at a later date. Evening and weekend readings are often the most valuable. A recording hygrothermograph records temperature and relative humidity for a week on a single sheet of graph paper, but is more expensive than devices which do not record.

ACIDITY, pH, AND PAPER

Acidity, a word which is often spoken of in regard to paper preservation, is a complex subject. Acidity is usually measured and expressed in terms of pH, the negative concentration of hydrogen ions on a logarithmic scale. The pH scale ranges from 1 to 14, where 7 is neutral, 1-7 is the acidic range, and 7-14 the alkaline range. A pH of 3 is ten times more acidic than a pH of 4, and one hundred times more acidic than a pH of 5.

It is now well established that acidic conditions are harmful to cellulose, the main constituent of paper. Acid catalyzes the breakdown of the cellulose fiber, producing shorter fiber length and therefore weaker paper.

Paper can develop an acidic nature because of many factors. Inherent vice, caused by materials added during the papermaking process, such as alum-rosin size or groundwood pulp fibers, is one factor. Atmospheric conditions such as sulfur dioxide gas can produce acidic substances in paper.

A very common method of introducing an acidic condition into paper is by storing it next to other acidic materials such as acid paper, cardboards, and wood. This is the easiest problem for the custodian of any collection to remedy. Non-acidic storage materials are necessary in libraries and archives, a fact well stamped on the minds of most librarians and archivists through articles, lectures, and advertisements. Non-acidic folders, boxes, labels, matboard, and papers of varying qualities and sizes are available from a variety of vendors.

Every so-called acid-free product is not alike. Some products are simply not quite as acidic as a lesser quality item made by the same company. Such products should be avoided. A product made of a pure chemical pulp, a non-acidic size, and the addition of an alkaline buffer to counteract the build-up of acidity over time is a good product. Archival file folders, envelopes, and papers can easily be found which conform to this high quality. Matboard is often made of 100 percent rag fibers creating a high quality product if there are no harmful additions such as alum. Conservation board, which is also used for matting, is not rag but made of high quality pulp, and is recommended if buffered with an alkaline salt. Some manufacturers produce acid-free colored matboard.

Measurement of pH is also not an easy topic. In order to get an accurate measurement, a sophisticated pH meter is usually used in laboratory situations. In addition, the sample must be properly prepared, usually by measuring it to a given weight, cutting it into very small pieces, and then soaking it in either cold or hot water. This type of process is too time consuming and expensive for most small institutions and, of course, not possible when testing an item from the collection.

The easiest way to measure pH on an item which is expendable (such as a folder, box, or label, but not an item from the collection) is with an archivist's pen. An archivist's pen contains a chemical which turns a different color depending on the pH of the item being tested, It is easy, but accurate within only a broad range. However, this range is good enough to tell whether or not a storage material might be considered archival. The pen should have the ability to register the alkaline and acidic range, not only the acidic, as some archivist's pens do.

To test an item in the collection, non-bleeding pH strips are a good choice. A small drop of water is applied to an inconspicuous place on the item. The strip is placed over the water and weighted for a few minutes. The color of the strip is then compared to a color chart. The strips are more accurate than the pen and safe to use.

HANDLING BY CURATORS AND PATRONS

When a staff member or a reader wants to use an item, the following precautions should be taken. Always handle the item with clean hands and on a clean work space. Carry items with two hands and never carry more than can be comfortably accommodated. Large items and heavy boxes should be moved on carts. Ballpoint pens, ink pens, and felt tip pens should not be used near valuable items. Use only pencil, which can be easily erased. No food or drink should be allowed in reading rooms or storage facilities. Items which are handled a great deal should be given to readers either in a mat or encapsulated.

COLLECTION SURVEYS

One of the best ways for a curator to come to know a collection better is to do a conservation survey. A conservation survey can be as elaborate or simple as the curator feels is necessary. If a piece by piece survey is warranted, an examination form can be completed for every item. A more informal survey will not reveal as many particulars, but will give a good idea of problem areas or collections which are in good condition. *Curatorial Care of Works of Art on Paper*, by Anne F. Clapp, contains an example of a detailed examination report form.

During a survey, the curator should note or set aside all items which are too fragile to be handled by untrained staff members or the public. Notes can be made on items needing treatment so that as funds become available a quick and intelligent decision on what should be treated first can be made.

The curator can then also decide what items should not be handled by users in original format, perhaps due to condition or value. A photograph, microfilm, or acid-free photocopy can be made ahead of time, so that when a request for a restricted item is made there will not be a delay in handling the request. Copy machines can be used with acid-free paper to produce an archival copy.

PROCESSING COLLECTIONS

A basic method of upgrading the condition of collections already in the possession of an institution, as well as making sure that new collections meet minimum standards, is proper processing. Processing, from the preservation point of view, means removing all items which are harmful to the collection and arranging for proper housing and storage.

All paper clips, rusting staples, rubber bands, acidic folders, and unnecessary pieces of paper such as old labels and newspaper clippings should be discarded. If an old label, newspaper clipping, sales slip, or annotation is important, put it in an acid-free or polyester wrapper or folder and store it next to the item.

HOUSING MANUSCRIPT AND SINGLE LEAF PRINTED ITEMS

An institution which has the resources and manpower to house each item in its collection separately should do this. The most common way of storing single leaf items is to insert each item into an acid-free letter- or legal-size folder. No item should be unnecessarily folded to fit into such an arrangement. Oversize items should be stored separately. Each box should be filled so that no item sags or bends, but should not be so crowded that removal or return of a folder is a problem. If a box is not to be filled for some reason, use pieces of acid-free cardboard to pad the unused space, removing pieces when new folders are added. Folders should be labelled with pencil or typed labels.

Oversize Items. Items larger than a legal-size folder should be put into a home-made folder of acid-free folder stock. These folders can then be placed in map cases or on shelves that are large enough to accommodate them without sagging.

Matting and Unmatting. All items that enter an institution housed in acidic mats should be removed from their mats if this can be done without harming the items. Acidic mats harm the items they are supposed to protect in two ways. Acid can transfer to the item, causing discoloration and embrittlement. Secondly, acidic mats are themselves often very brittle. If handled carelessly they can break, often tearing the item within as well. If the item is simply hinged to the mat, the hinge can be slit with a scalpel or sharp knife. However, if the work of art has been glued down to either the back or front of the mat, or in some cases to both back and front, then the job of removing the mat should be left to a conservator. If a mat does not open easily, it is probably glued shut. Do not try to pry it open, because it might be glued to the work of art as well as to itself.

Mats are widely recognized as one of the best ways to store and exhibit works of art on paper. It is therefore important for the custodian of a collection to understand what the components of a mat are so that matting can be done in-house if desired, or proper standards can be set for any work done by a commercial matter and framer.

All work sent to an outside firm should be rigorously checked to be sure that high quality materials are used throughout the matting process. It is easy to make a mistake but difficult and expensive to rectify one, especially if a mistake is not recognized until years after the fact, when damage has already been done.

Anyone who wants to set up an in-house matting operation should order the recently published National Preservation Program publication called *Matting and Hinging of Works of Art on Paper*, which is available from the Library of Congress. It describes, with illustrations, various mat designs for different needs. It also includes the necessary wheat starch recipe for making the paste used in hinging and a list of supplies and suppliers needed for the various processes.

Only acid-free matboard should be used. Matboard is usually sold in 2-ply (thin) and 4-ply (thick) weights (see Figure 2.1). The back of the mat (1) should be 4-ply because it supports the work of art. The window mat (2) can be 2-ply, which is less expensive, or 4-ply, which gives a more pleasing bevelled edge when properly cut. An item which is to be framed should have a 4-ply window mat to keep it from touching the glazing. The window mat for a very large item should be made of two 4-ply boards to allow for the possibility of cockling during the time while the item is framed. A 4-ply window mat and 2-ply back mat is a dangerous combination. The back of the mat will sag when handled because it is less stiff than the window. This will allow the work of art to bend, which can be harmful.

The window mat and back mat are attached with a strip of gummed white cloth tape (3) cut slightly shorter than the length of the mat. It is best to adhere the mat along the left or top, depending upon which is the longer side.

Proper hinging is crucial for good matting (see Figure 2.2). There are two basic types of hinges: pendant hinges, which are used when the edge of the mat covers the work of art, and folded hinges, which are used when the mat does not cover the work of art (sometimes called ''floating'' a work of art). Pendant hinges are stronger and should be used when possible. Both pendant and folded hinges can be reinforced with an additional piece of paper if the item is heavy.

Hinges should always be placed at the top, never at the side. Hinging along a side will allow the paper to sag. For most prints and drawings, two hinges will suffice. For large ones an extra hinge in the middle can be added.

The first step in the hinging process is to make the hinges and paste them to the work of art. Instead of cutting the hinges, made of Japanese paper, with a scissors or knife, take a small brush and wet the paper along the outline of the hinge, then tear the paper, pulling fibers out as you tear. This produces a feathered edge which will not imprint a sharp line when pasted to the work of art. Paste one third of the hinge using cooked wheat or rice starch paste. Apply the pasted part of the hinge to the work of art and weight it until dry. Once both hinges are dry, the second step is to position the work of art in the mat, weight it lightly so it will not move, and paste the upper two-thirds of the hinge to the back mat. Weight until dry. If you add the extra reinforcing piece, paste over the upper part of the hinge after it has dried. If three hinges are used, adhere the middle one to the back mat first and then adhere the two side hinges.

Framing. Good framing is as important as good matting (see Figure 2.3). A proper frame unit consists of the following components: the frame (1), glazing (2), the mat unit (3 and 4), the backboard (5), and a sealing layer (6). The frame is a matter of personal taste. It should be strong enough to support whatever will be put into it. The choice of glazing is important. Glass is heavier and bends less easily than Plexiglas. Glass filters less ultraviolet light than UF 4 or UF 3 Plexiglas. Plexiglas, because of its electrostatic properties, attracts dust. It will also pull particles off of chalk, pastel, and charcoal drawings, so it should not be used on these media. Do not ship frames with glass unless absolutely necessary. Use Plexiglas for shipping whenever possible. If it is necessary to use glass, tape the whole glass surface so that if breakage occurs the sharp edges will not be able to harm the framed item. Do not tape Plexiglas, because the tape is difficult to remove and may mar the plastic. It also scratches very easily.

The mat unit is discussed above. It provides an air space between the work of art and the glazing as well as supporting the work of art. The window mat must be thick enough to keep the matted item away from the glaz-

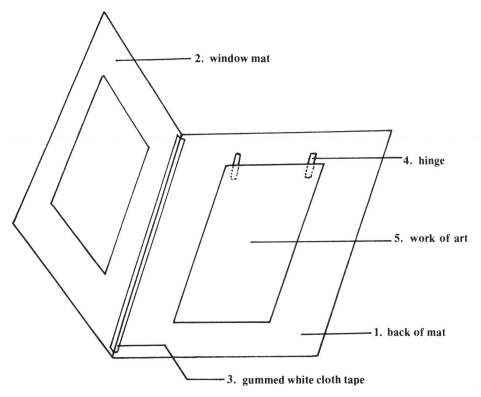

2. window mat

4. hinge

5. work of art

1. back of mat

3. gummed white cloth tape

Figure 2.1. Mat. Diagram by Karl Buchberg.

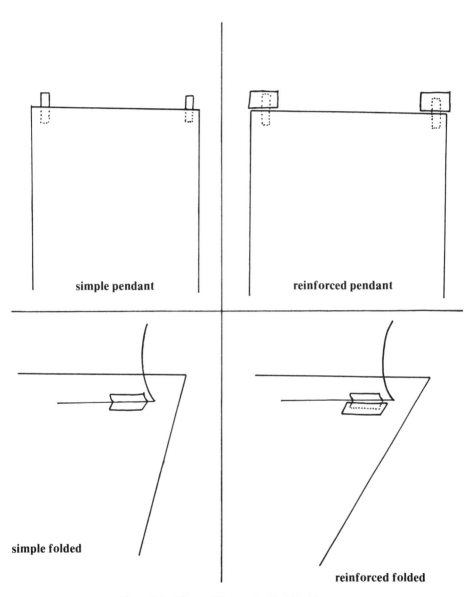

simple pendant

reinforced pendant

simple folded

reinforced folded

Figure 2.2. Hinges. Diagram by Karl Buchberg.

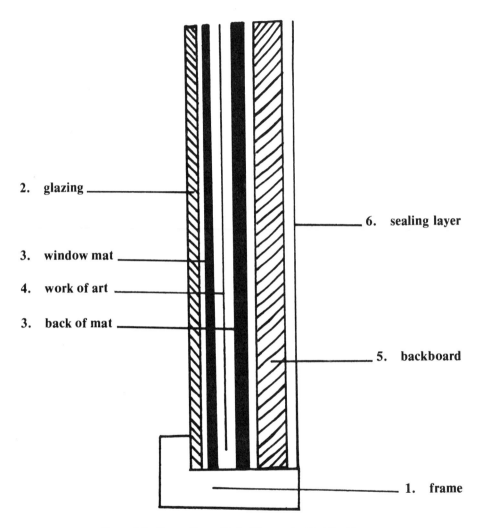

2. glazing

3. window mat

4. work of art

3. back of mat

6. sealing layer

5. backboard

1. frame

Figure 2.3. Proper Frame Unit. Diagram by Karl Buchberg.

ing. When the temperature drops rapidly, condensation can occur on the glazing. If paper is touching the glazing it will be stained by the water droplets which have formed on the glass or Plexiglas. Over time, mold will begin to grow on the glass due to the high relative humidity. If the window mat is sufficiently thick to keep the matted item away from the glazing, no damage will occur if the problem is handled quickly. The mat should be removed from the frame, the glazing should be thoroughly cleaned, and then the mat can be reinserted if there has been no damage to it. If the mat is wet or moldy, remove the work of art, discard the damaged mat, and make a new one.

The backboard protects against damage from the rear and also blocks dust and dirt. The backboard should be a good quality acid-free board, but need not be ragboard. If good quality board is not available, place a sheet of acid-free paper or a sheet of polyester between the mat and the backboard to act as a barrier. The backboard is held to the frame with stainless steel or brass nails. A picture framer's tool, a hand-held squeeze device, inserts nails without the force of a hammer. The backboard is then sealed with gummed tape, a piece of paper glued to the frame, or a sheet of polyester taped to the frame.

To hang pictures, metal plates with loops should be screwed to the frame instead of using screw eyes, except on very small frames.

MOLD AND PEST CONTROL

A major problem in institutions, especially those which are not climate-controlled and which acquire new material, is the control of insects and mold.

Mold will grow at relative humidities above 68 percent, appearing as fluffy white or black patches on paper and leather. If mold growth is not stopped, it can weaken, stain, and eventually destroy paper. Purple-brown staining on paper is often evidence of serious mold growth.

If mold is discovered, survey the collection to see how extensive the infestation is. Remove all affected pieces from storage.

A thymol chamber, a wooden cabinet with shelves for the affected items and light bulbs to volatilize the thymol (the fumigant) is an effective in-house tool to combat mold. A design and description can be found in *Curatorial Care of Works of Art on Paper*, by Anne F. Clapp. It is best used in a well ventilated area. Thymol is a carcinogenic chemical and should be used with caution.

Insects are a more complex problem. A variety of insects attack cellulosic materials, usually leaving a lattice-work pattern of destruction as evidence. Often the insects themselves cannot be detected. If insect damage is discovered, remove all affected items to a remote area away from other materials. In a small institution it is probably wisest to call a professional exterminator. In-house equipment is expensive, and the fumigation gases, which are lethal, have to be safely vented outside the building.

ENCAPSULATION

Encapsulation is a very easy and useful preservation technique. This simple method consists of sandwiching single sheet items between two layers of an inert plastic; one such trade name is Mylar. The two layers of plastic support the item and allow it to be handled, seen from both sides, and easily removed if need be.

The two pieces of plastic are joined on all four sides with double-sided tape. Recently a machine which will secure the plastic ultrasonically has been developed but expense will probably limit its use to large institutions and regional centers. Explicit instructions on how to encapsulate can be obtained from the Preservation Office of the Library of Congress.

Ideally, all paper should be deacidified before encapsulation, as the closed atmosphere in the plastic may tend to increase degradation of an acidic item. However, many small institutions which do not have the capability to deacidify may still find encapsulation useful. Another useful tool is a polyester folder which is taped on two sides; the air can still circulate but the electrostatic charge will hold the item in place. If an item is very rare and valuable, an institution should consider consulting a conservator about deacidification before encapsulation. If a curator has quantities of very fragile but not very valuable materials which are handled by staff or patrons, or will be retained for a limited length of time, encapsulation is probably justified even without deacidification. However, items that are encapsulated without deacidification should be clearly marked as such.

The electrostatic charge of plastics will pull off particles from the paper surface. This means that particulate media, such as charcoals and pastels, should never be encapsulated. In general, works of art on paper should be matted in preference to encapsulation.

MENDING

Mending is one of least complicated conservation procedures and can probably be done in-house on selected items. If an item is very rare or very fragile, it is best to send it to a conservator. This is especially true if the item is a work of art and is torn in the design area, because making an invisible mend requires a great deal of skill and practice. If an institution wants to set up an in-house mending area, it would be wise for one member of the staff to attend one of the many workshops which are now given around the country to learn simple conservation techniques. Once some basic skills are learned, this person should practice on material of no value before attempting to work on something that is rare.

If the item is of archival value, a mend that is reversible can be made without risking damage to the item. Needless to say, no repair should ever be made with commercial adhesives such as Scotch, masking, or wet gummed paper tapes.

The proper adhesive for a mend is a cooked wheat starch paste or methyl cellulose. Wheat starch must be cooked in a double boiler and then strained. It has a short shelf life unless refrigerated, and even then will not last for more than a month. Refrigeration may weaken wheat starch paste. Methyl cellulose is easy to mix and has a long shelf life. *Curatorial Care of Works of Art on Paper*, by Anne Clapp, has formulas for wheat starch paste.

Making the mend is a two-step procedure. First the mend is aligned so that the tear overlaps in the proper way. Unless a tear is made by a scissors, knife, or some other sharp instrument, or is on a very brittle sheet of paper, a tear will have an upper and lower edge. Both edges should be pasted, aligned, and put under a light weight until dry. Then a strip of Japanese paper should be torn about 1/8 " wide and in 1 " lengths. Instead of cutting the strips, take a small brush, dip it in water, and run it along the Japanese paper where you want to tear. Then pull on both sides of the water line. The paper should pull apart, leaving paper fibers hanging out like small feathers. This feathered edge insures a good bond from a small mending strip and also insures that a hard line will not show on the front of the item. Paste the strip and apply it to the tear. Then weight the tear until dry to make sure that it will remain flat.

Acceptable archival heat-set tissues, mending papers with heat activated adhesives, are available. Sheets of heat-set tissue are cut into thin strips and applied to tears with a heated tacking iron. However, some conservators feel that these are not as strong or permanent as pasted strips.

TREATMENTS TO BE UNDERTAKEN AT A CONSERVATION FACILITY

Some treatments should not be undertaken by untrained staff members. Any treatment, no matter how easy it might seem to perform, takes a certain background in order to insure success. This background includes the theory behind how and why a treatment is chosen, how the actual treatment is done, how an item is tested to make sure it can undergo a given treatment, and how to react if something unexpected happens. Insufficient preparation can cause a disaster, and a disaster is usually more costly and time-consuming to rectify than the original problem. In general, untrained persons should avoid any treatments involving the use of water (except, of course, in making paste) and chemicals.

Washing. Washing a paper item, although it sounds as though it might be easy, can often be tricky. All pigments and inks must be tested to make sure they will not run in water. Even the most experienced conservator tests pigments because there is rarely a foolproof case. The washing procedure and subsequent flattening of the item also require care and should not be done by an unskilled person.

Washing can often be of great benefit to paper. It helps remove impurities, often lightens the color of discolored paper, and is usually a first step in the deacidification process.

Deacidification. In many conservation laboratories, deacidification follows washing. Deacidification neutralizes acidic components in paper and deposits alkaline compounds into it, providing an alkaline buffer to counteract acidic build-up in the future. Deacidification has been proven to prolong the life of paper.

There are three basic types of deacidification processes: aqueous, non-aqueous, and vapor phase. Aqueous deacidification involves the immersion of the paper in an aqueous solution or brushing the sheet with an alkaline compound dissolved in water. Non-aqueous, as its name implies, involves immersion, brushing, or spraying of an alkaline compound dissolved in an organic solvent other than water. Vapor phase deacidification involves an alkaline compound in the gas phase, and is of most importance for use on bound volumes which do not have to be unbound to undergo the vapor phase process, and to institutions with very large collections which could never be treated on a one-by-one basis. Vapor phase processes in development will be able to handle large quantities of material, bound or single sheet, at a time. Aqueous deacidification can only be used on items that can stand contact with water. This would rule out many watercolors, ink and wash drawings, gouaches, and items with powdery media such as pastels, charcoals, and pencil drawings. When aqueous deacidification can be used safely, usually with printed items, it is often the process that conservators prefer because initial washing in water aids greatly in removing acidic components from the paper sheet. In addition one is relatively sure of uniform deposition of alkaline salts when the paper sheet is immersed in an aqueous deacidification bath.

Non-aqueous deacidification has several benefits. It can often be used on items that cannot be touched by water, and as organic solvents do not cockle paper nearly to the extent that water does and also evaporate much more quickly, the whole process is much faster. If an item is immersed in a non-aqueous bath, some acidic components will be washed out, although less than in a water bath. If the deacidification solution is brushed or sprayed on, no "washing" effect takes place. Most non-aqueous deacidification solutions contain some toxic components, so all work should be done under a fume hood or in a very well ventilated area.

Vapor phase deacidification offers the hope that one day large quantities of material will be able to be handled relatively inexpensively. As of yet, however, no mass procedure is commercially available.

Bleaching. Bleaching is sometimes a necessary procedure in conservation treatments but should only be carried out on certain items by a conservator. Although washing lessens discoloration of paper, sometimes an item remains badly disfigured even after washing. This is often true of papers that have foxing—brown patches of varying sizes—which is probably caused by the action of mold on iron salts in the paper. Matburn, caused by acidic mats, and staining from acid cardboard or wooden backings, usually cannot be washed out. If these discolorations occur on works of art, bleaching is often the only recourse to restore proper color balance to the paper. On works of archival interest only, such discoloration may be left; stabilization of the paper is usually the important concern.

Bleaching is a very tricky procedure. In addition to the hazard of weakening the paper through improper technique, overbleaching, resulting in stark white paper, is common and all too easy to achieve.

Tape Removal. Tape removal, especially of adhesive and masking tape, should be left to a professional conservator. Organic solvents, all of which are toxic to humans to some degree, are necessary to remove tape and the stains it leaves behind. In inexperienced hands, the tears that tape covers can tear even more seriously and the sticky adhesive residue can spread and become even more firmly entrenched in paper fibers, causing serious problems.

PLANNING A CONSERVATION STRATEGY

Careful and thoughtful planning is a necessary first step toward a successful preservation program. The needs of every institution are unique, as are the resources in terms of personnel and money.

As has been stated earlier, providing a good environment should always be a first step in any preservation program. Equally important is formulating a disaster plan which can be implemented swiftly if a disaster should occur. Even though the chances of a disaster striking an institution are low, quick response is the key to success. Fire and water damage, which almost invariably occurs with fire damage, are the two major hazards faced by most institutions. *Procedures for Salvage of Water-Damaged Library Material*, by Peter Waters, and *Disaster Prevention and Disaster Preparedness*, by Hilda Bohem, are two good books on this topic. Many large libraries now have disaster plans which give specific advice on materials and services available in the area of the given library. Smaller institutions might profitably ask larger libraries to share such information.

Storage, discussed in an earlier section, should be the next priority in a preservation program. In the past, some have felt that it is most important to restore famous items in a collection while letting lesser known, and to some, therefore, less important collections remain in terrible condition. Often this was done because the resources to completely restore a large collection did not exist within a given institution while the money to restore a single glamour item could be more easily raised.

Recently, however, the concept of *phased conservation* has been gaining favor among conservators and curators. Phased conservation means that although complete restoration of a collection might be an ultimate goal, a step-by-step approach, based on resources on hand, is taken. This means that proper housing would come first, followed by simple conservation procedures, followed by more elaborate and complete treatments. A phased approach seems the only sensible one in times of financial limitations.

After proper storage has been provided, obtaining the services of a professional paper conservator, discussed below, is a good step. Establishing a good working relationship with a private conservator or a regional center, usually made up of a large staff of professional conservators, is necessary for an effective use of limited funds for preservation.

Education of staff members and patrons on the preservation world and needs of the institution through books, slide shows, and workshops is an excellent way of heightening awareness of the problems of the institution and benefits to be gained through proper conservation. Creating an enlightened preservation attitude among all users of library, archival, and historical society collections will reap long-lasting benefits.

THE RELATIONSHIP BETWEEN INSTITUTION AND PRIVATE CONSERVATOR

If an institution feels the need for the services of a professional conservator and that one object, a select number of objects, or the whole collection is worthy of particular attention, then such a professional should be consulted. One good way to start is to hire a conservator for a day as a consultant to do a survey of the entire collection, piece by piece if it is small or in a more general way if it is large. A conservator will then write a report on environment, housing, and the condition of individual items. From this overall condition report the curator will better understand what needs to be done. If the curator has already done a survey of the collection and does not feel that another opinion is warranted, such a survey would not be necessary.

Then, if funds permit, the curator can begin to select individual items to be conserved by an appropriate conservator. The conservator is equipped to tell the curator which items need conservation by virtue of their condition. The conservator will not appraise. It is the curator's decision, or a joint decision, as to what items are most important in the collection. Consideration will, of course, include monetary value, but will also cover historical importance, local importance of a collection, and importance by virtue of the completeness of a certain collection.

When a conservator receives an item, he or she will write a condition report, unless this has already been done in an earlier survey, and give an estimate of the cost of treatment. If the curator agrees, the conservator will then proceed, taking photographs before treatment, sometimes during treatment depending on how elaborate the process is, and after treatment. A treatment report will accompany the completed item. This will be a record for the curator and for any future curator, reader, or conservator who wishes to know how the item was treated.

Usually, the conservator will charge for the initial condition report and proposal. This charge is normally deducted from the price if treatment is carried out but must be paid even if it is not. Remember, the report and the testing which it entails are time consuming and require the expertise of a professional.

The institution and the conservator should not only have an understanding as to which objects should be treated, the price of treatment, and what will be done during treatment, but also what the possible outcome of the treatment will be. This means that not all items will come out looking new. Old items look old and should look old.

The curator must decide what type of information he wants to preserve. For many manuscripts and printed items it is the intellectual information. Therefore, the conservator should stabilize the item so no more damage can take place. Replacing lost words, lines, and color would not be appropriate. But if the value is aesthetic, and this is usually the case with works of art on paper, not only stabilization but also replacement of missing areas would be a valid consideration.

The better the curator understands the collection, the easier the relationship with the conservator will be. The conservator can tell what is possible and desirable from the point of view of condition but the curator must know the importance of the item in the collection to be able to respond effectively.

BASIC STORAGE AND HANDLING TECHNIQUES

Broadsides, printed maps, and single leaf book remains. Printed items, without printed or hand applied color, are limited to two variables in their construction: the paper support layer and the ink media layer. The date of manufacture and previous storage conditions will usually determine the condition of the item. Rag papers made prior to 1866 will usually be in relatively good condition, although exceptions will be found, especially among papers containing alum and those which have been improperly stored. The condition of post-1866 papers will depend upon their fiber content and other additives, as described in the section on paper history and paper quality. Printing ink is usually of good quality; it is more stable than the paper is and does not present great preservation problems.

Items printed in color or with handcolored additions are more fragile. Some colors are more light-fast than others; all exposure is detrimental in some measure. Storage of this class of materials depends upon size and how the materials are catalogued within a collection. If an item can fit into a legal- or letter-size folder without being folded, it can be easily stored that way and put in an acid-free manuscript box. Oversize items can be put in handmade acid-free folders cut to fit the item and placed in map cases or on broad shelves.

If single leaf items are to be stored upright on bookshelves, they must be adequately supported. A stiff acid-free folder with flaps inside to protect the contents from dust should be used. The folder should tie or fasten at the fore-edge (Velcro tabs are often used). Such folders can be purchased commercially or made in-house.

Newspapers. Storage and preservation of large quantities of newsprint is a problem. For small clippings and important sheets deacidification and encapsulation is a particularly good technique. However, this would be expensive and time-consuming for long runs of newspapers. Copying, usually onto microfilm, and restricted use of originals is usually the best approach.

Posters. Posters should be stored flat in map cases whenever possible. Rolling posters will introduce a permanent curl into the paper and also invites injury if the roll is flattened accidently. Encapsulation is a good way of storing and allows for easy handling. Very rare posters can be matted and exhibited in the same manner as works of art on paper. Fragile or damaged posters can be reinforced by lining with Japanese paper, a procedure to be done by a conservator.

Manuscripts. Manuscripts, including typescripts, can include a variety of media. Inks, typewriter inks, and pencil are the most common, although more exotic media will be encountered. As with printed items, the quality and condition of the paper will usually determine the overall condition. Most writing inks have proven to be stable. One exception is iron gall ink, a brown-black ink made from gall nuts, which seriously deteriorates paper, often eating all the way through a sheet.

Storage of manuscripts is best accomplished by inserting individual items in acid-free manuscript boxes. Oversize manuscripts should be stored in large folders and placed flat on wide shelves or in map cases.

Stamps and ephemera. Stamps should be stored in acid-free glassine envelopes. If they are found glued to envelopes or postcards, it is best to leave them that way rather than trying to remove them. Ephemera can be matted, if sufficiently valuable or interesting, or stored in acid-free envelopes or folders. If ephemera have gummed backs, store them in glassine folders as you would stamps. Until recently, most glassine envelopes were made of highly acidic paper. Collections should be removed from such envelopes and stored in acid-free ones.

WORKS OF ART ON PAPER

Prints. This category of artwork includes intaglio prints (engravings, mezzotints, etchings, drypoints, aquatints), and planographic prints (woodcuts, monotypes, lithographs). Unlike a manuscript or book where the text is the most important consideration and condition somewhat secondary, works of art are valued according to their condition. Therefore, utmost care in handling and storage of works of art is paramount. Do not touch the surface of a print or drawing, let anything drag across it, or stack one upon another.

Matting is the best protection for works of art on paper. The window mat provides space between the glass and the artwork; the back of the mat provides support for the item. Groups of mats which are not stored in frames should be placed in Solander boxes or acid-free boxes that are the same size as the mats. For extra protection, a piece of polyester or acid-free glassine can be placed under the window mat and over the work of art to help prevent dirt from settling on the image.

Watercolors, charcoals, pastels, and pencil drawings. Watercolors are very fragile because watercolor pigments are often highly fugitive. Exhibition of watercolors should be kept to a minimum, behind UF-3 Plexiglas, and under dim lights. Charcoal, pastels, and pencil drawings are equally fragile because the media layer is held very loosely to the paper. Charcoals, pastels, and pencil drawings should not be exhibited behind Plexiglas or stored with a polyester sheet over them; the electrostatic charge of the plastics will pull particles off the paper. These works of art should be matted and stored in boxes as described with prints.

SUGGESTED READING

Bohem, Hilda. *Disaster Prevention and Disaster Preparedness.* Berkeley: University of California, 1978.

An outline for a disaster preparedness plan with a disaster prevention checklist and sources of assistance.

Clapp, Anne F. *Curatorial Care of Works of Art on Paper.* 4th ed. Oberlin: Intermuseum Conservation Association, 1980.

A discussion of curatorial problems and procedures for handling works of art on paper.

Dolloff, Francis W., and Roy L. Perkinson. *How to Care for Works of Art on Paper.* Boston: Museum of Fine Arts, 1971.

A short history of paper with discussion of preservation and of the factors that cause deterioration.

Duckett, Kenneth W. *Modern Manuscripts: A Practical Manual for their Manage-*

ment, Care and Use. Nashville: American Association for State and Local History, 1975.

A basic manual for archivists, with a chapter devoted to the care and repair of manuscripts.

Hunter, Dard. *Papermaking: The History and Technique of an Ancient Craft.* New York: Dover, 1978.

The basic history of papermaking. Reprint of the 1943 edition.

Ivins, William Mills. *How Prints Look.* New York: Metropolitan Museum of Art, 1943; Boston: Beacon, 1958.

An introduction to the appearance of prints.

Library of Congress. Preservation Office. *Polyester Film Encapsulation.* Washington, D.C.: 1980.

A twenty-three page instruction manual.

S. D. Warren Company. *Paper Permanence: Preserving the Written Word.* Boston: S. D. Warren Co., 1981.

An illustrated history of paper manufacture and a discussion of the problems of producing permanent durable paper.

Smith, Merrily A., and Margaret R. Brown. *Matting and Hinging of Works of Art on Paper.* Washington, D.C.: Library of Congress, 1981.

A comprehensive set of instructions for conservation work.

Waters, Peter. *Procedures for Salvage of Water-Damaged Library Materials.* 2nd ed. Washington, D.C.: Library of Congress, 1978.

The basic instruction booklet. This belongs in the library and as an integral part of the library's disaster plan.

Zigrosser, Carl, and Christa M. Gaehde. *A Guide to the Collecting and Care of Original Prints.* New York: Crown, 1965.

Describes print techniques and curatorial considerations. Chapter 7 by Gaehde outlines in detail how to conserve fine prints.

3

Books and Bindings

ANGELA FITZGERALD

The book is a multipurpose object: its presence has become so familiar to us that it is taken for granted today. However, it is only within the past hundred years that books have become such commonplace objects. Before the industrial revolution, books were produced for the moneyed, cultured, and religious elite. It was almost four hundred years from the time that movable type was developed until the book became a commonplace object. The more abundant books are, the more frequently they are used; the more profound their impact, the more invisible they become. A book can serve as an object of commerce, an instrument of social change, an article of practical use, a work of art, or an instrument of faith. The ubiquitous presence of books is an integral part of the communications revolution, a causative factor in the shaping of twentieth century life.

Today we are faced with great numbers and varieties of books in various states of repair. In order to appreciate the variety that makes generalized solutions unwise, one should be familiar with the history of book production and the materials and structures that make the physical object.

HISTORY OF BOOKS AND BINDING

Books as convenient gatherings of related material physically held together have been with us for more than two thousand years and have had protective coverings for almost as long. The earliest materials for the recording of human affairs were clay tablets and papyrus scrolls. The King of Nineveh's library of clay tablets is believed to date from about 700 B.C. It had a librarian, a system of classification, and a shelving plan. The library was part of the King's palace and appears to have been guarded by a god.

Vellum and papyrus scrolls were the common form of the book until a series of brilliant breakthroughs by ingenious anonymous craftspersons gave us the book as we know it today. Papyrus, from which the word paper is derived, is a giant reed which was split, flattened, and formed into sheets similar to paper. By the fall of Rome, circa 385 A.D., vellum, or the less elegant parchment, had become more common writing materials. The codex, originally wax-covered wooden or ivory tablets joined together, developed into a collection of manuscript sheets of papyrus or vellum, later paper, held together by sewing or gluing and placed between boards. The codex format of the book remains the most suitable for reading. The precise date that the codex came into popular use is unknown, but by 500 A.D. codex volumes were routinely produced in the Near East.

Outside the Mediterranean area the book developed differently. The Saxons wrote runes on slabs of beech wood. The word *book* derives from the Anglo-Saxon word for beech, *boc*. In Central America, the Aztecs developed their own form of the codex. In the Far East, printing and binding of books developed earlier, independently from the Middle East, but similar in appearance to the codex in the West.

The basic characteristics of the book have remained unchanged from the fifth century to the present day. To put a book together, sheets are folded to make a gathering, or signature, and are then sewn through the center of the fold. The thread passes around central cords which hold the various signatures together. The spine, the back of the text block, is glued, then the cover, or boards, are attached. The great advantage of the codex is that, unlike a scroll, it can be easily consulted at any place from front to back, and is portable.

Each country has developed its own style of binding; the evolution of a national taste in the general society influenced book production as well. The type of book produced and the uses to which it was put also changed its appearance, as did outside influences, such as the arrival of Netherlandish binders in England in the late fifteenth century. The recognition of various bookbinding techniques and styles is a specialty in itself, which requires the study of the elements of design, structure, and materials. Several of the references given at the end of this chapter explore this field. Over the centuries, as the book evolved into its current form, there have been many changes and improvements in its structure and decoration, and in the speed and method of its production. However, the basic form of sheets bound together between protective covers remains unchanged.

The Copts in Egypt were probably the first to cover books with leather. The earliest known bindings, on the Nag Hammadi codices, date from the fourth century A.D. Islamic binding practices, including decoration with gold and mosaics of colored leather, became highly developed and spread to Europe by the seventh century. The Islamic style was adapted to the tastes of book owners and to the abilities of the bookbinders.

Books were individually written and illustrated by hand until the fifteenth century. The development of wood block printing was contemporary with the development of printing with movable types, and grew from the same social conditions. By 1456 the printing press with its metal cast movable type enabled books to be "mass produced." The books printed before 1500 are called *incunables* or *incunabula*, terms derived from the Latin word for cradle, for these are the products of the infancy of printing. While manuscript production in workshops continued until the early sixteenth century, by the year 1500 the Western cultural explosion was under way and printing presses appeared in every major city on the Continent and in Great Britain. Printing reached the New World by 1535, when a European-style printing press was established in Mexico. Bookmaking and printing did not begin in the United States until the 1630s, and followed contemporary European trends toward mechanization.

BOOKMAKING FROM 1500 TO THE PRESENT

Innovative changes in book binding, printing, and the distribution of books generally occurred first on the Continent and spread to Great Britain; in their British form they influenced North American book production. The period of British domination of American book production lasted until the late nineteenth century when technological innovations in the United States put America ahead in the field.

From the fifteenth to the eighteenth century, the printed book was offered to the public in various forms and prices. Plain calf or sheep were the most popular leathers for binding but, unfortunately, time has proven them not as durable in most cases as the more expensive goatskin, vellum, or tanned pigskin. Spines of books were rarely lettered until the sixteenth century. Until the early nineteenth century, readers purchased their books unbound with plain paper wrappers to protect them. The text was held together with a simple stab sewing. The owner of the book then had it bound to his or her own specifications. The binding put on a book at the time of its publication, whether by the printer or for the owner, is called a contemporary binding since it is contemporary with book's publication. However, documents proving when, where, and by whom a binding was executed rarely exist for the majority of books produced in this period.

The nineteenth century was a period of rapid technological advances in many industries, including book production. The impetus for these advances is apparent—the greatly increased population and the beneficial effects of popular education had created a reading public whose appetite for books could not be satisfied by existing methods of production. Mechanical production was the only possible response to the need for greater quantity, speed, and economy. This was an era that saw the rise of the great publishing houses and, with the invention of the steam-powered press in 1815, the creation of a new industry.

Paper production methods were also revolutionized to meet the voracious demand, as has been discussed in the previous chapter. Unfortunately, the mass produced short-fibered ground wood pulp papers used in the contemporary production of books have embrittled rapidly, giving us a preservation problem of massive proportions.

Binding methods were mechanized to keep up with the printers' output and the public's demand. The nineteenth century marked the advent of cloth covered case-bound edition bindings, or publisher's bindings. Cloth was first used as an inexpensive binding material in England about 1825, and its use spread rapidly to the United States. Case binding, a binding made separately from the content of the book and then attached, replaced the slower method of lacing on the boards. By the end of the century, each step of the bookbinding process had been successfully mechanized and binders became technicians rather than craftspeople.

The inherent weaknesses in early mechanized methods of binding and paper production have taught us through experience the principles of sound book construction and paper manufacture. Today the modern book manufacturer cannot plead ignorance as an excuse for producing a poor quality book. Books can be mass produced today to equal all but the best handmade and hand-bound volumes and this can be done at a reasonable cost. Public demand for good quality books can lead to the improvement of their structure.

Adhesive bindings, also known as perfect bindings, began to be used about 1900. In this method of binding, the pages are not sewn together; the single sheets are held together with adhesive alone, which is placed along the back edge of the text. Although adhesive binding is widely used today, it has generally been an unsatisfactory method of binding a book together and the technique is in disrepute among readers, librarians, and authors. However, adhesive binding can be done well, by hand or machine. Book producers assure us that the technology exists to make adhesive binding perfectly acceptable for circulating books. The correct method requires roughing the back of the text after it has been trimmed and fanning the sheets while applying a cold glue which dries quickly and remains flexible. Adhesive bindings should not be rejected out of hand. Like anything else, this technique can be done either poorly or well.

A new advance in automated bookbinding, electronically welding together the back edges of specially made paper, presents the possibility of developing into a superior method of construction. However, no machine binding can, at this point, approach the permanence and flexibility of a well-made hand binding. This remains the best choice of binding for rare and invaluable books.

The great increase in the popularity of paperback books is a recent phenomenon which has developed since World War II. Precursors exist; paper covered books date back to the earliest period of book publication. The nineteenth century series of inexpensive popular reprints known as "yellow backs," published in England and sold in railway stations, is an early example. However, the production of huge runs of books with mass appeal in low-cost editions, with a paper cover adhered to the text, is a new development, dominated by the United States publishing industry.

In 1935 a group of commercial binders specializing in the binding of periodicals and the rebinding of worn library books formed a trade association, the Library Binding Institute (LBI), to develop standards, to guarantee quality, and to protect the interests of libraries, their principal customers. The LBI claims that books bound according to their standards can be expected to last through a hundred circulations. Library binding is appropriate in circulating collections where it is expected that books will be discarded when worn. A book that will remain a part of the library's permanent collection, one that cannot readily be replaced, should be restricted in use and should not circulate. Standard library bindings are inappropriate for such material.

Librarians who are responsible for circulating collections should have the LBI's useful and clearly written *Library Binding Manual* (Boston: 1972) and a copy of the LBI's *Standards* (1981). Binding done at a certified library bindery is guaranteed to meet LBI standards. Books given a library binding by a nonmember firm may be sent to the LBI's Book Testing Laboratory at the Rochester Institute of Technology, Rochester, N.Y., for a free examination. The laboratory tests materials and new methods of bookbinding. "Usability" is their catch-word and standards are designed with the number of circulations in mind. However, the LBI's standards may not be the most appropriate for a research or special collection. The librarian should work closely with the library binder to develop specifications for the library's collections. A number of new binding techniques that do not meet the strength-oriented LBI standards may prove far more appropriate and less costly than following a standard which was designed to be general in scope.

At present there are four main categories of bound books of concern to librarians. They are: (1) edition bindings, which are also called trade or publisher's bindings and are the standard commercial product found in bookstores everywhere. An edition binding is machine-made, usually with a glossy dust jacket, and it is not made for durability. It is put together in a variety of ways, with materials and structures chosen for economy or suitability for production needs. (2) Library bindings, which were discussed above. (3) Hand bindings, which are often unique artistic productions by designer-binders. They are frequently costly, and the level of craftsmanship varies. (4) Conservation bindings, a relatively new category, in which books are carefully bound or rebound for permanence and durability, often with some consideration for the book's artifactual value. Within each of these categories there is a wide array of types, making generalizations difficult. This chapter attempts to give a useful outline of a complex field; librarians may then be able to recognize general categories of books and bindings and to research further according to their specific needs.

Computer assisted book production is so new that its effect and applications are as yet unclear. Since 1965, printers, paper manufacturers, and edition binders have begun using computers to monitor various phases of their operations. Doubtless computers will be used more and more widely to further increase speed and efficiency in book production. Computers are causing a revolution, one that can result in a product of higher quality, if developed correctly.

The twentieth century has seen the rise of a widespread and effective concern for conservation. Within the past decade the preservation specialist has arrived on the library scene, with a professional approach to the prevention of deterioration of materials in library collections. Some of the conclusions of these specialists are presented in the discussion on the physical nature of the book that follows.

MATERIALS AND STRUCTURE

The causes of deterioration in books lie in the nature of the materials of manufacture, the structure of the book, and the environment in which it is housed. Obviously, with time all things decay, but understanding what hastens deterioration enables us to prolong the useful life of a book. The function of the structures and materials used to bind a book is to protect, preserve, and support the written material within. They must also allow the book to be opened and read. The life of a book depends upon the mechanics of its construction and the physical and chemical nature of the materials used to make it.

PAPER

Paper is the major component of the book. The causes of paper deterioration are covered in the preceding chapter and will be discussed here as they relate to the book and its binding.

Brittleness is the most common problem in book conservation. The presence of acid in the paper greatly accelerates the molecular disintegration of the cellulose, reducing the life of a sheet of paper from many centuries, as we see in existing incunabula, to only twenty years in some currently produced books. Brittle paper breaks or crumbles even when it is handled delicately. It is often dull yellow and gives off a nose-prickling acrid odor. It can be identified by bending a corner of a page several times. If the corner breaks off, the paper is too brittle to be commercially rebound. Paper pro-

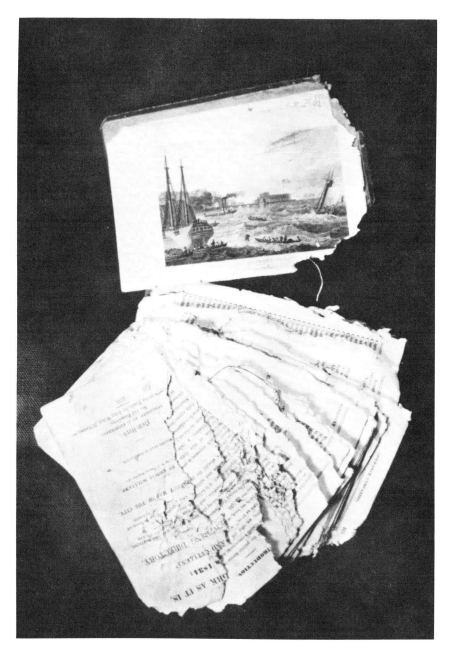

Figure 3.1. Deteriorated Book. Photograph courtesy of Gay Walker.

duced since the 1860s is notorious for its brittleness. A page of extremely brittle paper no longer functions as it normally would as part of the book. A brittle page often breaks in several places at once. Brittle pages are most frequently found at the beginning and end of a book.

In some cases the deterioration is limited to the edges of the page, while the text-bearing portion is still relatively firm and flexible. This is caused by airborne gases and particulate matter that affect the exposed edges. At this point the book still may be rebound. The disintegration of the page can be considerably retarded if the cause of the problem is removed by improving the storage conditions.

Often the end sheets of a book are of a paper more acid than the text. Thus, the first and last pages of the book will become quite brittle while the center remains in good condition. It is tragic when this has occurred during the "restoration" of a rare or valuable book, when irreplaceable frontispieces, title pages, and colophons become brittle, discolored, and broken due to the poor quality of the endpapers and/or binding placed upon the book with the hope of protecting it. During wartime, paper was in short supply and manufacturers used paper from a number of lots, producing books that contain some sections that are more acid than others.

LEATHER

Due to its flexibility, durability, and availability, leather was the most widely used material for the covering of books until the mid-1800s. Leather lends itself well to decoration in gold and to attractive blind-stamped patterns. The early methods of tanning leather frequently produced a product resistant to decay. These bindings have endured, while poorly tanned leathers have rotted away. The more efficient methods for tanning leather, which began to be used as early as the seventeenth century, held within them the seeds of rapid decay that resulted in split joints, loose backs, and powdery leather covers.

Many of the books produced during the great book deluge which began in the nineteenth century are bound in crumbling, deteriorated, useless leather bindings. Leather in this condition provides no support or protection for the book; it contaminates any other book it touches; it stings the hands when touched and can cause skin rashes; it can neither be repaired nor restored. Such books are omnipresent in library collections today. Their rapid deterioration is apparently caused by chemicals in the leather and in the air which trigger a series of reactions that are not clearly understood. Oiling such a book will only blacken the powdery leather and mingle grease with the leather dust. Leather specialists have no solution for its repair; it is beyond help.

Physical weakness in the leather can also lead to breakage and the loss of support. Leather can break because it is too dry, of poor quality, or so thin that it has no strength. The librarian with a collection of leather-bound volumes will need to turn to the conservator for assistance in determining the types of leathers present in the collection. The conservator will choose the appropriate procedures for the preservation of the books within the collection.

VELLUM AND PARCHMENT

Skins of vellum or parchment are prepared today as they were in early times; the skin is degreased and treated with lime, but it is not tanned. Vellum is made from calf skin and parchment from sheep skin, although the terms are often used interchangeably. Both vellum and parchment are extremely durable and may be the longest-lasting protective coverings available for binding. However, they absorb moisture easily and must be stored under conditions of rigorous humidity control. They are not widely used today and few binders know how to work with them, but they are very handsome and strong.

ALUM-TAWED SKIN

Alum-tawed pigskin is competitive in price with leather and vellum and may be a better choice of book covering, since tawing is an alkaline process and leather is acidic. Therefore, when neutralized, pigskin will gain a longer life. Oiling will darken the light color of alum-tawed skin, but the increased flexibility may be more important than maintaining the original color.

BOOK CLOTH

About 1820 a cloth suitable for bookbinding was manufactured in England. It rapidly replaced leather as the major covering material for books. Cloth had two irresistible advantages over leather: its low cost pleased both the manufacturer and book buyer, and it could be produced uniformly in large quantities and handled in a roll of several hundred yards. This made large-scale case binding a reality. Since leather skins vary in size, shape, and thickness, and are only a few feet long, leather could not be adapted to high-speed mechanical processes. Today the market is dominated by cloth covers. Only luxury productions and extremely valuable books are covered in leather today.

Book covers are woven fabrics, usually cotton. Their various names refer to the weave or finish of the book cloth, not to a different fiber composition. Thus, "linen" often has a linen look; "buckram" is a heavier, stronger weight of cloth. All cloths are impregnated with a filler to stiffen them. Starch, used as a filler for a hundred years, gives an attractive feel and appearance but is easily damaged by water and can attract mold, mildew, and insects. The fillers most commonly used today are plastics, pyroxylin or vinyl, which will withstand wiping with a damp cloth. Today pyroxylin is the preferred filler for books in circulating library collections.

Pyroxylin coatings have been challenged by the Environmental Protection Agency (EPA) for generating an unacceptable level of toxicity during manufacture. Vinyl coatings are so far an unacceptable substitute. When they are shelved next to a pyroxylin coated book the plasticizers in the vinyl will migrate to the pyroxylin, causing it to become sticky. Nontoxic acrylic coatings are being developed that appear to be tough, flexible, and visually indistinguishable from pyroxylin-coated cloths. Poly-cotton book cloths which are light but tough are being developed.

All book cloths are produced in grades from F, which is the highest and strongest grade as well as the most expensive, down to A. Librarians can turn to the *Library Binding Manual* and the library binder for guidance in selecting appropriate book cloths; all books do not require grade F covering. The National Association of State Textbook Administrators (NASTA) has also prepared specifications, *Manufacturing Standards and Specifications*, 1976, which are available from the Book Manufacturers Institute, Stamford, Conn. They are usually referred to as the BMI specifications. The Library Binding Institute will accept nothing below grade F, while NASTA requires at minimum a grade C plastic-impregnated cloth. Any bindery will supply swatch books of sample book cloths in the various grades they use. This book is bound in pyroxylin-impregnated grade C cloth. Some book cloths are plastic-coated instead of being sized or impregnated. These are unacceptable, as the coating quickly cracks and peels. They deteriorate rapidly, becoming soft and sticky.

Nonwoven binding materials began to appear on the market in 1965. They are usually made of vinyl-impregnated paper. Because they are cheaper to produce than cloth, they will doubtless find a growing market as product improvements are made. They cannot be recommended for library use until time has shown how they will age.

SIZE

Size is a dilute adhesive material added to paper by the paper manufacturer to fill the pores and to make it suitable for writing, drawing, and printing. Until recently glue or gelatin were most commonly used for sizing. Today paper manufacturers use clay fillers and alum rosin size, while conservators prefer vegetable-based size.

BOARD

Board is the general name for the stiff support used under the covering material on the sides of the book. Boards have been made of wood, pulped rope, straw, paper, and sheets of paper pasted together to make a board of the required thickness and rigidity for the job at hand. Their durability and degree of acidity vary. Very dense, acid-free board suitable for binding of the finest quality is available commercially. The thickness and denseness of the boards must be determined for each book, depending upon its size and weight, how it will be used, and its value. The boards on this book, for example, are 88-point genuine binder's boards. Usually book board thickness is between seventy and ninety points; a point is equivalent to one-thousandth of an inch.

Until about 1500 books were normally covered with wooden boards, usually oak. However, such boards provide too heavy a covering for an object that is meant to be portable, thus pasteboard boards became more practical. Pasteboards were common in Near Eastern book production for several centuries and were not uncommon in the Middle Ages in Europe, where they were frequently made from bits and pieces of older manuscripts of vellum and parchment.

Pasteboards are made by pasting together several sheets of paper to form a firm "board" suitable for binding. In general, pasteboard covers last until the covering material wears off, usually at the corners (the dog-eared volume), when lumps of board start to disintegrate. The layers of poor quality board come apart easily, especially when the book is kept in a damp environment. Generally, the materials are of an inferior quality, with destructive effects on both the covering material and the endpapers.

A better grade of board, called millboard or binder's board, is made much like paper, in a solid sheet of wet fibers. Until World War II, rope millboard was available and was very tough. Today's binder's board is dense and strong. It is more expensive than pasteboard but it is the best material for the covering of books. Its use is required in the Library Binding Institute's *Standards*. Millboard can be made acid-free.

Chipboard is a flimsy material made from straw or paper shavings. It is too weak and unstable to serve as a satisfactory supporting material. However, because it is inexpensive, it is still used occasionally.

ADHESIVES

There are three main classes of adhesives that are of concern to librarians: paste, glue, and synthetic polymer. Each has different characteristics, making one more desirable for a particular application than another. Each adhesive exerts a different contractile force as it dries. The adhesive is an important element of a book's structure. A strong adhesive, or a thick layer of adhesive, can break fragile material at the adhesive's edge. The adhesive which fails no longer holds the book together. A perfect-bound book begins to lose pages; a case-bound book will fall out of its case; glued sections will begin to fall away from each other, straining the sewing.

Many different types of adhesives are available today. Their qualities differ widely, depending upon their chemical composition; consistency at application; the temperature; the nature of the surface to which they are applied; which additives, such as fillers, starches, and fungal inhibitors, are used; and whether one adhesive is used alone or in combination with another.

An adhesive must penetrate both of the surfaces that are to be stuck together and last as long as needed without straining or embrittling the materials that come into contact with it. An adhesive used upon an object of permanent value must be reversible; that is, it must be removable at any point in the future without damaging the object. Accelerated aging tests, which are undertaken by conservation scientists to determine the long-range behavior of adhesives and their safety for conservation use, can be misleading. Heat can significantly alter the chain reaction of decay from that which naturally takes place over time. Use of adhesives on valued objects must be left to a skilled professional binder/conservator.

All pastes are made from vegetable materials and are reversible. Traditionally, pastes are made from wheat or rice flours, which are cooked in water to produce a sticky colloid. Wheat or rice starches are purer, whiter, more finely milled substances and thus they are used more frequently for conservation purposes than flour paste. Both flour and starch pastes are nutrients for insects, molds, and rodents. Normally they contain a wide variety of additives.

Methyl cellulose, a purified plant carbohydrate with the nutrients removed, is powdery when dry and clear when it is mixed with water. It can be stored for long periods. It is an ideal adhesive for certain minor repairs in a library once a staff member has been taught how to use it. However, it can become brittle if it is applied too thickly or if the drying is not carried out under enough pressure.

All glues are made from animal products. The best are made from animal hides; bone glue is an inferior product because it breaks down very quickly. Gelatin is the main ingredient in glue. It becomes very hard when it is dry, is a nutrient for insects, and fails over time. Flexible glue has linseed oil or glycerine added to it in a not very successful attempt to retain its flexibility. Isinglass is a glue extracted from fish bladders and it decays rapidly.

Modern book producers often use the term *glue* to refer to the adhesive that affixes the cover material to the boards of the book and *flexible glue* to describe the adhesive used in backing (gluing-up) and in perfect bindings. These adhesives are usually made of synthetic polymers with additives. Synthetic polymers are white when liquid and semi-transparent when dry. The most widely used in binding is polyvinyl acetate, or PVA. It is available under trade names such as Elmer's, Sobo, and Velverette. Jade 407 and Elrace 1874 are safer adhesives for conservation purposes. While Elmer's and Velverette get stiff, the others seem to keep their rubbery nature indefinitely. None attracts insects or mold. Their misapplication has given them an undeserved notoriety. They cannot be removed after they have dried unless they are immersed in water for twenty-four hours, a treatment that few books can tolerate. Even this does not always work. PVA changes as it ages in ways that are not completely understood. It, too, can be difficult to remove. Recently applied PVA can sometimes be removed with ethyl alcohol and water or other chemical solvents.

The synthetic polymers are widely used in modern book production and are generally referred to as hot melts, resins, or plastic glues. Additives are normally found in these adhesives. Book manufacturers believe that they now have developed adhesives that are fluid enough to penetrate the paper fibers, dry fast enough to match the speed of their machines, are very strong, remain flexible when dry, and last three years on the average. They may be correct, but we must wait to be certain. It is too early to recommend any adhesive by name. Librarians and conservators need to discuss quality with book manufacturers and establish appropriate standards.

BOOK STRUCTURE

A book is a complex three-dimensional structure made from a dozen or more different materials, each of which is often chosen individually for each book. In addition, each part of the book's structure is multipurpose. For example, each page has several functions. As a single sheet, it is the medium upon which the text is printed. If pages are missing, out of sequence, or deteriorating, it is difficult to use the book. As a unit in a multi-unit structure, each page supports the page on either side as the leaves are turned. The page flexes when any part of the book is read; when the book is closed it returns to its original position so that the book can be read again. This seems simple, but failure to perform any of these functions can lead to structural failure of the whole. When any structure fails, the book begins to come apart and becomes unreadable.

The materials of any structural element also affect performance. Structure and materials must be considered together, but for clarity they have been presented separately in this section. The materials and structure combine to protect a book effectively and attractively and to maintain its use and value, whether as a circulating volume or as an artifact.

When a binding fails, the covers of the book come off or the pages fall out. The book cannot be repaired by sticking the pages back into the binding again, for the structural design of the book is unsatisfactory. In order to understand how the structure of a book can fail, it is necessary to have some understanding of how a book is constructed. There are many ways of putting a book together by hand or machine. Some are old, some new, and some experimental. Each has advantages and disadvantages, depending upon size, the number and the weight of the pages, and the intended use. To repair a book it is necessary to recognize how the book was assembled and to evaluate whether the breakage was caused by faulty structure or deteriorated materials.

The pages in a book are not single leaves placed in a binding, but are parts of signatures, a gathering of folded sheets that make up a section of a book. The book is printed in large, flat sheets and each sheet is folded to make a signature. A folio volume is one that consists of sections of four pages each; each sheet has been folded once. In a quarto volume, the sheets have been folded twice; in an octavo volume, they have been folded three times (see Figures 3.2, 3.3, and 3.4). Modern books are printed on large sheets of paper with sections of thirty-two or more pages per sheet.

SEWING TECHNIQUES

The leaves of the signatures are held together by sewing through the folds on the inner margin, or gutter, of the book. The signatures are attached one to another in commercial binding by linking chain stitching on the outside of the folds. If bound by hand, the signatures are held to each other by cords or linen tapes, around which the sewing passes. The cords or bands create the raised bands on the back of the text block (see Figure 3.5). Sometimes raised bands are created for a deluxe effect. The ridges are formed by sticking strips of leather or twine under the covering material. This is called "false raised bands" since the ridges are not an integral part of the structure of the book.

The cords can be sunk into recessed grooves cut into the back of the book, a style known as "sawn-in." This gives the spine a smooth surface and allows the thread to lie straight. Sawn-in books have a reputation for falling apart, but this is due to poor execution of the binding rather than to any inherent unsoundness in the technique. If the grooves are kept shallow, it can be the ideal sewing for a particular book. On books with stiff paper or thick signatures, it is not appropriate; these books will fall apart.

Each section is sewn together "all-along" or "two-on." When sewing two-on, two sections are sewn at the same time, with the thread alternating between one section and the other. Thus there is one-half as much thread in each section. Sewing all-along means that the thread passes all along the length of the section, passing around the cords or tapes.

Overcasting, or oversewing, is a technique with a deservedly poor reputation, but oversewing by hand may be effective in certain situations. It is a technique for holding single sheets together. Overcast sewing was often used from the mid-nineteenth to the mid-twentieth century to strengthen end-sheets. It is not satisfactory, for when the book is opened its pages will strain against the sewing and break where they are stressed, especially if the pages are thick or brittle.

Books that are manufactured today are sewn by machine, not by hand. The thread is stitched by machine through the fold or gutter of each section and passed through the other stitches on the spine to join the sections to one another. Machine sewing is usually done with cotton or nylon thread which should last the life of the volume in a circulating collection.

ROUNDING AND BACKING AND LINING-UP

After it has been sewn, the book is thicker at the back than at the fore-edge, due to the addition of the thread. This extra thickness is called swelling and enables the book to be rounded. The amount of swell must be neither too great nor too small or rounding and backing will be unsuccessful; an improperly rounded and backed book will collapse unless other experimental methods of hand binding are employed. The binder must calculate the thickness of the sewing thread used so that it matches the strength of the pages and the amount of swell that is necessary. Unbleached linen thread is the most suitable for hand sewing.

After it is sewn, the book is given a coat of adhesive, which holds the sections to each other and allows the book to be shaped. This is known as "gluing-up." The back is rounded by hand or machine so that it assumes its familiar half-moon shape and the fore-edge becomes concave. The adhesive is tacky and the sections slide past each other as the rounding is done. When the glue sets, the sections hold this position. An unrounded book soon becomes concave at the back and this strains the hinges and the sewing.

Backing forms ridges or shoulders at the edge of the back. The height of the ridge must exactly match the thickness of the boards, which in turn is determined by the book's size and weight. The shoulders form the lip, which locks the shaped spine into position against the boards. They return the back to its rounded form after each use, which helps the book keep its shape.

At this point the back is "lined-up" by gluing one or several layers of reinforcing material to it. This additional support enables the book to arch upward in a half-moon shape and open freely. It also transfers stress from the point of opening across the entire back of the book. If too many layers are added to the back, the book will not open well; its pages will arch up stiffly and will not lie open properly. Too few layers will not support the book back; it will crack and lose its pages. If poor quality material is used for lining-up, it will accelerate the deterioration of any materials that come into contact with it.

The processes of rounding, backing, and lining-up form the essential structure of the text block. The rounded shape of the spine supported by the

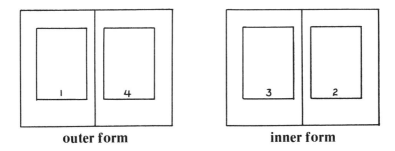

outer form   **inner form**

Figure 3.2. Imposition of Type Pages for a Sheet in Folio. Diagram by Henry Cioch. Redrawn from Ronald B. McKerrow, *An Introduction to Bibliography for Literary Students* (Oxford: Oxford University Press, 1927).

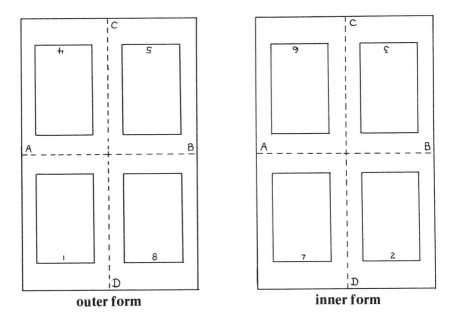

outer form   **inner form**

Figure 3.3. Imposition of Type Pages for a Sheet in Quarto. Diagram by Henry Cioch. Redrawn from Ronald B. McKerrow, *An Introduction to Bibliography for Literary Students* (Oxford: Oxford University Press, 1927).

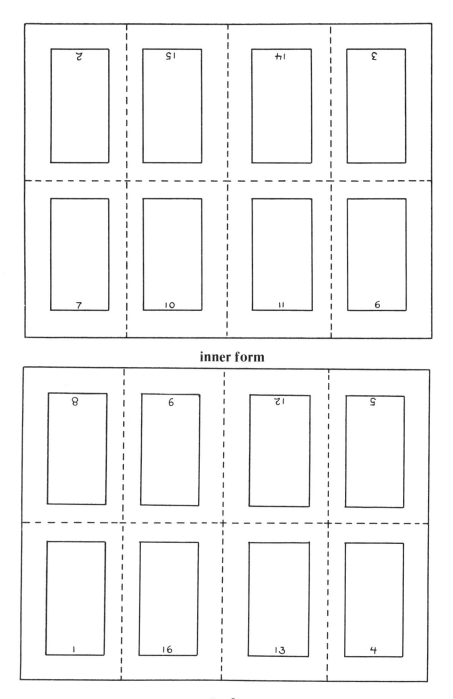

inner form

outer form

Figure 3.4. Imposition of Type Pages for a Sheet in Octavo. Diagram by Henry Cioch. Redrawn from Ronald B. McKerrow, *An Introduction to Bibliography for Literary Students* (Oxford: Oxford University Press, 1927).

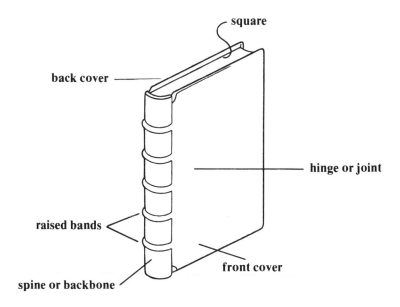

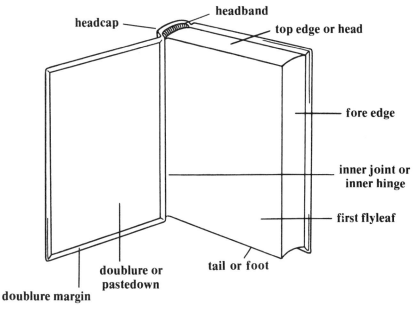

Figure 3.5. The Anatomy of the Book. Diagram by Henry Cioch. Redrawn from Ronald B. McKerrow, *An Introduction to Bibliography for Literary Students* (Oxford: Oxford University Press, 1927).

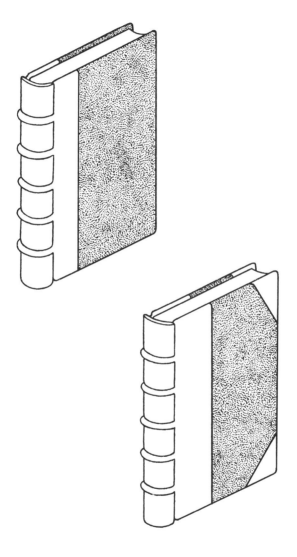

Figure 3.6. The Covering of the Book: *top*, Quarter Bound Volume, *bottom*, Half Bound Volume. Diagram by Henry Cioch. Redrawn from Ronald B. McKerrow, *An Introduction to Bibliography for Literary Students* (Oxford: Oxford University Press, 1927).

layers of paper allows the book to flex open easily and to return it to its original shape when it is closed. The boards fit into place at the joints, or shoulders, holding and supporting the book. The importance of these procedures cannot be overemphasized. If they are done correctly, they give the book flexible, long-lasting support. Repairs that do not make allowance for these functions will not work. The margin for error in these steps is so small as to be almost nonexistent.

The boards, or covers, of the book are cut slightly larger than the text block. This overhang is called the square and must be large enough to protect the pages but not so large that the book tends to fall forward out of its binding, which will distort the spine and break the binding.

BINDING IN BOARDS VERSUS CASING-ON

Boards can be bound-on to a book or cased-on. When a book's cover is bound-on, the uncovered boards are attached to the text block one by one. The cords, or tapes, are either laced through the boards, inserted into a split, or stuck to the upper or lower sides of the boards. The cords for this last operation are frayed-out to a fan shape to reduce bulk without sacrificing strength. Historically, lacing-on was the method of attaching the boards, but this technique adds no real strength to the book. Book cords break at the joint, never over the board. They break when the cords decay.

The cover, or case, for a cased-on book is made separately from the contents, then the contents are attached to the completed case. All machine-bound books are made this way. Provided that the materials and execution are sound, cased bindings are very strong, but no machine-made book can be as strong as a well-executed handbound book. However, there are few hand binders today who thoroughly understand the principles of book construction, though in the past decade there has been a rapid development of the field of conservation binding, leading to increased knowledge and more trained professionals.

The weakest point in a case binding is at the joint, or hinge. Usually a piece of super, the cloth that is put on before the back liner, is wrapped around the back before attaching the back liner and then glued to the boards. In addition, the outermost endpaper, the pastedown, is stuck to the inner side of the board. Sometimes an internal cloth hinge is added for strength. If the super or the endpaper is flimsy, it will break at the joint and the book will fall out of its cover. This can also happen if the adhesive fails.

The fit of the boards to the joint of the text block can either be close (tight joint) or set-off (French groove). Case-bound books, books sewn on tapes, and books bound in vellum and parchment will generally have a French groove. Books bound in leather will more often have a tight joint. The choice is up to the binder.

Today, most books are bound with a hollow back; that is, the spine of the cover is not attached to the back of the text, but flexes away when the book is opened. This may help the cover's spine last longer than it would on a tight back because it changes shape less often. A hollow back works well provided the text's back is adequately supported by layers of paper called "lining-up papers." The strongest hollow back is made by gluing a flat hollow tube of good quality paper to the back of the text and the hollow tube's upper side to the spine of the cover.

Until the mid-1800s, the cover material was usually affixed directly to the back of the text block in a style known as "tight back." It is not advisable to use this method with cloth or vellum. Leather will flex open with the book but it breaks down sooner than a hollow back because of the extra bending it must do. A book that has been previously bound with a tight back can be rebound with a carefully constructed hollow back which may last longer. The book will look the same on the shelf and the hollow back provides a sounder construction.

The endpapers of a book help to attach its text to the cover. They are often decorative, as well. Aesthetically, they act as a transition from the cover to its contents. If they are weakly attached or of poor quality, they will not perform well. The best endpapers are sewn on to the text as it is sewn together. If endpapers are attached with adhesive after the text is sewn, they may pull off. Usually they break at the hinge because the paper is not of sufficient strength.

EDGE DECORATION

The outer edges of a book may be gilded or dyed with ink. Experience has shown that this decorative coating often protects the book's interior from decay-causing dust and grime, although it is not a routine part of modern book protection.

COVERING

A book may receive a full, three-quarter, half, or quarter binding. This refers to the pattern of the covering (see Figure 3.6). The book cover needs the most protection at the spine, joints, and corners. A strong binding that also uses expensive leather economically is one of quarter leather with vellum tips at the corners. Full leather looks very handsome but the leather on the boards adds no strength to the binding.

MECHANICAL BINDING

There are many kinds of mechanical binding, whereby books are held together by metal or plastic. Spiral binding is the most familiar. Such bindings are used for books that must lie open perfectly flat. All have a device that joins single sheets by passing through one edge. The cover consists of two separate sheets. The process of producing spiral bindings is actually less automated than the production of cased-on books; the term *mechanical* refers to the device that holds the sheets together. A quick and inexpensive style of mechanical binding, with the trade name Velo-bind, uses a plastic strip that is heat sealed to a back strip through the book. This binding is good as long as the plastic lasts and is very useful for disposable information. However, since the book will not lie flat, the inner margins must be large so that the reader can easily use the book, and it can only be photocopied on a machine with the camera at one edge.

PRESERVING BOOK COLLECTIONS

Preservation is the maintenance of objects as close to their original condition as possible for as long as possible, or until they are no longer needed. Book preservation means prolonging the useful life of a book. Not every volume needs to be preserved forever, although each community should undertake the preservation of its own recorded culture and history. Some library collections become valuable over time; what was once a current manual or novel can later become one of the few surviving copies and thus must be preserved for its scarcity and specimen value.

The needs and budgets of libraries vary widely from well-endowed, meticulously cared for special collections and rare book libraries to the smallest, most neglected local accumulations. However, no matter what the size or the budget may be, keeping collections in a favorable environment is important for all institutions.

The ingredients of good care for a library collection are cleanliness, stable temperature and humidity, clean air, minimal exposure to harmful light, and proper handling techniques practiced by all members of a library's staff. Preservation in this sense need not require a great amount of money, but it does require good sense and consistent application.

Basic housekeeping as it applies to books means careful handling, good shelving, using supports that do not damage books, and regular cleaning. It involves nontechnical, practical, and inexpensive procedures for prolonging the useful life of books and paper. They are briefly outlined here.

SHELVING AND STORAGE

Books should be shelved on baked enamel shelving, if possible, and archival materials should be housed in similar file cabinets. Books should never be shelved closer to the floor than six inches, to reduce their contamination by dirt and dust, and to help prevent possible water damage if flooding should occur. Books should never be packed tightly on the shelves; open space around a shelf of books allows for air circulation and reduces the possibility of mildew.

Bookends should be sturdy, nonskid, and without sharp edges that cut both books and people. They must be high enough to support the books, especially oversize books.

HANDLING

Open books carefully. Books must never be forced open in any one place as that may break the spine and loosen pages. New books should be opened on a flat surface. Let down the boards one at a time. While holding the text block upright in one hand, gently smooth down a few leaves at the front and then at the back. Continue to do this until the center of the book is reached.

Books and paper should be handled with clean hands. Hand lotion should not be applied before opening and using a valuable book, for the oils are destructive to the paper and the covers. Food, beverages, and smoking should not be permitted in work areas where books are processed.

Metal clips and rubber bands are harmful to books and paper. If clips are absolutely necessary for a short period of time, plastic clips can be purchased that will not harm paper. Rubber bands will of themselves decay and affect the book in contact with them. In addition, the band will cut into fragile, brittle paper and bindings. If deteriorating books need to be held together, even temporarily, linen ribbon should be used; even a soft cord is far less harmful than rubber bands. Pressure-sensitive adhesive tapes are even more harmful to books. They are exceedingly difficult to remove and it is nearly impossible to remove their stains. Such tapes should not be used in libraries, but if they are, only on materials with no permanent value.

SHELF CLEANING AND BOOK VACUUMING

Two workers can vacuum about a thousand books and clean about one hundred shelves in a day, following a half day of training from a book conservator. The equipment needed is minimal: silicone-treated dust cloths, a flat-topped book cart, and a shoulder-carried vacuum cleaner. When vacuuming fragile books, cover the nozzle of the vacuum cleaner with fiberglass screening and wrap it with a cushioning material to protect the books from abrasion or loss of loose bits.

REPAIRS

Books with torn spines, loose boards, and broken sewing are obvious candidates for repair. Circulating books in need of repair are most easily spotted as they are returned from circulation. Some minor repairs can be done in-house, provided that the individuals who attempt the work are neat and dextrous, and receive proper instruction from a conservator or conservation technician before attempting to undertake repairs on library property, for even the simplest repair can, upon occasion, go awry. There are numerous seminars and workshops for library personnel on in-house repair techniques. They are sponsored by agencies such as the American Library Association Resources and Technical Services Division Preservation of Library Materials Section (PLMS), the Society of American Archivists, the American Association for State and Local History, as well as by state or regional agencies, library schools, or by book conservation centers such as the Northeast Document Conservation Center (NEDCC), Andover, Mass.; the Conservation Center for Art and Historic Artifacts (CCAHA), Philadelphia; and the New York Botanical Garden Book Conservation Center, New York City. Information about conferences, seminars, and workshops on conservation can be found in *Conservation Administration News*, a quarterly newsletter for library administrators responsible for preservation; the ALA/PLMS *Preservation Education Directory*; and *Opportunities for Study in Hand Bookbinding and Calligraphy*, issued by the Guild of Book Workers, which will point the way to book conservators in the region who can be of assistance. Two other sources of information are *The Abbey Newsletter*, edited by Ellen McCrady, which is issued about six times a year, and the *Newsletter* of the American Institute for Conservation of Artistic and Historic Works (AIC), issued four times a year.

Most book conservators will provide simple, clearly written instructions for the operations that they teach in their workshops. In addition, Jane Greenfield, head of the Book Conservation Laboratory at Yale University Library, has prepared a series of pamphlets with step-by-step instructions for *Wrap-Arounds*, *Tip-ins and Pockets*, *Paper Treatment*, *Hinge and Joint Repair*, and *Pamphlet Binding*, which are available upon request. Robert De Candido, of the New York Public Library Conservation Division, has published a helpful article in *Library Scene* on how to set up a small in-house repair shop. Jane Greenfield has also written a pamphlet on how to set up a small bindery, which is a part of the pamphlet series mentioned above.

Many library books, however, will require professional help. Book conservation is a relatively new field; treatments are often experimental and somewhat limited. Acidic paper can be deacidified, bindings can be restored, but there is little that can be done to return brittle paper or rotted leather to internal strength. And in the literature of conservation written for libraries there is little discussion of the dangers involved to the books if repairs are undertaken haphazardly; a little knowledge can be dangerous indeed.

Some of the procedures involved in book repair are simple. The secret is to diagnose and prescribe the correct treatment. This requires knowledge and experience. The librarian should consult with the binder/conservator and make a survey of the library's collections. The survey will reveal books that have come loose from their cases, books with loose boards, books with brittle paper, and books with dry or rotten leather bindings.

The librarian or curator in consultation with the binder/conservator should be able to draw up a program of repair. It will probably consist of phases, which are put into action as funds permit, and might include the hiring of a full-time or part-time specialist, or arranging to hire one on commission. The specialist can conduct workshops for staff members on selected procedures.

A book conservator can identify which dry leathers might benefit from a leather treatment and conduct a half-day workshop for staff personnel on the procedures for oiling those selected books. Oiling must be taught in person. It is very easy to damage books by careless or excessive oiling or by oiling the wrong books.

The library's budget and the value of each book together determine whether a complete restoration or repair should be done. If it should, the binder/conservator will prepare a condition report and treatment proposal on each book, stating present condition, what will be done, and the cost. The condition report is not only useful; it is essential to the life of the book, just as for other objects. If a complete repair cannot be undertaken immediately, the various elements of a phased solution come into play, including tying the book together, placing it in protective wrappers, or boxing. Books with loose boards can be tied up with soft white library ribbon. If the tied volume is so large that it slumps on the shelf, it must be placed on its side. If the boards are valuable in themselves and fragile as well, the book should be wrapped.

Wrapping is done with acid-free paper. The book is wrapped like a package; conservators have developed a number of different styles. It is a good solution for books with rotten leather because it prevents them from contaminating their neighbors or irritating the hands. Wrappers also provide adequate protection for broken bindings as they await repair. Sturdier wrappers can also be constructed easily. This preservation technique is often taught at conservation workshops. Wrapping or boxing is usually suitable only for books in a restricted access area; in an open area, there is nothing to prevent a patron from taking a volume and leaving only the empty container for future users.

Boxes can be bought ready-made, or they can be made to order by a binder using acid-free, buffered materials. They can also be made in-house if the staff has been properly instructed, but the costs of constructing these boxes in-house may not be justified in collections where only a few books will require them. Boxes are a good solution to the problem of housing fragile material and, while they are expensive, they cost far less than full restoration. There are various styles of boxes; the clamshell, strip, and folder boxes are perhaps the best known. Instructions for making various styles of boxes are available from conservators who offer instruction on their construction, as well as from regional centers, such as the Conservation Center for Art and Historic Artifacts in Philadelphia, and the Northeast Document Conservation Center in Andover, Mass. A comprehensive guide, *Boxes for the Protection of Rare Books*, developed at the Library of Congress Preservation Office, is available from the Government Printing Office. In addition, a thirty-minute slide presentation of the strip box developed by John Hyltoft at the Smithsonian Institution is available for loan or purchase from the Office of Museum Programs, 2235 Arts and Industries Building, Smithsonian Institution, Washington, D.C. 20560.

Book boxes must be measured and cut precisely with an accuracy of plus-or-minus one millimeter. Books must fit snugly into boxes; if the box is too small, it will crush the book; if it is too large, the book inside will slide around, splay, and slump. Ready-made boxes rarely fit snugly and thus they are not as satisfactory as custom-made boxes. Slip cases are not recommended as they invariably wear the book as it is being slipped in and out of the case. Boxes must be checked regularly to verify that conditions within the box have not changed.

BOOK JACKETS

Glassine covers, made of highly acidic paper, are especially harmful to the book and should be discarded whenever they are found. Acid-free glassine is available and can be substituted, if necessary, to keep the appearance of the original wrapper, even though some conservators question the stability of these wrappers. Circulating libraries frequently keep the book jacket on current books and add a plastic cover to prevent short-term damage to the volume. This should only be done when it is clearly understood that the volume in question will be discarded within a year or so. Often the jacket paper is of poor quality as well. However, book collectors prefer books in their original wrappers. Rare book repositories that wish to retain dust jackets should remove them from their books and store them archivally.

MASS DEACIDIFICATION

Mass deacidification, the simultaneous treatment by chemicals of a large group of books and paper to neutralize the acids that can contribute to paper disintegration, may shortly be available commercially. Deacidification of individual papers is covered elsewhere in this volume, so this section will concentrate on mass treatment of library books. At present, three methods are being tested.

Since 1979 the Public Archives of Canada has been using a system installed there by the American inventor Richard Smith. This system uses liquefied gas (magnesium methoxide in methanol and liquefied Freon) to form a reserve of magnesium carbonate with the book. These compounds are believed to be stable and chemically safe for paper. The method deacidifies 150 volumes a day. There are still several unanswered questions about this method, such as the cost per volume and the amount of alkaline reserve that is obtained. Smith foresees no difficulty in constructing and operating larger or smaller units. He hopes to further develop methods for strengthening deteriorated paper and other protective methods for books.

Vapor phase deacidification (VPD) sheets, treated papers which are interleaved into books, and the morpholene deacidification process developed by William Barrow do not deposit enough alkaline reserve, so books and papers must be re-deacidified periodically. These treatments can also discolor paper and the Barrow method will make some book covers sticky. The vapor may be carcinogenic.

Since 1974 the Library of Congress has been developing the diethyl zinc process of deacidification, which is undertaken in a vacuum chamber with a capacity of five thousand volumes. Diethyl zinc is extremely explosive and flammable unless it is handled correctly. During transshipment it is stabilized with mineral oil. The mineral oil is completely removed prior to treatment. To date there have been no accidents, but for safety's sake, the process cannot be undertaken within a library or museum. The estimated cost of treatment (excluding shipping) is five dollars per volume. Vacuum chambers are available throughout the United States, an unused legacy from the space program. The Library of Congress will complete its tests in 1983 and hopes that the process will be available to all institutions for the treatment of non-rare books and materials. However, as of this printing the technique is still experimental. The Library of Congress plans to deacidify all new acquisitions routinely to reduce further deterioration of part of our cultural heritage, as well as deacidifying selected retrospective materials in their collections.

It must be emphasized, however, that deacidification cannot restore strength to brittle paper; it can only retard further deterioration. There are still many things that we do not know about the nature of library materials and the causes of their deterioration, and we are not always sure what effect conservation treatments will have in the long run. Ultimately, the preservation of the books in the library's collections rests in the hands of a sensible and informed curator who uses the knowledge that we now have to care for the collections and closely follows the rapid developments in the new field of library preservation.

SUGGESTED READING

De Candido, Robert. "What Repairs Can Be Done Easily and Economically Within A Library . . . " *Library Scene* 10:2 (June 1981): 22.

   Setting up a small workshop for less than one thousand dollars.

Diehl, Edith. *Bookbinding: Its Background and Technique*. 2 vols. New York: Dover, 1980.

A definitive history of bookbinding and techniques of the craft. A reprint of the 1946 edition.

Glaister, Geoffrey Ashall. *Glaister's Glossary of the Book*, 2nd ed. Berkeley: University of California Press, 1979.

A nearly comprehensive guide to the terms used in papermaking, bookmaking, and publishing.

Greenfield, Mary E. (Jane). *Wrap-Arounds, Tip-ins and Pockets, Paper Treatment, Pamphlet Binding, The Small Bindery, Hinge and Joint Repair*. New Haven: Yale University Library, 1980–1982. (Yale University Preservation Pamphlets, 1–6).

A set of basic instructions, clearly illustrated.

Horton, Carolyn. *Cleaning and Preserving Bindings and Related Materials*. 2nd ed. Chicago: American Library Association, Library Technology Program, 1969. (LTP Publication, 18).

Describes the organization and management of a systematic survey of stack conditions and outlines a program of care for books. A third edition is in preparation.

Lee, Marshall. *Bookmaking: The Illustrated Guide to Design, Production, and Editing*. New York: R. R. Bowker, 1979.

A clear guide to the materials and tools used in the book production industry.

Library Binding Institute. *Handbook for Library Binding*. Boston: LBI, 1971.

Covers the topic of library binding.

_____. *Standards for Library Binding*. Boston: LBI, 1981.

The standards for the industry.

Roberts, Matt, and Don Etherington. *Bookbinding and the Conservation of Books: A Dictionary of Descriptive Terminology*. Washington, D.C.: Library of Congress, 1982.

Covers the history of preservation, materials used, notable binders. It is extensively illustrated.

Roberts, Matt T. "The Library Binder," *Library Trends* 24:4 (April, 1976): 749–62.

A discussion of the different needs of librarians and the services that a library binder can and should provide.

Roberts, Stephen H. "What the Library Binder Expects from the Librarian," *Library Scene* 7:3 (September–December 1979): 2–4.

A discussion of library binding operations and how the librarian can work with the binder.

4

Photographs

GARY ALBRIGHT

Photography has had a tremendous influence on our perception of the world, both past and present. Throughout our lives we have been deluged with photographic images in all forms of printed media. As a result of photographs we are familiar with foreign lands, personalities, and historic events. Photographs also provide us with glimpses of our families and forebears, presenting insight into their surroundings and modes of living. Only recently have public institutions and the public itself realized the documentary importance of photographic images. With this increased interest there has been a resultant growth in the use of photographic collections. As a consequence, those in charge of these collections are becoming concerned with the maintenance and care of images and are asking questions regarding their preservation. Much research needs to be completed before these questions can be definitively answered, but a basic understanding of the problems and of possible solutions does exist. The information which will be presented here should prove useful to those interested in the preservation of our photographic heritage.

Photographic conservation derives many of its fundamental principles from the traditions of paper conservation. Yet it must be understood that a photograph and a nonphotographic paper artifact are different. This is obvious if the photograph is on a support other than paper, such as metal, glass, or a flexible film, but even with a paper support there is the added complication of the photographic image. This image is very sensitive to atmospheric conditions and is likely to have inherent chemical instabilities. Stains, tears, and losses can often be reduced or repaired, but the techniques are complex and the results sometimes less satisfactory than the corresponding treatments on paper artifacts.

There are many different processes which can result in a photographic image. Each process has its own characteristics, its own problems of permanence and deterioration, and its own requirements for storage and conservation. For a custodian to be able to properly maintain and care for a collection, he or she must have a basic understanding of photographic principles and be able to identify the various processes with their respective problems.

PHOTOGRAPHIC PRINCIPLES

A photograph, by definition, is a fixed light-sensitive image on a support. It may be black-and-white or color, positive or negative, and silver or non-silver. Until the 1950s most photographs were black and white as opposed to color. The term *black-and-white* describes any monochromatic photographic process, the tone varying greatly depending on the process employed. Often black-and-white images will appear colored, as it was and still is common practice to hand-tint images. Tinted photographs, however, should not be confused with colored photographs. In a color photograph, the color material is inherent in the process, not added after a black-and-white image has already been obtained.

Two of the most basic terms in photography are *negative* and *positive*. A negative has a tonal range which reverses the original brightness range of the subject—shadows appear as highlights and highlights appear dark. In a positive photograph, the light and dark areas correspond directly to the lights and darks of the original subject. A positive may be made by exposure through a negative or directly from the subject. A "direct" positive is a unique image and is only duplicable by rephotographing the subject or by copying the original image.

In the process of producing a photograph, a light-sensitive material is applied to a sheet of paper or other support. This support is then exposed to light, either (1) to form a latent (invisible) image to be revealed later in a chemical developer (develop-out paper), or (2) to obtain a visible image directly from the reaction with light (print-out paper). In both cases the light-sensitive component of the image must then be removed or the image will continue to darken. This procedure is called fixing and, for most processes, consists of washing the photograph in a bath of "hypo" (sodium thiosulfate). Once fixed, the photograph is washed to remove residual fixer. Any fixer remaining in the support will lead to future fading and staining of the image. Usually, print-out paper (POP) undergoes an additional step before fixing called *gold toning*. During gold toning, the silver in the image is partially replaced by a deposit of gold, resulting in an image with a more pleasing color, and at the same time providing some protection for the image from atmospheric deterioration. Toning is also practiced on develop-out papers (DOP), but the procedure occurs after or during fixing of the image. As a result of differing mechanisms of image formation, POP and DOP papers exhibit dissimilar characteristics. POP prints are warm in tone, tending towards a brown, purple, or reddish color. DOP prints are cool—blue, neutral, or black. POP processes take much more light to print than DOP processes, therefore POP prints are almost always made in contact with a negative, whereas DOP prints may be either contact-printed or enlarged from a negative. Almost all negatives are a develop-out process. One other important consequence of processing is that POP processes are much more susceptible to degradation from atmospheric influences than are DOP processes. This is especially true for the earliest prints (1840–1850) before the importance of fixing and washing was understood.

In most cases the light-sensitive material in a photograph is a silver halide (silver chloride, bromide, iodide, or a combination thereof). During exposure and development, the silver in these salts is reduced to form metallic silver. The quantity of silver formed determines whether an area appears as a highlight (very little silver), midtone, or shadow (largest amount of silver). Silver-based processes comprise the great majority of photographs; however, there are processes that use other light-sensitive materials or metals. In these, the image may be composed of pigments, dyes, or nonsilver metals such as platinum, palladium, and iron. Platinum prints and cyanotypes (blueprints) are examples of two of the more common nonsilver processes.

POSITIVE PHOTOGRAPHIC PROCESSES

Photographic history begins with the announcement of the daguerreotype on January 7, 1839, by François Arago to the Academy of Science in Paris. Louis Jacques Mandé Daguerre, the discoverer of the process, was only one of a group of individuals experimenting with photography at the time. He did not invent photography, but as Peter Pollack has written in *The Picture History of Photography* (New York: Harry Abrams, Inc., 1969): "He made it work, made it popular, and made it his own." (p. 42). The daguerreotype is one of only two major photographic processes to have a metal support. (The other is the tintype.) It was used from its discovery in 1839 until circa 1860 when its popularity declined.

The daguerreotype image consisted of a mercury-silver amalgam on a silver-plated copper sheet which was produced in standard sizes by commercial firms. The images were mostly portraits and, being direct positives, were one of a kind. To enhance their effect and make them resemble painted miniatures, they were usually presented to clients in velvet-lined cases. (Other processes presented in these cases included ambrotypes and tintypes.) Hand-tinting of the image was fairly common, this being another method of increasing the resemblance of the daguerreotype to a miniature painting. Daguerreotypes are easy to recognize from their mirror-like surface and their rendering of minute detail. Unlike any other process, they can appear as either a positive or negative depending on the viewing angle and reflecting surfaces.

In the mid 1850s, the daguerreotype was superceded by the ambrotype. Introduced in 1854, the ambrotype was at the height of its popularity in

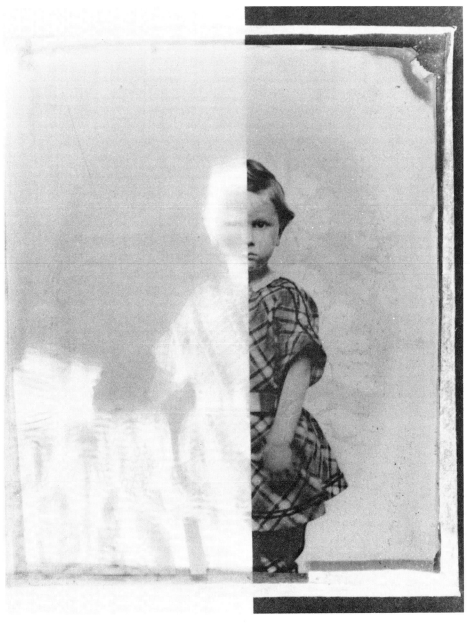

Figure 4.1. An ambrotype is viewed as a positive because of its black backing, *right*. If this backing is removed or damaged the image appears as a negative, *left*. Photograph by Donald Linne.

1856 and 1857, and continued in use through the 1870s. The image consisted of an underexposed collodion negative on glass with a black backing. Collodion had been discovered in the mid-1840s and was composed of nitrated cotton, known as gun-cotton, dissolved in a mixture of ether and alcohol. The backing was black varnish, cloth, paper, tin, or dark glass. Like the daguerreotype, the ambrotype was a direct positive, was used mostly for portraiture, and was presented to the client in a velvet-lined case. Ambrotypes were easier to make and cheaper than daguerreotypes, but they did not have the richness and sharp detail that the daguerreotype exhibited. They were often varnished for protection from the atmosphere. These images had a grayish green tone and often were enhanced with hand-tinting.

The tintype, also called the ferrotype or melainotype, was the last of the major direct positive processes. The tintype was patented in 1856 and was popular throughout the remainder of the nineteenth century. Its use continued into the 1930s when it was a novelty item at fairs and summer resorts. The tintype was identical to the ambrotype except that a black-lacquered iron plate was used for support instead of glass. Tintypes came in the standard daguerreotype sizes, were mostly portraits, and were usually varnished for protection and better viewing. They were mounted not only in velvet-lined cases, but also in paper folders, die-cut paper mats, and jewelry. Many were never mounted at all, but were stored loose. The image was a dull gray, the whites appearing creamy in color. Behind glass they can be confused with ambrotypes, but with the help of a magnet which would be attracted to the iron, even through the glass, the two can be easily distinguished. A magnet should not be used directly on the image surface as this could result in scratching of the emulsion.

The processes described so far were all direct positives and usually produced a right-to-left reversed image, for no negatives were involved in their production. The remaining prints to be discussed were all printed from negatives, and therefore were not reversed. They also had paper supports. These prints fall into two basic categories, print-out papers (POP) and develop-out papers (DOP). POP papers were the predominant photographic papers from 1835 through 1905, at which time DOP papers became the dominant form. POP papers were typically a sepia, warm brown, or purple tone. The most widely used POP processes included the salted paper print (1835–1855), the albumen print (1855–1895), and collodio-chloride POP and gelatino-chloride POP papers (1895–1905).

The salted paper print was invented by Henry Fox Talbot in 1835. It was used until circa 1860 and revived in the 1870s. The process consisted of washing a piece of paper in a salt (NaCl) solution, and after drying, bathing it in a solution of silver nitrate. Once dry the paper would be exposed to light, usually through a negative, and then gold-toned, fixed, and washed. The salted paper print did not render the detail characteristic of the daguerreotype, especially when exposed through a paper negative. Because of this and stringent patent controls, the process was not widely practiced. The image tones ranged from brown, to yellow-brown, to purple. The image was matte, as it existed within the paper fibers and not on the surface in a coating or emulsion. Often these images display fading to a pale yellow color, especially around the edges.

Albumen paper was first introduced in 1850 by Blanquard Evrard and was used into the twentieth century, although its popularity had waned by 1895. During its period of dominance, millions of albumen prints were produced, making them by far the most common form of photographic print in the nineteenth century. Albumen prints went through various crazes and formats, including cartes-de-visite (4¼ × 2½ inches), cabinets (4½ × 6½ inches), stereoviews (3 × 7 inch cards with two images for 3-D viewing), and larger formats. Albumen paper was made by floating a very thin but strong paper on a bath of egg white (albumen) mixed with ammonium or sodium chloride. This paper was purchased by the photographer who then sensitized it by floating it on a silver nitrate solution. After drying, the paper would be exposed in sunlight in contact with a negative until a strong image was obtained. It was then washed, toned, fixed, and washed again. Usually these images were mounted on a heavy card stock for presentation and to keep them flat. These mounts were an important part of the object, often containing useful information about the photograph. Since the image of an albumen print is the albumen layer and not in the paper, it is much sharper and clearer than the image of a salted paper print. Being a print-out process, the image tone is warm, varying from brown to purple and sometimes black. The surface is glossy and often exhibits a fine crackle pattern, especially in the shadows. Upon deterioration, these prints show highlight yellowing, fading around the edges, and a tone change to a dull brown-yellow.

Collodio-chloride and gelatino-chloride POP papers were first produced in the early 1880s. Collodio-chloride POP papers were very popular for portraiture and were used until circa 1910. Gelatino-chloride POP papers are still available today. These two processes dominated photographic printing between 1895 and 1905. Both are machine-made, have their image in an emulsion on top of the paper support, and have a warm tone. They can be matte or extremely glossy, and were purchased already sensitized from the manufacturer. The two processes are very hard to tell apart except with chemical spot tests. Collodio-chloride papers show excellent resistance to staining and fading, especially if platinum-toned, a common procedure. Gelatino-chloride papers are much more susceptible to atmospheric deterioration and often fade and change color to a light brown-yellow.

Develop-out papers are machine made and consist of a gelatin halide emulsion on a paper support. They were first produced in the early 1880s but because of their great speed and the corresponding necessity for a dark-room, they did not become popular until after the turn of the century; since then they have dominated the black-and-white print market. They can be matte or glossy, and for a long time have been available with textured surfaces. Usually they are a cool tone, either black or blue-black; however, with proper toning they can be made warm in color. These prints often exhibit silvering (bronzing), a result of unfixed-out silver salts decomposing and the silver migrating to the surface. Although silvering does occur in other processes, in DOP prints it is much more common and intense.

There were several important nonsilver printing processes in use during the nineteenth and early twentieth centuries. Most of these were popular with art photographers, used in the production of prints for books, or employed in the reproduction of art works. Some of these processes included platinum prints, cyanotypes (blueprints), gum prints, carbon prints, and woodburytypes. By far the most common of these, and the only one which will be discussed, was the platinum print. This process was invented in 1873 but was not used until platinum paper became available in 1880. The print was a silvery-gray color, had a matte surface, and was considered by many critics and photographers to have been the richest and most beautiful photographic process ever invented. The prints made by this procedure are virtually indestructible, except for the deterioration of the paper support. The rising cost of platinum at the beginning of the First World War spurred the use of an alternative process using palladium, which gave a slightly warmer tone. Both processes were out of commercial production by the early 1930s.

NEGATIVE PHOTOGRAPHIC PROCESSES

The presently popular negative-positive system of photography was first developed by Henry Fox Talbot. In 1840, Talbot discovered that a silver-based light-sensitive material, when exposed to light for a short period, formed an invisible or "latent" image. This latent image was then made visible through the use of a chemical developer. Talbot's process was known as the calotype or Talbotype. The support was paper, often waxed or oiled to make it more translucent. These negatives were dark brown to black in color, and required long printing times due to the opacity of the support. The prints produced (salted paper prints) were often fuzzy, showing evidence of the paper fibers in the negative. Calotypes were used from 1841 to circa 1855. (Examples of American calotypes are rare.)

The next major photographic breakthrough occurred in 1851, when Frederick Scott Archer introduced the wet collodion negative. This process remained predominant for the next thirty years until it was supplanted by the gelatin dry plate. Wet plate negatives were made by pouring collodion containing an iodide salt (or an iodide-bromide salt mixture) over a clean glass plate, the plate being twisted and turned to produce an even coating. Once the collodion had set, the plate was dipped in a silver nitrate solution and while wet exposed, developed, and processed. Whenever wet plates were produced, a darkroom had to be in the immediate vicinity, thus a photographer carried his darkroom with him at all times. Identification of these negatives is not very difficult. The support is glass, the image has a grayish green tinge, and the emulsion coating is uneven. Also, due to hand coating, the emulsion rarely covers the entire plate. Finally, the edges of the glass were usually ground to facilitate handling and to give better adhesion of the collodion to the plate.

Production of gelatin dry plates began in the 1870s and by 1880 they had practically replaced the wet plate process. Dry plates, unlike wet plates, were bought already sensitized and could be stored after exposure for later development. Their use continued into the 1920s. Gelatin dry plates had a glass support and appeared black in color. These plates were machine manufactured, resulting in a complete and even coating of the emulsion on the glass. The glass was coated in large sheets which would then be cut to standard sizes. Therefore, dry plates exhibit cut edges in the emulsion and glass, unlike wet plate negatives.

In 1889, Eastman Kodak began the production of nitrate-base film, the first practical flexible-base film. This flexible base made possible roll film for camera use. The film was exposed, advanced by winding on a spool, and after exposure of the entire roll sent back to the company for processing. No longer was it necessary for the photographer to develop his own negatives or make his own prints. Photography now became practical for the amateur. The first roll film (1889–1903) was very thin and curled easily. In 1903 a thicker gelatin-backed, non-curl roll film was introduced. Production of nitrate-base roll film continued until 1950. Nitrate-base sheet film was introduced in 1913 and manufactured until 1939. Identification of nitrate-base film is straightforward. First, it is often marked "Nitrate" on one edge. Second, a small clipping of the film will sink to the bottom of a solution of trichloroethylene. (This test should be performed where there is good ventilation as breathing trichloroethylene fumes is dangerous to one's health.) Third, nitrate film degradation products smell very acrid, and the film becomes yellowed, very brittle, and often sticky. Finally, although not recommended as a test, nitrate film is very flammable.

Safety-base film was developed as a result of the fire hazards associated with nitrate film. Safety-base roll film was introduced during the 1920s, but did not become popular until the mid-1930s. Safety-base sheet film was introduced in 1934. The earliest safety film consisted of a cellulose acetate base with a gelatin emulsion. By 1937, an improved safety film was being produced using cellulose diacetate, and about 1947 cellulose triacetate was introduced. Each film was more stable to atmospheric fluctuations than the previous one, but all had a cellulose nitrate subbing (adhesive) layer between the emulsion and the base. As with nitrate film, identification is fairly simple. Usually "Safety" is marked on the edge of the film, the film burns with difficulty, and it will float in trichloroethylene. As with nitrate film, the deterioration of safety film can be used for identification. Upon deterioration, safety film smells of acetic acid (vinegar), and forms channels between the emulsion and the base. Also, the nitrate subbing layer can break down, forming tiny bubbles within the negative.

The most recent flexible negative material is polyester (polyethyleneterephthalate). Introduced in 1965, it has found favor due to its strong dimensional stability. It burns with difficulty and will float in trichloroethylene. If it is made by Kodak, it is marked "Estar" on one edge.

DETERIORATION AND CONSERVATION OF CASED PHOTOGRAPHS

Photograph stability is influenced by several factors: the image structure, the support material, the quality of processing, and storage conditions. The deterioration of an image varies greatly with the photographic process involved, each process exhibiting characteristic patterns of deterioration. These patterns can be helpful in identifying a technique and at the same time can be used to specify the storage conditions needed to prolong the life of an image.

Due to their unique supports, cased photographs (daguerreotypes, ambrotypes, and tintypes) exhibit deterioration products unlike other photographic processes. The daguerreotype often has blue tarnish on its surface, formed by the reaction of the silver layer with sulfur in the air. Usually this tarnish occurs at the edges of the plate, spreading in from the mat. Another form of daguerreotype deterioration is evidenced by green deposits which can occasionally be found on the surface of the image. These deposits are copper salts, a result of corrosion of the copper plate at breaks in the silver layer. Also, clear amorphous droplets can often be found on the image surface. These are corrosion products from the cover glass and can absorb moisture which would promote corrosion of the copper plate.

When handling a daguerreotype, certain precautions should be observed. The daguerreotype surface is very sensitive to abrasion and therefore should never be touched. Even brushing the image to remove dust is likely to leave scratches. Most daguerreotypes were originally sealed into a packet consisting of the daguerreotype, a brass mat, and a cover glass. A paper seal was attached to the glass and overlapped onto the back of the plate. This seal held the packet together and prevented air from reaching the image, which could cause tarnishing. This seal, if not broken, should be left unaltered as it is an original member of the packet and proof of age. However, if the seal is broken, the unit can be separated, the glass cleaned, and the package resealed using good quality paper and adhesive. This procedure is fairly easy to learn and prolongs the life of the image.

One of most frequently mentioned restoration procedures in photography has been the cleaning of daguerreotypes. Many articles outline daguerreotype cleaning procedures and show stunning before and after examples of treatment; however, few of the articles discuss the dangers involved. First, it should be realized that any hand-coloring on the image will probably be removed during cleaning. The adhesion of the color to the plate is very weak and bathing the plate in water solutions is liable to wash it away. Another danger to the daguerreotype is the possible peeling of the image layer from the copper plate. This can occur if there is bad bonding at the copper-silver interface. Finally, cleaning procedures are known to remove silver from the image layer, cleaning being essentially a chemical reaction which dissolves silver from the plate. The number of times this procedure can be repeated without visibly changing the image is uncertain. It has been determined, however, that even one-time cleaning of the plate alters certain of its chemical and physical properties. Because of the dangers and the many unknown influences involved, most photographic conservators prefer not to clean an image unless absolutely necessary.

Ambrotypes, because they are on glass, deteriorate differently than daguerreotypes. Their deterioration usually occurs in one of the following forms: tarnishing of the image, breakage of the glass support, discoloration of the clear varnish used over the image, flaking of the image from the glass support, and deterioration of the black layer responsible for the positive nature of the image. When this black layer breaks down, the result is an image that appears as both a positive and a negative. Luckily, this form of deterioration is the most common exhibited by ambrotypes and the easiest to remedy. It can be corrected by simply placing a good-quality black matboard in back of the image and returning the photograph to its case. Except for tarnishing, the other forms of deterioration can usually be treated by a trained conservator.

Fortunately, tintypes are fairly stable as their construction makes treatment very difficult. Rust is their major problem, and if it occurs on the image side, will eventually cause flaking of the emulsion from the metal support. Treatment of this form of deterioration is very difficult, and it may be best simply to store the image so that it will not be subjected to pressure or rough handling, which would cause flaking. Other deterioration problems in tintypes include surface dirt, discoloration of the surface varnish, bending of the iron plate, and flaking of the image from causes other than rust, such as high temperatures. All of these forms of deterioration are hard to correct and should be referred to a professional conservator.

Daguerreotypes, ambrotypes, and tintypes are all found in small velvet-lined cases. These cases often show signs of wear, such as abrasion of the covers or broken spines. Also, the brass mat, the cover glass, and the thin brass preserver that surround the photograph can deteriorate. The brass parts can form green corrosion products. The glass may become dirty or exude the clear droplets mentioned earlier. If the cover glass is cracked or missing, the photograph package should be disassembled and a new glass installed. Any treatment of the case should be performed by, or after consultation with, a photographic conservator.

DETERIORATION AND CONSERVATION OF PAPER PHOTOGRAPHS

The deterioration of photographic paper prints has concerned photographers from the beginnings of photographic history. As early as 1855, the London Photographic Society established a committee, appropriately named the "Fading Committee," to investigate the stability of photographic prints. Their findings cited four reasons for print instability: the imperfect washing of prints; the use of old or exhausted hypo baths; the use of improper adhesives in mounting photographs; and excessive sulfur and moisture in the atmosphere. Imperfect washing of prints leaves residual hypo in the emulsion and paper base which reacts with the silver image, causing yellowing and fading. Old or exhausted hypo baths form complex silver-hypo compounds which are impossible to wash out of the paper. These react with air and moisture, causing fading of the image, yellow and brown stains, and silvering on the surface. Silvering is a thin film of silver sulfide which appears as an opaque veil, giving a metallic reflective sheen. Adhesives that contain sulfur or are acidic can cause fading or yellowing of the image. Such adhesives include rubber cement, animal glue, and pressure-sensitive tapes. Also, the mount itself or other materials in contact with the photograph can lead to deterioration. Very acidic materials may result in yellowing and breakdown of the emulsion. Image deterioration from atmospheric considerations is usually due to the presence of oxidants, sulfur compounds, or high relative humidity. Sulfur dioxide or hydrogen sulfide in the air will react with a photograph, causing fading or the formation of silver sulfide. Moisture acts to speed up detrimental chemical reactions in a photograph, leading to fading or discoloration. High relative humidity softens gelatin, which can cause dirt to become embedded in the gelatin image, promote mold growth on the image, and lead to ferrotyping (a glossiness on an emulsion which results from the contact of the emulsion with a smooth surface in the presence of moisture.) Moisture also affects albumen prints. Recent studies with albumen prints have shown that high relative humidity is the major cause for their highlight yellowing. There are other environmental factors that can lead to deterioration as well. Light can cause fading of the image, deterioration of the base, and embrittlement of the emulsion. Airborne particulate matter will settle on a photograph and cause abrasion or may act as a site for mold growth. Noxious fumes from such materials as fresh paint, plywood, cardboard, insecticides, or janitorial supplies can cause staining or fading of photographic images.

Processing and environment play an important role in determining a photograph's stability, but other factors influence it as well: the image structure, support material, and handling it has received. Careless handling is the main cause of physical damage to a photograph. Tears in the support, losses of the emulsion, and creases can all result from improper handling procedures. Photographs should always be carried so as not to touch the surface. Fingers not only leave oily residues which cause staining and silvering, but also acids which can result in pitting of surface. Photographs should not be picked up at one edge as the paper support may be brittle and breakage of the support can occur. Also, care should be taken to avoid abrasion of the image when handling several images at one time without some sort of interleaving layer. This may be a problem especially when photographs are stored vertically in filing cabinets without sleeves or envelopes.

The image structure and the support material are intrinsic properties of a photographic process. Whether the image is composed of silver or some other material, whether it is a POP or DOP process, both of these factors influence stability. Also, the nature of the support material is important. Paper, cellulose nitrate, cellulose diacetate, and other substrate materials all play crucial roles in the lifespan of a photograph. These can best be described by considering the individual processes.

Salted paper prints are made on paper, have a silver image, and are POP prints. They are very susceptible to environmental damage, as most POP processes are, and the paper support is affected by acidity and other factors that cause deterioration of paper. Salted paper prints (depending on their processing) can be unstable in light. The negative process, the calotype, being a DOP process, is much more stable and generally exhibits less fading and yellowing.

Albumen prints are a silver POP process, and, as expected, are very susceptible to high relative humidity. Above 60 percent RH, these prints yellow in the highlights and shift in tone to a yellow-brown. Below 50 percent RH they appear to be fairly stable. In many photographic albums albumen prints can be found which demonstrate this sensitivity to atmospheric conditions. Edges of the photograph and other areas more exposed to air are often faded, whereas the center of the image, which is protected, will many times still have its original purplish tone.

Collodio-chloride POP prints, unlike other POP prints, appear to be very stable to atmospheric conditions, especially if they have been gold or platinum toned. However, the similar gelatino-chloride POP paper is not stable. These prints are often severely faded, for they are susceptible not only to atmospheric deterioration, but also to improper processing.

Albumen, collodion, and gelatin POP prints are often found on original mounts. These mounts usually consist of a poor-quality core sandwiched between two thin good-quality papers. Many times this mount is very acidic and brittle, posing a serious danger to the photograph. If this is the case, extra care should be taken in the handling of the image and consideration should be given to its treatment.

Gelatin DOP papers, being a develop-out silver process, are more stable to environmental factors than POP papers. However, they are much more prone to deterioration caused by improper processing. They also exhibit much more silvering than do other paper photographs.

Platinum prints are a nonsilver process. Unlike silver processes, platinum forms an image completely immune to environmental factors. However, the paper support is not. Often platinum prints are very brittle, acidic, and discolored due to unremoved acids used during processing. This discoloration can be removed, the prints deacidified, and the paper lined if necessary for added strength.

The restoration of nearly all photographs is experimental and somewhat limited. Images can be removed from mounts and remounted onto new materials. Tears can be mended, abrasions inpainted, and occasionally stains reduced. However, little can be done with a faded image to return it to its original tone. In the literature of photographic conservation there are references to bleaching and redevelopment as a technique for restoring these images. This procedure is very risky and will only work with certain images. When "successful," the result can be an uneven mottled surface or a print with an image tone unlike the original. Also, there is always the threat of losing the image entirely. When conserving a photograph, the conservator must realize that it should not be treated as a paper artifact. For example, washing of photographs is often an acceptable treatment; however, one has to know when and where. Certain photographic processes cannot withstand exposure to water and would be damaged if subjected to such a treatment. Also, deacidification, while a common paper treatment, is harmful to many photographic images. Both gelatin and albumen are more stable in a slightly acidic state and if deacidified their emulsion becomes soft. Deacidification can also cause yellowing of the emulsion. One treatment used with photographs but not with paper artifacts is the refixing and rewashing of an image to remove any residual processing chemicals. Under the proper circumstances this technique can prolong the life of a photograph, but more experimentation must be done before the safety of the treatment can be assured. All of the conservation techniques described have their dangers and limitations. None of these procedures should be undertaken by anyone other than a photographic conservator.

DETERIORATION AND CONSERVATION OF NEGATIVE MATERIALS

Negative processes exhibit the deterioration characteristic of silver prints. They fade and yellow if improperly processed or stored in a hostile environment and are subject to careless handling. Usually negative processes are less prone to damage from improper processing. The support material, be-

Figure 4.2. Prints in photographic albums often exhibit fading at the edges where they have been more exposed to air and humidity. Photograph by Donald Linne.

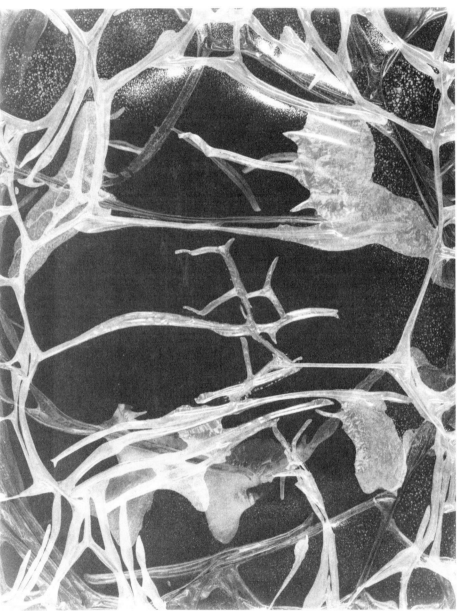

Figure 4.3. Channels between film layers are typical of safety film deterioration. Small bubbles often form when the cellulose nitrate adhesive used within the negative decomposes. Photograph by Donald Linne.

ing glass or plastic, does not readily absorb the processing chemicals, therefore they are easy to wash out. However, due to their high silver content, negatives exhibit much more silvering than do paper prints.

Glass plates have two main dangers, breakage and separation of the emulsion from the base. In either case the object should be stabilized by placing a 4-ply acid-free matboard on the emulsion side of the plate. For a broken plate, a piece of glass should be used against the glass side in addition to the matboard over the emulsion. The added layers should be the same size as the original support and may be held together using magic mending tape or Filmoplast. The objects should then be set aside and stored horizontally awaiting treatment by a conservator.

Cellulose nitrate negatives are often the most pressing problem confronting a photographic collection. Cellulose nitrate is known to be an unstable compound which deteriorates over time, and as it disintegrates, the destruction of the silver image occurs. J. M. Calhoun has identified five stages of nitrate deterioration: (1) there is formation of amber discoloration with fading of the image; (2) the emulsion becomes sticky; (3) the film generates gas bubbles and emits a noxious odor; (4) the film becomes soft and welds together; and (5) the film deteriorates into a brownish acrid powder. Films in the second and third stages of deterioration are often brittle. Film in the first, second, and sometimes the third stages is able to be copied onto new photographic material. Those negatives in the fourth and fifth stages should be destroyed because of their extreme flammability and the danger they pose to other films nearby. All nitrate negatives should be separated from the main body of the collection in order to keep the gases they generate from harming other materials. They should be copied as soon as possible, as their stability is unpredictable. Also, they should be stored in a well-ventilated, cool environment, with a relative humidity below 50 percent.

Early safety film has a cellulose acetate or diacetate base with an adhesive layer of cellulose nitrate. Upon aging, the base shrinks, causing separation of the gelatin emulsion, usually in the form of channels. Also, the cellulose nitrate adhesive deteriorates, forming small gas bubbles within the negative between the base and the emulsion layers. Eventually, deterioration results in yellow staining of the image. As with nitrate negatives, copying seems to be the only reasonable alternative for preservation of these images. There has been a stripping method developed for both nitrates and safety films. With this process, the gelatin emulsion is stripped from the base material and reattached to a more stable support. Whether this procedure is viable for mass conservation has yet to be determined.

THE STORAGE OF BLACK-AND-WHITE MATERIALS

Proper storage of a photographic collection incorporates several basic concepts, some of which have been previously mentioned. When storing photographs, it is best that each item has its own enclosure. This diminishes the migration of residual processing chemicals from image to image, and lessens the amount of handling a photograph will undergo, thus reducing the chance of physical damage. Ideally, print materials should not be stored with negatives, especially not in the same enclosure, because of the possible transfer of harmful chemicals from one image to another.

Usually horizontal storage is preferable to vertical storage as this helps keep the images flat. If vertical storage is used, each image should have enough physical support to prevent bowing or warping. There are exceptions to this rule; glass plate negatives and positives should be stored vertically. When stored horizontally their accumulated weight can cause breakage or serious abrasion to the plates located at the bottom of the pile. For vertical storage, a rigid separator should be attached to the sides of the container every few inches so that the plates will not lean too heavily against each other and cause damage. The plates should be stored compactly but not so tightly as to cause scratching or make the removal of the plates from the files difficult. With horizontal and vertical storage, photographs are often contained in narrow boxes. These boxes should be constructed of buffered paper stock. They should not be packed too deeply and too tightly as this could lead to abrasion or breakage of the images. Materials of similar size should be stored together, for the mixing of different sizes can cause damage or increase the risk of misplacing the smaller items. For horizontal storage drop-front boxes are recommended as these greatly facilitate retrieval of individual photographs.

Nitrate negatives and early safety film negatives should be separated from the collection and stored away from all other material. It is best to store these materials in well-ventilated areas at low temperatures and low relative humidity. This is especially true of nitrate film, which should be checked periodically to determine its state of deterioration. Nitrates that have become sticky or that are completely faded should be properly disposed of. Both nitrate negatives and early acetate film should be stored in buffered paper envelopes. Plastic enclosures seal in the deterioration products, which then react with and further deteriorate the image. If a large amount of nitrate film is to be stored, a film vault is strongly recommended, mainly as a fire safety precaution.

Storage enclosures acceptable for photographs fall into two basic types, paper and plastic. Paper preservers are porous and therefore do not enclose gases or moisture. They are opaque, protecting the material from light, but of course this makes it necessary to remove the object for viewing. Presently, the use of buffered materials in contact with photographic emulsions is being questioned, as there are indications that buffered materials may damage photographic images. Therefore, for most materials, nonbuffered, acid-free enclosures are preferred. However, alkaline buffered enclosures should be used for nitrate negatives, early safety film, brittle prints, and prints on acidic mounts. All of these materials are acidic and the buffer is needed to counteract the acidity.

Paper enclosures are available in several forms, including envelopes, folders, and mats. It is best to purchase envelopes without the finger cut in order to discourage the placement of fingers on the image during removal of the photograph from the enclosure. Also, for added protection, the use of envelopes with a top flap is desirable as the flap keeps dust from entering the envelope and causing abrasion to the image. When using paper envelopes for storage, make sure the seam is on the side and always insert the emulsion away from the seam. Under pressure the overlapping seams can cause depressions in the emulsion. Also, adhesive purity is always suspect, and improper adhesives will lead to fading or silvering of the image. Preferable to seamed envelopes are seamless enclosures. These avoid an adhesive, provide a top flap, and encourage the placement of the object on a flat surface in order to open them. The construction of these envelopes is shown in Figure 4.4.

The plastic materials suitable for photographic storage include polyester (Mylar), triacetate, and polyethylene. Plastic enclosures have the advantage of allowing an image to be viewed without handling, thus reducing chances of abrasion or scratching. Their disadvantage is the possibility of trapping moisture inside the enclosure, which can lead to ferrotyping of the image under certain circumstances. Polyester is the most inert and rigid of the three plastics mentioned. Its disadvantage is the generation of static electricity, which can attract dust. Triacetate is softer than polyester, is more easily scratched, and is not as strong a support. Polyethylene is the softest and least rigid of the three. If used, plastic enclosures often need additional support included in them, such as permatan bristol or some other board of good quality.

Two other products are useful for storing photographs. The first is Tyvek, an opaque, random-spun polyethylene. It is inert, neutral, porous, and has no tendency to ferrotype. This material is flimsy and offers little mechanical support to the object; however, it appears to be a safe alternative for use in the storage of photographs. The second product consists of a paper folder with a polyester sheet attached along an inner edge with double-sided tape. The polyester holds the object in place, yet allows for easy removal. The image is viewable without handling, and the paper backing gives support and permits the transfer of moisture.

Guidelines for the matting and framing of photographic images follow the standard procedures developed for works of art on paper. Preferable to hinging the photograph might be the use of photocorners made from an inert plastic or acid-free paper. Photocorners allow for easy removal of the image (this could pose a security problem) and do not have the cockling problems that paper hinges sometime present. These corners can be adhered with wheat starch paste or taped with magic mending tape.

Cased objects, because they are three-dimensional, present different storage problems than flat photographs. They can be stored horizontally in padded drawers, or vertically, if placed in small boxes made with acid-free heavy paper. Microfilm boxes can be purchased or boxes can be custom-made. Microfilm boxes tend to be a little large for the object and, if used, it might be necessary to stuff the box with acid-free tissue to prevent movement of the case. Custom boxes fit tightly and are made by following the directions in Figure 4.5. If many cases are needed, it is best to prepare templates for use as patterns. The attachment of a 35mm contact print of the image to the exterior of the box would greatly reduce the need to open the box and would make locating an image much simpler.

As mentioned earlier, photographic materials should be stored in a cool environment with a relative humidity under 50 percent. The importance of relative humidity in determining a photograph's stability cannot be stressed enough. When storing photographs, remove all rubber bands, paper clips, and staples. Keep in mind that fumes from janitorial supplies, new paints, etc., can be detrimental to an image. Sources of dust, such as unsealed cinderblock walls, will lead to abrasion of the photographic emulsions. Finally, when writing on a photograph, use a graphite pencil. For the newer "RC papers," a good-quality felt tip might be necessary. If using a felt tip pen, be careful not to store images in contact with each other as these inks can offset onto adjacent materials.

THE CARE OF COLOR MATERIALS

The conservation of color photographs is a complicated subject about which there is very little information. As of now, almost all conservation measures for these images are of a preventative nature. Once an image has become stained or faded, little can be done to restore it.

Ironically, the earliest color systems are often more stable than many of the modern processes. Early color photographs were a combination of a black-and-white silver image with some form of color screen. The first commercially successful color process, the Lumière Autochrome (introduced in 1907), consisted of a black-and-white panchromatic gelatin emulsion on a glass plate coated with a series of small red-, blue-, and green-dyed potato starch grains. It was developed as a direct positive and viewed with back lighting or by projection. In dark storage, the stability of the early color transparencies (Autochromes as well as others) has proven to be very good as the colored particles are stable if not exposed to light. However, this does not mean all early color photographs are in good condition, for this depends greatly upon their history of storage and use. Light causes fading of these images, therefore they should never be projected and exhibition should be strictly limited. It is best for viewing to occur at the lowest possible light levels.

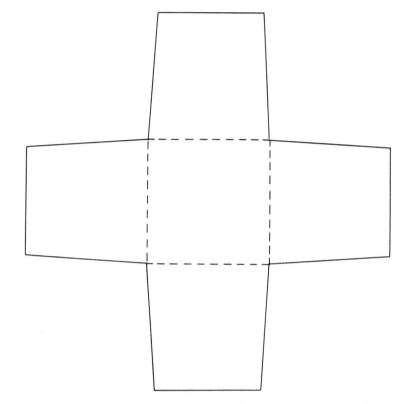

Figure 4.4. Making a Seamless Envelope. Diagram by Gary Albright, redrawn by Henry Cioch.

Beginning around 1935, new color processes were introduced. Color prints and transparencies were produced by bleaching the silver image formed during exposure and replacing it with color dyes, resulting in more brilliant colors and better clarity than were available before. The dyes were selected primarily for their chemical suitability and not necessarily for their permanence. As a result, most modern color processes are prone to fading from light. More serious than the light stability of these images are their dark storage characteristics, for even in the absence of light these images change color and fade.

Preservation of color images is a major concern. Most of our photographic heritage from the late 1950s to the present is on unstable color material which will fade, often in a relatively short period of time. Essentially, there exist two alternatives for color preservation. The first method involves the production of color separation negatives. For each image, one makes

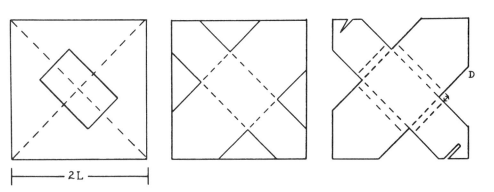

1. Cut a square whose sides are two times the largest dimension (L) of the photograph case.

2. Find the center of the square by drawing lines from the corners.

3. Place the case diagonally at the center and mark the sides (allow space for the hinges).

4. Extend the case lines to the edges of the square (as shown in the middle drawing) and cut out the triangles.

5. Fold the arms at the inner rectangle and from these folds measure out a distance equal to the depth (D) of the case (as shown in the right drawing). Fold the arms at this distance.

6. Place the case in the box and fold over the wide arms followed by the narrow arms. Mark the narrow arms where the two meet. At these marks cut a notch on one arm and a slit on the opposite side of the other arm. Both cuts must extend slightly over halfway through the width of the arm. When closing the box, fold the slit arm under the notched arm.

7. Depending on the thickness of the material used to make the box, it may be necessary to score the lines before folding.

Figure 4.5. Making Boxes for Cased Photographs. Diagram by Gary Albright, redrawn by Henry Cioch.

three different negatives on black-and-white film, each negative being taken through a different color filter. These negatives can then be stored and later used to produce a new color print. As can be guessed, the procedure is difficult and expensive.

An alternative and much more economical system for preserving color images is low temperature (cold) storage. By storing color photographs at low relative humidity (40 percent) and low temperatures, their life expectancy is prolonged considerably. The following example is an illustration. Assume that a color image has a useful lifetime of five years if it is kept at room temperature (75 °F, 24 °C) in the dark. This same image stored at 40 °F (4.5 °C) would last for eighty years and if stored at 0 °F (-18 °C) its projected life would be approximately seventeen hundred years. Several institutions have already installed cold storage vaults for their color holdings. Those who can't afford a vault should consider the use of a refrigerator. However, refrigerator usage does have problems. Relative humidity within the refrigerator must be maintained at approximately 40 percent or color deterioration will continue even in cold storage. Certain refrigerators meet this specification, but if one cannot be located, photographs may be stored in moisture-proof sealed packages, such as Kodak storage envelopes. One obvious problem of sealed packages would be the difficulty of retrieving images for use. A disadvantage of any cold storage system is the necessity for the materials to acclimate to room temperature and relative humidity before they can be unwrapped and used. Most of the vaults that have been built have "warm rooms" at their entrance for this purpose. If considering cold storage, become familiar with the literature available before proceeding.

There are times when the preservation methods mentioned are not possible. If this is the case, color images should be treated essentially the same as black-and-white images. Light levels should be kept low, relative humidity should be around 40 percent, and temperatures should be as low as possible. Color materials should not be stored in buffered paper as the buffering compounds are thought to be harmful to color dyes. Exhibition of color materials should be severely limited. It should be realized that the stability of a color photograph varies greatly depending on the process with which it was formed. Cibachrome, dye-transfer, and Kodachrome processes are much more stable than are the Ektachrome and instant color processes. Also, the processes that are most stable in dark storage are not necessarily the same as those that are most stable in light.

COPY NEGATIVES AND PRINTS

The copying of negatives has previously been mentioned in connection with nitrate and early safety films. With these materials, copy techniques are essential for preservation. However, copy negatives and duplicate prints can be useful in other ways. Duplicate prints can save originals from tremendous amounts of handling. Also, the use of duplicates minimizes the risk of theft of valuable vintage prints from a collection. The recording of images on microfilm or some other reduced format is another alternative. This would enable a researcher or publisher to quickly scan a collection to determine which images are of interest. Microfilm can also be distributed to other institutions, thus expanding the usefulness of a particular collection.

USE OF PHOTOGRAPH COLLECTIONS

Although the physical handling of original photographic materials can be greatly curtailed through the availability of copy negatives and prints, there are occasions when the researcher must examine originals. It is advisable to prepare typed guidelines for handling the images that are desired, and the curator of the collection should remind the user of the instability of the medium. The best precaution against abuse, however, is an orderly archive that demonstrates the concern of the curatorial staff.

Photocopies (such as Xeroxes) provide a quick duplication method. Though they are of poor photo-quality, they do give recognizable images. Under certain circumstances these could prove very useful, such as for cross-indexing in a subject filing system or for identification of items in cold storage.

There are many methods for copying photographs, each having its own particular applications, advantages, and disadvantages. Before making a commitment to any particular system, become familiar with the processes available and discuss them with a knowledgeable photographer or institution.

SELECTED READING

The following reading list is meant to be a basic introduction to photographic preservation. Within this chapter it was not possible to cover all photographic processes or to give detailed instructions. This reading list will fill in many of the gaps. Whenever reading information on photographic conservation, keep in mind that the field has only existed for a few years and that information is constantly changing. An article published today could be out of date within a year. Therefore, be careful when implementing the suggestions these sources provide. It is always advisable to contact someone abreast of the field before making any important decisions.

SUGGESTED READING

Calhoun, J. M. "Storage of Nitrate Amateur Still Camera Film Negatives," *Journal of the Biological Photograph Association* 21:3 (August 1953).

Crawford, William. *The Keepers of Light.* Dobbs Ferry, N.Y.: Morgan & Morgan, 1979.

   The material covered includes a basic history of photography and photographic processes, with a chapter on conservation.

Eastman Kodak. *Preservation of Photographs.* Rochester, N.Y.: 1979 (Kodak Publication F-30).

   A very basic text on fundamental photographic conservation.

Eaton, George T. *Photographic Chemistry in Black and White and Color Photography.* 2nd ed. Hastings on Hudson, N.Y.: Morgan & Morgan, 1965.

   An introduction to photographic chemistry on an elementary level.

Gill, Arthur T. *Photographic Processes: A Glossary and Chart for Recognition.* London: Museum Association, 1978 (Museum Association Information Sheet, 21).

   A useful publication for understanding photographic processes.

Hobbie, Margaret. "Paper and Plastic Preservers for Photographic Prints and Negatives," *History News,* October, 1980.

   A summary of photographic preservers and of their advantages and disadvantages.

Reilly, James. *The Albumen and Salted Paper Book.* Rochester, N.Y.: Light Impressions, 1980.

   An excellent book on early POP processes. Included are a history, techniques, and preservation.

Rempel, Siegfried. *The Care of Black and White Photographic Collections: Identification of Processes.* Ottawa: Canadian Conservation Institute, 1979 (CCI Technical Bulletin, 6).

   Detailed procedures for identification of black-and-white photographs.

_____. *The Care of Black and White Photographic Collections: Cleaning and Stabilization.* Ottawa: Canadian Conservation Institute, 1980 (CCI Technical Bulletin, 9).

   Detailed instructions are given for handling and storage of black-and-white photographs.

Weinstein, Robert A., and Larry Booth. *Collection, Use and Care of Historical Photographs.* Nashville: American Association for State and Local History, 1977.

   An excellent and essential book for the conservation of photographs.

Wilhelm, Henry. "Color Print Instability," *Modern Photography* 43:2 (February 1979), pp. 92ff.

5

Slides

NANCY CARLSON SCHROCK AND
CHRISTINE L. SUNDT

Slides are photographic materials, and their preservation demands the same attention to proper processing, handling, and environmental controls described in the chapter on photographs. However, the format of slides, the preponderance of color images, and the requirement that the transparent images be projected pose special problems. Moreover, the current emphasis on slides as teaching tools in media centers as well as in the traditional art history collection necessitates a separate discussion.

BACKGROUND

The use of slides predates the discovery of photography. As early as the seventeenth century, "magic lanterns" were used with candles to project hand drawn or painted images onto a flat surface in darkness. By 1850, photographic slides were produced from glass negatives onto albumen-coated glass. Like stereographs, lantern slides were popular as home entertainment. They also became an essential part of the lectures on the Lyceum and Chautauqua circuits, as this 1885 advertisement from *Scientific American* indicates:

> MAGIC LANTERNS AND STEREOPTICONS, all prices. Views illustrating every subject for PUBLIC EXHIBITIONS, etc. A profitable business for a man with a small capital. Also, Lanterns for Home Amusement. 136 page Catalogue free. McAllister, Mfg. Optician, 49 Nassau St., N.Y.

Lantern slides were produced commercially as early as 1860 when the Langenheim Brothers of Philadelphia marketed views of American cities, now quite rare. Slides produced by German companies were also sold in the United States. During the 1920s, the Keystone View Company in Pennsylvania produced teaching sets of lantern slides which were used in public school systems. By 1930, there was a national association of "visual educationists," but widespread use of slides in all levels of public schools did not occur until the 1960s.[1]

The growth and expansion of public museums and the development of art history as an academic discipline created new markets for slides. By the late nineteenth century, some museums provided slides for illustrated lectures as a public service. The leader was the American Museum of Natural History in New York City. By 1900, universities such as Massachusetts Institute of Technology, Cornell, Princeton, and Harvard had slide collections covering the fields of art and architecture, natural history, and science.

During the 1930s, the introduction and perfection of the Kodachrome three-color film process made inexpensive 35mm color slides available. The simultaneous growth of art history programs in colleges as part of liberal arts curricula promoted the establishment of a large number of collections. Despite an initial reluctance to abandon lantern slides, most collections had made the transition to 35mm slides by the 1950s. The early slide libraries were typically part of an art history department or specialized museum. During the 1960s, as media centers replaced more traditional libraries, slides became part of the teaching program throughout public school systems. The major feature of these instructional collections is the integration of all media into a single classified sequence that allows the user to find information on any topic in a range of formats. These libraries are more likely to regard slides as sets to be kept together as a unit, whereas the specialized slide libraries treat each slide as an entity to be separately catalogued. Public libraries, which may have inherited lantern slides, also actively collect slides and slide/media sets.

Today slides are found within integrated collections in public and school libraries as well as in specialized slide libraries in museums and university departments. Many graduate art history collections consist of over one hundred thousand slides. Not surprisingly, the slide curators of art collections have been in the forefront of efforts to promote professionalism in the organization, management, and preservation of slide collections. The standard text for the field, Betty Jo Irvine's *Slide Libraries: A Guide for Academic Institutions, Museums, and Special Collections*, was published in 1974 and was followed, in 1979, with a greatly expanded second edition. Under the leadership of Nancy De Laurier, the Mid-America College Art Association (MACAA) instituted concurrent sessions for slide curators at its annual meetings in 1971. The *MACAA Slides and Photographs Newsletter* began publication in 1974 as a communication organ for curators of art and architecture visual collections and expanded its scope in 1980 as the *International Bulletin for Photographic Documentation of the Visual Arts.*[2] Although the *Bulletin* focuses on art slide collections, it includes general information of value to all librarians handling slides, with sections on conservation and copy photography and a column containing summaries of articles about slides in photographic journals. Each *Bulletin* includes order forms for MACAA guides on topics in visual librarianship. For slide conservation, the two most useful are *Guide to Equipment for Slide Maintenance and Viewing*, edited by Gillian Scott (1978; revised edition in process for 1983), and *Guide to Copy Photography for Visual Resource Collections*, by Rosemary Kuehn and Zelda Richardson (1980). These inexpensive booklets are wise investments for librarians responsible for the care of slides.

PHOTOGRAPHIC PROCESSES

The term *slide* indicates a photographic format rather than a single photographic process. The base must be transparent, either glass or film stock, so that the image, either black-and-white or color, can be viewed when projected.

The original $3\frac{1}{4} \times 4$ inch lantern slides were printed from a negative onto a sensitized glass plate coated with albumen and later with gelatin. After processing, the emulsion side was covered with a glass plate of similar size and bound on its edges with black paper or fabric tape. Often the image was given a paper mask before binding (see Figure 5.1). The first lantern slides were black and white, but beginning about 1907, color slides were produced by Lumière Autochrome, Dufaycolor, and other processes paralleling the early stages of color print photography. Hand-tinting black-and-white images was another method used to produce color slides until the market was taken over by color films.

Most slides in the 2×2 inch format are produced on a film base which is usually acetate. Original slides are direct positives (reversals rather than negatives) developed from the film that was in the camera at the time the actual object or scene was photographed. Most, but not all, slides purchased from commercial dealers are reproductions of original slides produced by either of two basic techniques: (1) duplicates rephotographed from the original slides, or (2) slide "prints" reproduced from original negatives as slide positives, or from internegatives taken from a positive original. Original slides are, of course, closest to the original subject. With each successive generation of duplicates or copies, there will be a regression of color accuracy along with heightened contrasts between the highlights and shadows.

Slides may be produced by relatively simple black-and-white film processes or by the more complex color techniques. The technical aspects of both processes are described in the previous chapter. The most common slide in current usage is the 2×2 inch mount enclosing a piece of 35mm film. Other sizes can be mounted in the 2×2 inch format, including film from the 110 pocket Instamatic camera, the older Instamatic (size 126), and the now obsolete 127 "super slide."

Figure 5.1. W. Butcher & Son Advertisement for Lantern Slides, Projectors, and Accessories from *The Photogram* 6:72 (December 1899), Published by Dawbarn and Ward, Ltd., London. Photograph by C. Sundt.

CAUSES OF DETERIORATION

The materials and processes used to create slides can also be linked to their gradual or, in some cases, rapid deterioration.

Nearly all lantern slides are black-and-white images in which glass is the support for the photographic emulsion. Since residual chemicals are less likely to be retained on nonporous surfaces such as glass than on porous materials such as paper, the image on a lantern slide plate is usually stable. However, residual chemicals in the papers and glues used to mask the image and bind the edges of the glass plates could be responsible for damage, especially if the slides have not been stored in a controlled environment.

With lantern slides, the major problem is often the glass itself, which is fragile and easily broken when mishandled or improperly stored. If it is only the cover glass that is cracked or shattered, the slide is easily repaired by replacing the cover glass and rebinding the plates. A cracked or broken photographic base may render the slide unusable. However, if the breakage is slight, the slide can sometimes be salvaged by sandwiching the broken pieces between two glass plates and rebinding the unit.

Old slides are rarely replaceable since negatives or reprints are seldom available. Furthermore, most of the commercial firms that produced these slides have been out of business for many years. Another problem commonly associated with glass-supported emulsions is the separation of the emulsion from the glass base. This is most frequently caused by exposure to extremes in temperature and relative humidity in the storage area. Such damaged materials should be sent to a conservator.

In marked contrast to the glass-supported image, the survival of color images rests more with the photographic process than with the material used to support the emulsion, which for most Kodak and competitive color slide films is cellulose triacetate. Fading is by far the most serious problem encountered today. Color, the product of organic dyes, will eventually fade from exposure to ultraviolet radiation or other environmental factors. The inherent degree of instability in the dye layers that comprise the film's emulsion is one of many reasons why fading occurs at different rates in different films. Usually the results are the same in all instances where fading is identified: altered contrasts and a shift in the color balance.

The lifespan of color images also varies with film types. During the 1950s, 1960s, and most of the 1970s, many commercial art slides were produced on Eastman Color Motion Picture Print Film which was later found to have a very short lifespan—usually six to eleven years. A predominantly magenta image typically remains once the cyan and yellow dye layers in the film have faded. While a more stable equivalent of this film is now on the market, purchasers should be aware that some dealers may continue to sell slides produced on the older film stock. It is important when ordering slides to specify that they be on fresh film stock. Current films have been improved considerably, and from the data now available, their life expectancy should be appreciably longer than films used in the 1950s through the late 1970s. Kodachrome, Ektachrome, and the new Eastman Color films, if handled and stored properly, could last up to fifty years, perhaps longer.

The lifespan of all slides is dependent upon the environment in which the materials are housed. Light causes fading, but slides also fade in the dark as well because of chemical reactions accelerated by high temperatures and excessive humidity. A shift in the color balance and a loss of detail and highlights occur as deterioration progresses. Slides can also be destroyed by fungus or insects that feed on the gelatin emulsion, another reason why proper storage of slides is so important.

PRESERVATION PROGRAM

Slide libraries should develop an integrated preservation program that shares the concerns of book collections. Where slides are part of a multimedia facility, their special requirements should be included in the total preservation policy of the institution. In all cases, such a program should address the following issues:

1. Acquiring images on the most stable films
2. Binding, technical processing, and preparation of the slides in a manner appropriate to intended use
3. Storing the slides in containers and equipment made of safe and stable materials
4. Providing environmental controls that are specifically designed to meet the special demands of film collections
5. Providing guidelines for handling and projection
6. Preparing a disaster plan with specific recommendations for photographic materials

Such policies should also cover special items in the collection, especially those having importance. Just as a librarian identifies rare books for special collections, so too should a slide curator identify unique slides with archival value, such as lantern slides showing buildings or sites now altered or destroyed, slides that exhibit historically significant photographic processes, and slides that provide a record of a collection, exhibition, performance, etc., which cannot be replaced. These items should be isolated for special care. Unique slides, not restricted by copyright, should be copied and only duplicates projected. The originals should be placed in cold storage according to the stringent guidelines for archival preservation outlined in the previous chapter.

At the other extreme, there may be slides with only temporary value—instructional materials needed for a single semester or on a topic outside the main focus of the collection. These may not warrant the expense of special processing as their need is limited. Slides that are subjected to long projection times will show color losses in a short time. For heavily used items, it may be more cost-effective to invest in multiple copies initially, rather than to purchase replacements repeatedly as they fade or are damaged by use.

The majority of slides in a collection fall between these two extremes. Although slides may have long-term research value, they are often neglected because the enormous expense of cold storage cannot be justified for the collection. Yet the time and expense required for cataloguing, processing, and maintaining these materials demand that provisions be made to insure that the useful life of the slides be as long as possible.

ACQUISITIONS

There are several types of sources for slides: commercial suppliers, copy photography, original field photography, and duplication from personal collections. Regardless of the sources, librarians should learn to recognize various film types and try to purchase slides only on the most stable film stocks. The following list provides information about the keeping characteristics of some of the popular slide films. It contains unofficial Kodak data on dark fading time, at 75 °F (24 °C) and 40 percent RH, required to reach a density loss of .10 from 1.0 original density of one or more dyes.

More than 50 Years

Kodak Dye Transfer Prints

Kodachrome 25 Film (K-14)

Kodachrome 64 Film (K-14)

Kodachrome 40 Film (Type A) 5070 (K-14)

Kodachrome 25 Movie (Daylight) (K-14)

Kodachrome 40 Movie (Type A) (K-14)

21 to 50 Years

Kodachrome II (Daylight) (K-12)

Kodachrome II Professional, Type A (K-12)

Kodachrome-X Film (K-12)

Ektachrome 400 Film (5074) (E-6)

Ektachrome 200 Film (Daylight) (E-6)

Ektachrome 160 Film (Tungsten) (E-6)

Ektachrome 64 Film (Daylight) (E-6)
Ektachrome 200 Professional Film (Daylight) 5036 (E-6)
Ektachrome 160 Professional Film (Tungsten) (E-6)
Ektachrome 64 Professional Film (Daylight) 6117 & 5017 (E-6)
Ektachrome 50 Professional Film (Tungsten) 6118 & 5018 (E-6)
Ektachrome Slide Duplicating Film 5071 (E-6)
Ektachrome Duplicating Film 6121 (E-6)

11 to 20 Years

Ektachrome-X Film (E-4)
High Speed Ektachrome Film (Daylight) (E-4)
High Speed Ektachrome Film (Tungsten) (E-4)
Ektachrome EF Film 7241 (Daylight) (ME-4)
Ektachrome EF Film 7242 (Tungsten) (ME-4)
Ektachrome MS Film 7256 (ME-4)

6 to 10 Years

Instant Print Film PR10
Ektacolor 37 RC Paper (EP-2 + EP-3 Stabilizer)
Ektacolor 74 RC Paper (EP-2 + EP-3 Stabilizer)
Ektachrome RC Paper, Type 1993
Ektacolor Slide Film 5028
Ektacolor Print Film 4109

6 Years or Less

Vericolor II Film, Types S & L (C-41)
Kodacolor II Film (C-41)
Ektachrome Film 6115 (Daylight) (E-3)
Ektachrome Film 6116—Type B (E-3)
Ektachrome Slide Duplicating Film 5038 (E-4)
Ektachrome Duplicating Film 6120 (E-3)
Kodacolor-X Film (C-22)
Ektacolor Film, Types S & L (C-22)
Ektacolor Internegative Film 6008 & 6110 (Modified C-22)
Eastman Color Negative Film 5254 & 7254 (ECN)
Eastman Color Negative II Film 5247 & 7247 (ECN-2)

Eastman Color Print Film 5381 & 7381 (ECP)

Eastman Color SP Print Film 5383 & 7383 (ECP-2)

Ektachrome 40 Movie Film 7262 (EM-25)

Note: This data is from both published Kodak information and from several sources within the Kodak Company in Rochester; the names of the sources must remain confidential. We believe the information is accurate; however, much of the data has not been approved for public distribution by the Kodak Company. This data is for products in use through mid-1978. Historical collections will largely consist of the older materials listed.

Henry Wilhelm

Source: Gail Fisher-Taylor, ''Interview: Henry Wilhelm,'' *Photo Communiqué* 3:1 (Spring 1981). Reprinted by permission of Henry Wilhelm.

Film stability is affected by how the slides are used. Certain films will last better in the dark while others are better suited for projection. The following list indicates the relative stability of common color transparency films, where 1 represents the most stable films and 5, the least stable.

Dark Keeping

1. Kodak Kodachrome 25 (K-14)
   Kodak Kodachrome 64 (K-14)
   Kodak Kodachrome 40 Type A (K-14)

2. Kodak Kodachrome II (K-12)
   Kodak Kodachrome-X (K-12)
   Kodak Kodachrome Type A (K-12)
   Kodak Ektachrome 64 (E-6)
   Kodak Ektachrome 200 (E-6)
   Kodak Ektachrome 400 (E-6)
   Kodak Ektachrome 160 Tungsten (E-6)
   Fuji Fujichrome 100 (E-6)
   Kodak Ektachrome Duplicating Film (E-6)

3. Kodak Ektachrome-X (E-4)
   Kodak High Speed Ektachrome (E-4)
   Fuji Fujichrome R-100 (E-4)

4. Agfa Agfachrome 64
   Agfa Agfachrome 100
   GAF 64 Color Slide Film
   GAF 200 Color Slide Film
   GAF 500 Color Slide Film

5. Kodak Ektachrome Professional Films (E-3)
   Kodak Ektachrome Film (E-2)
   Kodak Ektachrome Film (E-1)
   Kodak Ektachrome Duplicating Film (E-4)

During Projection*

1. Kodak Ektachrome 64 (E-6)
   Kodak Ektachrome 200 (E-6)
   Kodak Ektachrome 400 (E-6)
   Kodak Ektachrome 160 Tungsten (E-6)
   Fuji Fujichrome 100 (E-6)
   Kodak Ektachrome Duplicating Film (E-6)
   Kodak Ektachrome-X (E-4)
   Kodak High Speed Ektachrome (E-4)
   Fuji Fujichrome R-100 (E-4)

2. Kodak Kodachrome 25 (K-14)
   Kodak Kodachrome 64 (K-14)
   Kodak Kodachrome 40 Type A (K-14)
   Kodak Kodachrome II (K-12)
   Kodak Kodachrome-X (K-12)
   Kodak Kodachrome Type A (K-12)
   Agfa Agfachrome 64
   Agfa Agfachrome 100

3. GAF 64 Color Slide Film
   GAF 200 Color Slide Film
   GAF 500 Color Slide Film

* For a typical amateur photographer, the light fading stability of most 35mm color slide films is adequate for the usually limited total times of projection (projection times longer than one minute at a time and a total of 20 minutes for Kodachrome films—45 minutes for Ektachrome films—should be avoided). Dark keeping stability is generally the most important consideration for a color transparency film. If prolonged projection is expected, duplicate slides should be made for projection purposes.

Dark keeping rankings are based on results from tests performed as outlined in *ANSI PH1.42-1969 Method for Comparing the Color Stabilities of Photographs*, modified to use 45% and 76% relative humidity with the results averaged. Agfa Agfachrome films in particular are very sensitive to high relative humidity during storage; the dark keeping stability of these films can be greatly improved by storing them in a low (25-40%) relative humidity environment.

Source: Gail Fisher-Taylor, "Interview: Henry Wilhelm," *Photo Communiqué* 3:1 (Spring 1981). Chart copyright © 1981 by Henry Wilhelm. Reprinted by permission.

Guidelines for evaluating the quality of commercial slides appear in the "Statement on Slide Quality Standards" prepared jointly by the Visual Resources groups of the College Art Association and the Art Libraries Society of North America (ARLIS/NA) and reproduced at the end of this chapter. Color slides purchased from commercial sources should be evaluated against these criteria and any unacceptable slides should be returned promptly to the vendor. It may be necessary to request information beforehand about whether the slides to be purchased are duplicates or originals, in addition to technical details about film type and processing. For art and architecture history slides, this information is available in the *Slide Buyers Guide* (4th ed., Kansas City: Mid-America College Art Association, Visual Resources Committee, 1980). This data, compiled by Nancy De Laurier with the assistance of other slide curators who have provided evaluations of purchased slides, includes technical details about the production techniques used by each dealer.

Many slide collections used for educational purposes are built with materials produced by in-house copy photography from books or other printed materials. Procedures for photographing images from printed sources are described in detail in the *Guide to Copy Photography for Visual Resources Collections* (Albuquerque: MACAA, 1980). For both in-house copy photography and for original slides taken in the field, fresh film is a requirement. It should be stored under the conditions recommended by the manufacturer, used as soon as possible, and processed immediately after exposure. Consider using silver halide film for photographing black-and-white images because of its greater permanence. Ideally, the librarian should supervise the photographer directly to maintain control over the work.

Another source of slides for the collection is the duplication of original slides owned by individuals. If this is done, be certain that the slides to be reproduced are free of dust and fingerprints. Otherwise fibers or smudges will be copied in the duplicates. Use a reputable commercial laboratory or send the originals to a Kodak processing laboratory and specify that the contrasts be controlled and that color accuracy be maintained. If the results are not satisfactory, return the material to the lab for reprocessing. Eastman Kodak currently has two Ektachrome-type 35mm slide duplicating films on the market: Ektachrome 5071 and SO-366. Both offer low contrasts and good color reproduction in most slide duplicating operations. Copyrighted slides from commercial dealers cannot be duplicated without the permission of the dealer or copyright holder.

Few libraries today actively acquire lantern slides. But in addition to acquiring what is only available in old collections, it is still possible to produce lantern slides. However, these are usually direct-positive images on cellulose triacetate or polyester base film rather than positive prints on glass. Negatives, when available, should be retained for future replacement copies; these should be stored according to the guidelines outlined in the previous chapter.

SLIDE BINDING

Once purchased, slides usually arrive in glassless cardboard or plastic binders, often requiring additional preparation for use. If slides are to be handled extensively over a long period of time, they should be mounted between glass to protect the film from dust, abrasion, and the heat of the projector. Slide sets that remain as a unit in a projector tray or are used infrequently may not need any extra protection, but eventually they too may become dusty. Fingerprints and fibers which would otherwise destroy an unprotected slide can easily be removed from the glass surface of a mount (see handling section). Film in open mounts also tends to react to the heat during projection by buckling or "popping," causing the image to appear out of focus after a few seconds on the screen. Although slide bindings are expensive and require staff time to prepare, they prolong the life of the slide.

Commercial glass mounts are made of plastic or metal and glass. Most are easy to assemble, thin enough to fit the majority of today's projectors and trays, and usually capable of withstanding the heat of an overheated projector without melting. A detailed evaluation of the available brands and instructions for preparation appear in the *Guide to Equipment for Slide Maintenance and Viewing* (Albuquerque: MACAA, 1983) and Irvine's *Slide Libraries.*

Slide bindings are available with two types of cover glass: regular, and anti-Newton glass, which is a special etched glass useful for counteracting spectrum rings known as "Newton rings." These are evident during projection and are caused when the shiny base side of the film comes in contact with another shiny surface such as regular glass. Newton rings are especially evident in light or white areas of the image.

In the past, it was considered preferable for the slide binding to allow some air circulation between the film and the glass so that the film could expand and contract during projection. This theory was effectively challenged by A. G. Tull, a Fellow of the Royal Photographic Society, who proposed "Glass Contact Binding."[3] With this method, the film is sandwiched directly between two pieces of glass which are held together by gummed paper strips (much like the old lantern slides) and masked on the outside of the glass (see Figure 5.2). This arrangement eliminates the air pocket inside the mount in which moisture can condense. While up and down movement of the film is thus restricted, it is still able to expand sideways, if necessary.

Christine Sundt, slide curator at the University of Wisconsin-Madison, came to a similar conclusion recently after additional research.[4] She suggests, however, that Tull's method should be somewhat modified to be more effective—that reflective polyester film tapes be used both for binding and masking instead of Tull's recommended black-paper tape, which tends to absorb both moisture and heat. The use of nonporous, reflective poly-

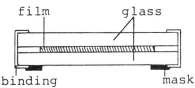

Figure 5.2. The Basic Principle Governing both Tull's "Glass Contact Binding" System and Sundt's "'Airtight' Glass-Film Sandwich." Sundt recommends using reflective polyester film tapes for binding and masking. Diagram by R. Sundt.

ester film tapes is beneficial, furthermore, since it creates an airtight enclosure for the film. In this enclosure the film will be safe from whatever moisture or pollution may exist in the storage area.

An alternative to glass mounts for little-used materials is the acetate sleeve which fits over the open-frame mount in which the slide usually arrives from processing. Acetate sleeve protectors are inexpensive and can be quickly fitted around the slide. They could be useful for materials kept in programmed sets. However, one should be wary of using sleeves over cardboard mounts in humid climates since cardboard absorbs and maintains moisture which may contribute to fungus or mold growth during storage or damage to the film during projection.

Whatever technique is selected, the films and supplies should be kept clean and the work carefully supervised. The work area should be dust-free and neatly organized, with good lighting, large work surfaces, and ample storage space for equipment, supplies, and work in progress (see Figure 5.3). If the film is processed in-house, it should be allowed to dry completely before mounting. When mounting film between glass, it is important that the area should not be humid, otherwise moisture will be trapped within the binding.

When handling the slides during mounting, always be careful to keep fingerprints off the film and the glass of the mount. Workers' hands should be clean, and preferably they should wear disposable cotton gloves. Lint and superficial dust can be removed from the film and glass surfaces with a soft lint-free cloth or camel's hair brush. Avoid using cloths impregnated with antistatic cleaner because the chemicals may harm the film. If the film or glass is very dirty, use one of the cleaning agents recommended in the MACAA *Guide to Equipment* cited previously. Denatured alcohol is particularly effective for removing greasy residues from glass. Seemingly insignificant dust particles or spots are annoying when projected onto a large screen.

Slides frequently need to be masked to eliminate extraneous information or distracting areas in an image. Use tapes only as recommended, preferably on the glass instead of on the film itself. Avoid using cloth tapes or "masking tape"; these will deteriorate under heat and ooze adhesive onto the film or glass. To complete processing, slides should be labeled accurately and

Figure 5.3. Binding Area of Work Room, Slide and Photo Collection, Department of Art, University of Texas, Austin, Fine Arts Building, Completed in 1979. Photograph by Ron Jameson.

given a signal dot in the lower left corner of the image to facilitate correct insertion in projectors. Labels and signal dots should have a permanent adhesive.

ENVIRONMENTAL CONTROLS

The most important measures a slide curator or librarian can take with regard to a slide collection are to control light, temperature, and relative humidity (RH) in the work and storage areas. Color materials are subject to two types of deterioration: light fading in reaction to exposure to visible light and ultraviolet radiation; and dark fading, which occurs in the dark in reaction to temperature and humidity. When temperatures over 75 °F–80 °F (24 °C–28 °C) are combined with RH of 65 percent or more, moisture will condense on the film or within the typical slide mount within a very short period of time—sometimes in no more than a matter of hours. If conditions persist for several weeks, fungus could begin to grow within the slide mount, first on the glass facing the base side of the film, then on the base side itself, and finally on the emulsion surface, causing permanent damage to the image.[5] To prevent these problems, slides should be stored at low temperatures with controlled humidity. Excessive dryness can also be a problem, causing the film to become brittle, warped, and even cracked.

Most slide collections are used as teaching or reference resources. They are created to meet the specific demands of patrons, teachers, or students who wish to browse, study, or select slides for presentations. Acceptable conditions for a circulating or active collection are 70 °F (21.5 °C) or less with RH of 25 to 45 percent. Fluctuations in temperature and RH should be kept to a minimum since this "cycling" can produce dimensional changes in the emulsion layers of the slides. Administrators of slide collections should apply for exemption from government regulations for energy conservation which restrict the use of heating and cooling equipment. Applications for exemption are usually available from the physical plant department of an institution. Administrators should be made aware that it is short-sighted to turn off environmental control systems at night or over weekends.

Ideally, slides should be housed in a building with an adequate heating, ventilating, and air conditioning system which circulates and filters air, maintains a constant temperature year round, and controls humidity. A total system, such as that found in areas where computers are housed, is preferable to window or household air conditioners that do not control humidity adequately. However, if this is not feasible, air conditioners in combination with room dehumidifiers should be used; something is definitely better than nothing. An electrical refrigeration-type dehumidifier controlled by a humidistat is best. The equipment should have an automatic shut-off to avoid flooding when the water collector is full, unless the unit can be installed to feed automatically into a drainpipe. When central heating causes excessive dryness, humidifiers should be used to maintain a safe level of moisture for the slides.

As an additional measure to protect film against excessively high humidity, silica gel or calcium chloride placed within individual storage cabinets may be used to absorb moisture. Silica gel lasts indefinitely, but it requires reactivation by heating when the moisture capacity is reached, usually when the color indicator changes from blue to pink. Eastman Kodak's pamphlet, *Prevention and Removal of Fungus on Prints and Films* (AE-22, Rochester, 1971), recommends one ounce of silica gel per fifty Kodachrome transparencies in Kodak "Ready-Mounts." However, Eastman Kodak, in its publication *Preservation of Photographs* (F-30, Rochester, 1979), does not recommend the use of silica gel or other desiccants as a permanent measure against excessive humidity. Abrasive or reactive dust from these chemical compounds may cause damage to the film.

Temperature and humidity can be monitored regularly by using a thermometer and (for RH) a psychrometer or hygrometer. Recording hygrothermographs provide a written record of fluctuations over long periods of time; although they are expensive, they should be considered for large or especially valuable collections.

Light is damaging to collections because it accelerates fading, especially of color images. Slides should be stored in darkness and exposed to the light only during use. Light can be controlled by drapes, blinds, ultraviolet (UV) film on window panes, UV roller shades, and UV shields on fluorescent lights. Slides are also exposed to light when they are sorted or reviewed on light tables, which are usually illuminated by fluorescent tubes. To limit UV radiation from light tables or from slide viewing (visual display) racks, the tubes can be covered by a UV shield, a sheet of UF3 Plexiglas can be installed under the surface covering, or tubes with lower UV emissions can be selected and installed.[6] Avoid viewing slides on the light table for long periods. The light table should be vented to prevent heat from building up. However, the intense light and heat of projection causes far greater damage to color slides than exposure to ambient lighting or heat from a light table (see section on projection).

Considering the special problems associated with slides, it may be advisable to reevaluate policies for integrated media collections. Since slides and films are prone to suffer extensive damage from high humidity, media centers without climate controls may want to segregate slides and other film materials in special areas where air conditioning and dehumidification can be provided.

Color slides of archival value should be kept in cold storage according to the same rigorous standards described for color negatives in the preceding chapter: in darkness, at 0 °F–10 °F (– 18 °C to – 12 °C) with relative humidity of 25–30 percent. If an institution already has a special cold storage vault for its microform masters, for example, this would also serve well for archival slides since the storage requirements are the same for both. As noted in the previous chapter, a frost-free refrigerator can be adapted to store color materials, provided that a humidity gauge is used to insure safe conditions at all times.

STORAGE

Besides monitoring the environment, librarians must also select the storage equipment for the slide collection. Their choice will be influenced by a variety of factors. Major considerations include space and whether media are to be integrated in a general collection or segregated. Storage should reflect patterns of use if it is to promote rather than hinder effective exploitation of the collection. Most important, storage materials and equipment should reinforce preservation efforts and not contribute to the untimely deterioration of the slides. The reading list at the end of this chapter provides more extensive information on this subject, and the Appendix lists suppliers, including names of manufacturers. Irvine's coverage in *Slide Libraries* is comprehensive, especially for file drawer cabinets which are used in the majority of academic slide collections. The *Guide to Equipment for Slide Maintenance and Viewing* is also helpful.

Within integrated media collections where slides are purchased and catalogued as discrete sets, shelved with other media, and circulated as units, slides are usually placed in standardized containers on regular library shelves. Among the types available from library supply companies are drop-front containers, zipped polyethylene wallets, pamphlet boxes, and loose-leaf binders. These usually provide flexible space for slides, cassettes, filmstrips, and their printed guides. The binders and containers offer protection during circulation, are compact and sturdy, can be labelled like book materials and stored on regular library shelves. These fall into two main categories:

Slide tray or magazine storage. Programmed sets of 35mm slides can be easily stored in trays or magazines. Because the slides are meant to be used in a prearranged order and not removed from trays during normal use, acetate sleeves may be all that is needed for extra protection. Trays are relatively inexpensive and usually come with their own cardboard or plastic storage box which can be labelled and interfiled along with their printed guides and other media on the same topic. Carousel trays and cubes are made of high impact plastic (polystyrene) which is safe for photographic materials.

Plastic sleeve storage. Groups of twelve to twenty-four slides often arrive as sets in transparent plastic sheets which provide an individual pocket for each slide. Such sleeves or wallets are particularly popular with media librarians and private collectors because they come in standard loose-leaf sizes and offer various options for incorporating or integrating accompanying materials. When slides are organized in a loose-leaf notebook, they can be filed on standard library shelves like books. They can be stored in conventional filing cabinets (see Figure 5.4) or suspended from specially designed filing cabinet racks. Because the sheets are transparent or translucent, the user has immediate visual access, making it easy to browse. However, preservation problems may arise if slides are kept in certain types of these sleeves for extended periods of time. If stacked tightly in highly humid conditions, the slides could stick to the smooth surface of the sleeve pockets, causing damage from ferrotyping.

Plastic materials used for storing photographic products should be chemically inert and nondestructive. Unfortunately, many of the sleeves that are provided with slide sets are made of polyvinylchloride (PVC) which can damage slides by releasing harmful gases during storage. Slide pages are now available in safe plastics, polypropylene, and rigid acrylic, for long-term storage of valuable slides. On the whole, sleeves are an inexpensive and convenient storage aid for slides, provided that they are made of safe materials.

When slides are catalogued, filed, and circulated as separate entities as in large collections, more compact and flexible storage is required.

Filing drawer cabinets. These are sets of drawers in a cabinet which can be placed on a bench, table, or custom-made base. Cabinets designed specifically for slides are available commercially (see Figure 5.5). Standard card catalogs can also be adapted for slides by installing custom-designed inserts to accommodate either single or group slide filing. This type of storage system has advantages: it is easy to add new material, guide cards, and shelf-list information, and groups of slides can be withdrawn with a single effort. One drawback is that browsing can be time-consuming; each slide must be removed separately for viewing and, in the process, can be easily misfiled when returned. Because this system encourages handling, slides should be mounted between glass to protect them from damage.

The storage cabinets should be made of metal, preferably baked enamel over steel, anodized aluminum, or stainless steel. Wood is a less desirable material. If used, wood should be properly aged and sealed with a synthetic resin to prevent the release of gases that are harmful to photographic materials. The storage drawers should be raised at least six inches above floor level to prevent water damage in case of flood.

Lantern slides are usually housed in specially designed wooden cases or cabinets. Other alternatives are certain types of metal cabinets, especially those used for microfilm, which can be adapted for lantern slides by installing custom-designed inserts.

For all slide cabinets, supporting dividers placed every five to ten slides or a back stop at the end of a row are essential, otherwise individual slides may fall and crack when groups are removed for viewing. Drawers with individual slots offer the best protection against breakage, but filing and integrating new material is often tedious.

Visual display racks. Up to 100 or more slides can be stored in a metal frame within a display rack. Each storage unit has several racks that can be pulled out individually and illuminated by the light source which is part of the unit (see Figure 5.6). Browsing is easy. However, like plastic page storage, this system is awkward for large or rapidly expanding collections because it requires more space per slide than drawer filing and it does not allow for easy integration of new material. This system works best for slides filed by consecutive number rather than by groups. Its drawback for slide preservation is that all 100 or so slides are exposed to light, usually a fluorescent beam, whenever a single item in the rack needs to be examined.

Other materials used in storage units, especially slide cabinets, are guide cards that must be made of neutral paper or of an inert plastic. Polyester guide cards or stock are available from library distributors. If humidity is a problem, then polyester cards would be preferable.

PROJECTION

Although continual exposure to ambient light contributes to the gradual fading of color slides, far more crucial and devastating is exposure to intense light and heat during projection. Since slides in a circulating library collection will probably be projected, it is important that librarians and users know how to minimize damage due to projection. To prolong the life of a slide collection, the following guidelines should be observed:

1. Slides having archival value should not be projected. Copies should be furnished (if permitted by copyright) for general use.

2. Only quality equipment should be used and should be serviced regularly to insure continued safe performance.

3. Illumination should be kept as low as possible within the wattage recommended by the manufacturer (high intensity xenon arc projectors should not be used).

4. The length of time the slide is projected should be kept to a minimum.

Information about projection equipment can be found in the most current edition of *Audio-Visual Equipment Directory* and in the forthcoming revision of the *Guide to Equipment.* The continued use of faulty or inefficient projection equipment will prove to be economically unwise if slides are destroyed because of it.

Libraries that maintain their own projectors and audio-visual equipment should establish and maintain their own standards for use. Where audio-visual equipment is maintained by a separate department outside the jurisdiction of the library, standards for maintenance and use should be established by the librarian in cooperation with the department in charge.

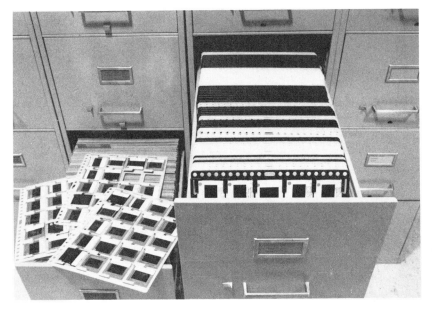

Figure 5.4. The open-frame design of the Plastican rigid Slide Frame makes viewing easy even without the aid of a light box. Visual aberrations are reduced and color distortion is eliminated. Photograph by C. Sundt, courtesy of Plastican Corp.

Figure 5.5. This sturdy metal cabinet made by Neumade holds six single-unit 2×2 inch slide cabinets. Neumade also makes single-unit cabinets for $3\frac{1}{4} \times 4$ inch (lantern) slides and filmstrips. Photograph courtesy of Neumade Products.

Figure 5.6. The Multiplex System 4000 provides viewing and storage all in one. This visual display rack system has a built-in light source. The modular design of the base accommodates a variety of film formats. Photograph courtesy of Multiplex Display Fixture Co.

Ideally, projectors should function within a temperature range of approximately 140 °F–160 °F (60 °C–71 °C). However, when not in proper working order, they have been known to register as high as 212 °F (100 °C)—boiling! A simple way to determine their condition is to measure their at-gate temperature with an Omegalabel, which is a self-adhesive temperature monitor that can be applied to any standard slide mount. Usually, if the temperature exceeds 175 °F (79 °C), this is a good indication that something is amiss in the projector. Typical trouble spots include the heat filter (is it in place and unbroken?), the fan (is it revolving properly or is its movement being obstructed by dislocated wires, foreign objects, etc.?), the exhaust vent/air intake (is anything blocking the vent, restricting the air supply?), and the motor (is it running smoothly; does it need cleaning or lubrication?). It is important that the projector include a heat-absorbing glass (or its equivalent) and an efficient cooling system. Ideally, slides should be allowed to warm up slowly prior to projection. This is most efficiently accomplished with carousel trays or magazines which allow the entire group of slides on the projector to be heated prior to illumination.

The length of projection time is critical to the lifespan of a slide. Film manufacturers recommend that this not exceed sixty seconds, while thirty seconds or less is preferable. Unfortunately, the length of time a slide is projected is usually one thing that cannot be controlled by librarians. At most, they can attempt to educate their users, perhaps through an exhibit of faded slides or "before and after" slide sets. If student projectionists are hired to show slides, they should be instructed in how to recognize an overheated projector. A list of suggestions for proper handling should be given to users when slides are being discharged.

HANDLING

Other aspects of handling are also important. At the circulation desk, users should be given a box or bag in which to carry individual slides to prevent loss, damage, or breakage. These can be the plastic boxes that often accompany new 35mm slides or which can be purchased in lots from photographic and some library supply companies. Heavy duty zip-seal plastic bags are especially useful for additional protection against moisture (rain, snow, and excessive humidity). Special carrying cases with individual slots are available and advisable for lantern slides. When the slides are returned, they should be cleaned. Glass that is dirty or covered with fingerprints can be wiped clean with a chamois or a soft cloth. A light application of denatured alcohol to the glass will remove grease effectively without introducing moisture. When sets are returned, be certain that all slides are present and in the proper order for the set. Rubber bands that contain residual sulfur should never be used to group slides in open frame mounts. A carpet on the floor may minimize slide breakage if a glass slide is dropped, but it may also contribute dust, fibers, and static, especially if the area is heavily traversed.

There is a tendency among users to regard slides as small, inexpensive items; they need to be reminded of their monetary value and their long-term research potential. A simple notice outlining basic guidelines could help to reinforce these values.

HELP SAVE OUR SLIDES!

Color slides are highly susceptible to fading and damage from exposure to light, heat, and high humidity.

PLEASE . . .

Keep the slides in darkness when they are not being used.

Avoid overheating them unnecessarily. Do not leave them in trunks, glove-compartments, or back windows of cars, on top of radiators, heaters, etc. A cool dry environment is best.

Be certain your projector does not overheat. Use the low-lamp setting and, by all means, check to see that the fan is working.

Do not project an individual slide for more than one minute.

Please tell us if you have noticed any problems with the slides when you projected them.

THANK YOU!

DISASTER PREPAREDNESS

All libraries should formulate a disaster plan. Water-damaged photographic materials require different treatment than water-logged books or papers. In the event of flooding, wet films and plates should be kept wet. Use plastic containers and keep the materials covered with cold running water—the colder, the better; add ice to keep the temperature down, if necessary. Seek professional advice at once. If local assistance (from a professional photofinishing laboratory) is unavailable during an emergency, call Eastman Kodak in Rochester, N.Y., at (716) 724-4000 for advice. Details about in-house treatment of water-damaged photographic materials are given in both Weinstein and Booth, *Collection, Use and Care of Historical Photographs* (Nashville, Tenn.: American Association for State and

Local History, 1977) and Eastman Kodak's *Preservation of Photographs* (Technical Publication F-30, Rochester, 1979).

In the disaster plan, the procedures for handling damaged photographic materials should be carefully outlined. The names and addresses of the closest professional photographic laboratories equipped to deal with damaged materials should be noted. It is advisable to discuss your plans beforehand with the laboratories named in your document so that they, too, will know what to expect if disaster strikes.

CONSERVATION TREATMENT

The treatment of deteriorated slides is a very complicated and costly procedure. It is preferable, therefore, to avert the need in the first place: to isolate valuable originals and other archival items; to provide properly controlled storage conditions; and to buy only the most stable films from commercial sources as new materials.

Today, lantern slides are nearly obsolete as teaching tools. While many institutions are now in the process of converting entire collections to the 2 × 2 inch format, it would be unwise and unfortunate if valuable early lantern slides were overlooked and automatically discarded. If a library has no space for its unused lantern slides, the material should be offered to a larger research institution with facilities to retain such items, or to a local historical society, rather than destroyed.

Because fungi on films deserve special and immediate attention, this problem is better treated by a photograph conservator. Eastman Kodak offers basic directions for treatment in its publications, *Prevention and Removal of Fungus on Prints and Films* (AE-22, Rochester, 1971) and *Preservation of Photographs* (F-30, Rochester, 1979). If fungus is present on the glass surface or on the non-emulsion (base) side of the film, the glass can be cleaned or replaced. If the emulsion of the film has been affected, the destruction is irreversible.

The repair and restoration of faded color slides is usually beyond the scope of all but the most specialized libraries or facilities. One method, developed by Eastman Kodak and currently being used, involves producing color masks to replace the color that has been lost to fading. This method is complex and is designed primarily for treating large format transparencies; it requires the specialized services of an expert.

Normal slide duplication, without color correction, may be a means of preserving slides on film stocks known to have a very short lifespan. In order to be effective, this should be done before any deterioration is noticeable.

SUMMARY

In conclusion, distinction should be made between expendable circulating slide collections and archival slide collections. The latter should be treated as precious and, perhaps, rare artifacts. For circulating slides, only films on durable stock should be purchased; thereafter, they should be stored in a controlled environment to maximize their useful life. High humidity should be avoided above all else because of the threat of mold and the accelerated rate of deterioration. Despite these precautions, the permanence of a circulating slide collection will always be relative to the type of use to which the slides are subjected, particularly the length of projection time. The type of mounts, storage materials, and equipment selected should be appropriate to the slide's anticipated lifespan, purpose, and intended use. Because of the impermanence of slide materials, replacement costs should always be taken into account in a budget. While patron use cannot always be controlled, it is possible for slide librarians to educate users and to be aware of sound preservation practices.

STATEMENT ON SLIDE QUALITY STANDARDS

Issued jointly by ARLIS/NA and CAA Visual Resources Groups

COLOR: The color should be as true as possible to the original work of art, neither over- nor under-exposed, nor off-color due to the lighting or the film type.

FILM: The film should have fine-grained resolution and color should be stable with a minimum shelf-life of ten years. Duplicate slides should be newly printed as far as possible to maximize their shelf life. High contrast in duplicate slides should be controlled. The film should be clean with no dirt or scratches on the surface nor duplicated onto the film from the master transparency or negative. The size 24 × 36 mm is preferable; the supplier should indicate other sizes if used.

PHOTOGRAPHY: The slides must be in focus and full-frame as far as possible without being cropped. Lighting should be adequate and even throughout, and without glare or reflections. In photographing paintings and buildings, distortion should be avoided.

INFORMATION: Accurate and complete information is necessary: artist's full name, nationality and dates, title of the work, medium, date and dimensions if known, and location. Cropped slides should be identified as such, and details should be described. An indication of the orientation is important, especially on details and abstract works of art. It should be clear which is the front of the slide.

It is important to indicate whether the slide will be an original or a duplicate: specific information on the source of the slide, film type and processing would be appreciated. Return and replacement policies should be spelled out.

PRICE: The price of the slide should fairly reflect the costs of production and distribution.

NOTES

1. Paul Saettler, *A History of Instructional Technology* (New York: McGraw-Hill, 1968), p. 79.

2. For subscription information, write to Nancy De Laurier, Art and Art History, UMKC, 204 Fine Arts, Kansas City, MO 64110.

3. A. G. Tull, "Film Transparencies Between Glass," *British Journal of Photography* 125 (1978): 322-23, 349-51, 353.

4. Christine L. Sundt, "Mounting Slide Film Between Glass: For Preservation or Destruction?" *Visual Resources: An International Journal of Documentation* II: 1/2/3 (1981-82): 37-62.

5. According to Pat Toomy of Rice University, who delivered a paper entitled "High Relative Humidity: A Threat to Slide Collections" at the annual meeting of the Mid-America College Art Association (MACAA) Visual Resources session in Houston in October 1980.

6. Raymond Lafontaine and Patricia A. Wood, "Fluorescent Lamps," Technical Bulletin #7 (Canadian Conservation Institute, 1980) lists fluorescent lamps with the levels of UV emission.

SUGGESTED READING

The following items include the most recent publications relating specifically to slide preservation. Irvine contains an extensive bibliography of pre-1979 publications on all aspects of slide librarianship. The MACAA publications provide up-to-date information on preservation and on storage and equipment. See also the reading list in the preceding chapter.

American National Standards Institute. *Practice for Storage of Processed Safety Photographic Film*. ANSI Standard PH1.43-1981.

Art Documentation, 1982–   . (Formerly *ARLIS/NA Newsletter*, 1972-1982.)

    See especially the columns on Preservation and the Visual Resources Special Interest Group for current information.

Audio-Visual Equipment Directory. Fairfax, Va.: National Audio-Visual Association. Annual.

Balsley, Gene, and Peter Moore. "How to File and Store Slides," *Modern Photography* 89 (January 1980): 104-7, 165, 168, 170.

    Aimed at orienting the individual collector to conservation. Includes a list of suppliers.

Eastman Kodak Company. *Kodak Color Films*. Technical Publication E-77. 1980.

    Information on color films and proper processing.

_____. *Planning and Producing Slide Programs*. Technical publication S-30. 1978.

    Sections on "Proper Care of Slide Film" and "Handling, Care and Preservation of Mounted Transparencies."

_____. *Preservation of Photographs.* Technical Publication F-30. 1979.

Basic introduction to photographic conservation.

_____. *Prevention and Removal of Fungus on Prints and Films.* Technical Publication AE-22. 1980.

Fisher-Taylor, Gail. "Interview: Henry Wilhelm." *Photo Communiqué* 3:1 (Spring 1981), 2–21.

Wilhelm discusses his current research into color stability.

Guide to Copy Photography for Visual Resource Collections. edited by Rosemary Kuehn and Arlene Zelda Richardson. Albuquerque: Mid-America College Art Association, Visual Resources Committee, 1980.

Guide to Equipment for Slide Maintenance and Viewing. edited by Gillian Scott. Albuquerque: Mid-America College Art Asociation, Visual Resources Committee, 1978.

Comprehensive guide to maintenance and viewing, including storage, projection equipment, and slide binding. List of suppliers is included. A revised edition is scheduled for publication in 1983.

International Bulletin for Photographic Documentation of the Visual Arts. 1980– . (Formerly *Mid-America College Art Association Slides and Photographs Newsletter.* 1974–1979.)

Although oriented to the curators of art and architecture collections in museums and colleges, the bulletin contains much of general interest on slide preservation. See particularly the columns "Conservation," "Ask the Photographer," and "Slide Market News." Also see "Photographic Journals" for articles of interest in professional photographic literature.

Irvine, Betty Jo. *Slide Libraries: A Guide for Academic Institutions, Museums, and Special Collections.* 2nd ed. Littleton, Co.: Libraries Unlimited, 1979.

The basic text on slide collections and their management, with an extensive bibliography. The second edition includes information on preservation and environment as part of the storage chapter.

Pacey, Philip. *Art Library Manual.* New York: Bowker/Art Libraries Society, 1977.

Chapter on slides.

Positive. London, Ontario: Brenda MacEachern.

This newsletter for Canadian visual collections librarians is edited and published by Brenda MacEachern, Slide Curator, Visual Arts Department, University of Western Ontario.

Tull, A. G., ed. *The Conservation of Colour Photographic Records*, Monograph No. 1, RPS Colour Group, The Royal Photographic Society of Great Britain, RPS Publications, Ltd., 1974, including among others, the following items: Ehrlich, J. "Heating of Slides by Light Absorption," *Colour Group Bulletin* No. 47 (1970).

Fabb, G. N. "Heat Generated in a Colour Slide by Light Absorption," *Colour Group Bulletin* No. 46 (1969): 10–12.

_____. "Summary of Sub-Committee's Investigation into Miniature Slide Projector Performance," *Colour Group Bulletin* No. 21 (1954).

Fereday, E. "Methods of Slide Mounting: Their Effects on Steaming-Up and Newton's Rings," *Colour Group Bulletin* No. 27 (1958): 7–10.

Wicksteed, Owen H. "More About Slide Projection," *Colour Group Bulletin* No. 46 (1969): 8–10.

_____. "The Overheated Slide," *Colour Group Bulletin* No. 34 (1961): 3–11.

Weinstein, Robert A., and Larry Booth. *Collection, Use, and Care of Historical Photographs.* Nashville, Tenn.: American Association for State and Local History, 1977.

For information on lantern slides.

6

Microforms

HELGA BORCK

Microphotography was first applied to documents in 1839 by John Benjamin Dancer, an English optician and maker of scientific equipment. Over the next ninety years, various uses were postulated and even made of Dancer's innovation, the best known of which was René Dagron's Pigeon Post, by which messages were sent into Paris in 1870, during the Franco-Prussian War. It was not until the 1930s, however, that interest became widespread and continued experimentation resulted in the development of practical microphotographic equipment. By this time, the rapid deterioration of materials published during the late nineteenth and early twentieth centuries, especially newspapers, was recognized as cause for substantial alarm, and the possibility of replacing brittle paper with microcopy became more and more attractive to libraries. While World War II slowed this trend briefly, the destruction it caused also demonstrated, all too dramatically, the need to provide security for valuable research materials. After the war, scholarly use of microforms increased dramatically.

The advantages and disadvantages of microforms have been argued practically since their invention. While few today would agree with early detractors who dismissed them as mere curiosities of some passing interest, but no practical use, accounts of the imminent demise of the printed book, so common during the 1930s and 1940s, were obviously exaggerated. Instead, microforms have joined books to create a larger and more complex scholarly atmosphere, and the prophets of doom have moved on to newer technologies.

The most obvious attraction of microforms is their compact size. While a great deal of space can be saved by using them, some of that space (sometimes a substantial amount) will be needed to house the reading equipment without which they are unusable. If the hard copy files to be replaced are bulky and little used, the savings can be great; heavily used collections, however, will require more reading machines, and space gains will diminish accordingly.

Dependence on machinery has certain drawbacks: a microform can be used only where there is reading apparatus, and staff and patrons alike must be trained to use the equipment. Staff must also learn routine maintenance techniques. Browsing through a microform is difficult, and simultaneous use of more than one title in order to compare texts, for example, can be sheer torture (if possible at all).

Why then, in the face of such adversity, do libraries collect microforms? The reasons should be apparent to anyone who has ever searched the out-of-print market without success, tried to read a stack of crumbling newspapers, or worried about the security of a rare item. Microforms are a relatively inexpensive means of preserving materials on poor paper, and permit widespread distribution of unique or rare items. They are much less likely to be stolen or mutilated than paper files, and can be used as working copy to lessen wear and tear on rare or delicate materials. They are easier to use than bulky files such as newspapers and are often less expensive in the long run because of savings in binding costs.

The technology of microform production is very similar to that used in other types of photography: sensitized film is exposed to light reflected from an object; the image thus produced is then made visible and fixed by chemical processing. Additional copies are made by bringing the processed film in contact with a length of unprocessed film or a sheet of treated paper and using light to transfer the image, or by projecting the image onto another surface. Whether the result is a snapshot or a reel of microfilm, the process is fundamentally the same. Computer output microform (COM) is produced the same way, beginning with a computer tape rather than a paper document or object. The taped data is converted to human-readable form and transferred to the film. This may be done directly, using an electron beam, or by displaying the data on a cathode ray tube screen, which is then photographed.

There are three types of film stock currently used in microform production: silver halide, diazo, and vesicular. Each is produced by a different process and has its own characteristics, strengths, and weaknesses. All three begin with a cellulose ester or polyester base. On silver halide film, one side of this base is coated with a gelatin emulsion containing a compound of silver plus one of the halogens (chlorine, bromine, iodine, or fluorine); the film is exposed to visible light and processed in a series of chemical baths. The emulsion on diazo film consists of a layer of nitrogen (diazo) compounds and a layer of amino compounds, called couplers, which react on contact to form an azo dye; these substances are separated by a thin layer of acid. Exposure to ultraviolet light destroys the diazo compounds in appropriate areas. The film is then treated with ammonia fumes which dissolve the acid layer, allowing the dye-producing reaction to take place, and the image is created. Vesicular film consists of a layer of diazo compound sandwiched between two layers of base. The destruction of the diazo compound by ultraviolet light produces nitrogen gas, which is trapped in the film. Applying heat causes the outer film layers to soften and the nitrogen gas to explode into bubbles (called vesicles) which form the visible image.

Silver film, because it is the most sensitive of the three, is generally used as camera or master film; subsequent copies may be of any type. Silver film is also the only kind that is considered archival at this time; that is, it can be expected to last indefinitely *if* processed and stored correctly. This is not to say that silver film is indestructible. Because of its gelatin emulsion, it is susceptible to fungal infestation at high humidity, is easily scratched by dirt and other particles, and becomes a sodden mess if wet. Diazo and vesicular films are not subject to these problems, although both can be damaged by deep scratches. They do, however, have other disadvantages. Diazo film is sensitive to light and prolonged exposure will cause the image to fade. This will happen eventually in any case but, if carefully handled, diazo film should last a fairly long time—up to one hundred years, by some estimates. Vesicular film fades if exposed to high temperatures, for instance, in an overheated reading machine.

Color microforms are more complex, and more expensive, than black-and-white, although the processes involved in their production are similar. Only limited use of color microforms has been made by libraries to date; this is due in part to the higher costs involved and in part to the fact that the color dyes tend to fade rather quickly. Color film is not considered archival at this time. It is also more likely to be stolen than black-and-white film; this is especially true of roll film, which can easily be cut up and mounted on slides.

Microforms exist in a variety of shapes and sizes, but there are really only two basic types: rolled and flat. Roll microfilm is available in a number of standard widths ranging from 8mm to 105mm; most film used in libraries is either 16mm or 35mm. In its simplest form it is wound on a spool or reel. More complex packaging units—cartridges and cassettes—have been designed to simplify use by eliminating the need to thread the film by hand through a reading device and by providing quick mechanized access; such packages also protect the film from dirt and minimize handling. Many reading machines are designed to allow use of more than one kind of roll film; machinery designed for use with a specific type of cassette or cartridge may not accept any other type, however, and caution must be used when buying such equipment.

The most familiar type of flat microform is the microfiche, which is produced either by stripping up (i.e., adhering) strips of 16mm or narrower film onto a clear 105mm × 148mm (about 4″ × 6″) carrier, or by using a step-and-repeat camera, which automatically films in a grid pattern to the same dimensions (i.e., optical stripping). The film is cut down to standard fiche size after processing. Ultrafiche is simply microfiche on which the image has been greatly reduced, to 1/90th or less of the document's original size, in order to fit more images on each card. Ultrafiche are generally created by filming the paper copy in the conventional manner and then filming the microfilm to compound the reduction. Special lenses are needed on reading equipment to render ultrafiche images eye-legible.

Other types of flat microforms include jackets, which differ from fiche in that the strips of film are inserted into clear plastic sleeves rather than pasted on a plastic surface; and aperture cards, which consist of one or more microimages set into a card carrying other data, usually keypunched. Micro-opaques (including Microcards and Microprint) consist of micro-images printed on heavy card stock by offset lithography or photographically printed onto photographic paper. Special equipment is needed for viewing and duplicating opaques because they rely on reflected rather than transmitted light.

Other important characteristics of microforms include polarity and reduction ratio. A microform may have either negative or positive polarity; negative consists of light (clear) print on a dark background; positive is dark print on a light ground. The camera film (generally called the master, since it is the best possible copy and is, or should be, used only for duplicating purposes) is usually negative; copies may be either negative or positive. Positive film was long thought to be easier to use, because of its closer resemblance to the printed page; many users prefer negative film, however, as it produces less glare.

The reduction ratio describes the degree of miniaturization of a microform and is generally written as a multiple of x. For example, a reduction of 14x of an 11 ″ × 14 ″ document would yield a microimage about 3/4 ″ wide and 1 ″ high, 1/14th the linear size of the original. Reduction ratios can vary tremendously, from 5x for work requiring great detail, to as high as 190x for ultrafiche.

Purchasing microforms and living with them afterward can be a harrowing experience, but, as with most things, it's a lot easier when one knows what to look for.[1] In addition to the usual questions of suitability for the collection, need, and cost, the following factors should be considered:

1. *CONTENTS:* Does the microform include everything wanted? If less, is it enough? If more, is it worth the additional expense? Many micropublishers offer large sets of related materials which may include thousands of titles, and it is not always possible to purchase individual items separately.

2. *FORMAT:* Is the microform in a serviceable format? If not, is the institution willing and able to purchase, house, and maintain whatever additional equipment is needed? This is where the reduction ratio becomes important: a microform at an unaccustomed reduction may require anything from an additional lens for equipment already on hand

to a new reading machine. Is the information suited to the format? Long serial and newspaper runs are often more easily handled on roll film; short items may be easier to deal with on fiche. Some materials, especially those which rely heavily on color for illustrations, charts, and the like, may not be suitable for any microformat.

3. *EASE OF USE:* Is the information arranged in a rational and usable fashion? Is it clearly labelled and targeted? What bibliographic tools (for example, indexes) are needed? Are they available? There are few things more frustrating than paying a lot of money for something only to find that the information it contains is all but impossible to get at.

4. *FILM STOCK:* With the exception of materials which are regularly updated, such as catalogues, most libraries will want their microforms to last as long as possible. Only silver halide film is currently considered archival, that is, able to last indefinitely under proper conditions; in fact, archival film has been defined as any film which will last as long as or longer than silver halide.[2] A great deal of controversy has been generated over the years by this definition and by the non-archival status of nonsilver film stocks. There are those in the library field who have advocated a "silver-or-nothing" policy, a position that has gradually shifted to "silver-whenever-possible" in the face of the continued use of diazo and vesicular films by the micropublishing industry. Silver film is more expensive than other types and, because of its emulsion, is more easily damaged by scratching; furthermore, no film is archival unless it is stored and used under proper conditions. Realistically, a decision regarding film stock should depend on what is available and on the nature of the file, expected type and level of use, storage conditions, budget, and reputation of the vendor. In all cases, it is important to determine beforehand the vendor's policy on damaged or inferior quality film; a reputable firm should stand behind its product.

Ideally, every microform should be thoroughly inspected upon receipt, and periodic spot-checks of the collection should be made to insure that no problems have developed. Full inspection of every item is time-consuming and may not be practical for most libraries, but an effort should be made to spot-check new receipts in order to weed out damaged or substandard film immediately. Some characteristics are obvious to the naked eye and can be easily checked: packaging should be sturdy and free of dirt, and the item should be clearly and fully labelled. Roll film must not be secured by means of tape or rubber bands containing sulfur. Film should be wound on plastic reels, which ought not to be so full that the film slips over the edges.

The remainder of the inspection will require a light box or, if none is available, a clean reading machine. The microform should be checked to see that:

1. No dust, dirt, blemishes, spots or scratches are present.
2. Images are sharp, clear, properly aligned, and in correct order.
3. Contents are complete, sufficiently described, and appropriately targeted.
4. Any splices on roll film are sound and of the welded type. Normally, no splices should appear on film intended for reader use. Pressure-sensitive cellophane tape is to be avoided at all costs.

Silver halide film should also be checked to see that it is acetate or polyester safety-base film; if it is, a small triangle or the words *safety film* (usually in English, French, or German) will appear at regular intervals along the edge. Until about 1950, some silver film was produced on nitrate-based stock; this was discontinued when it was realized that nitrate film is extremely unstable and is prone to rapid decomposition and spontaneous combustion. It is now relatively rare, but, because of its volatility, any film suspected of having a nitrate base should immediately be isolated and tested. This can be done by taking a small sample of the film and either burning it or placing it in a solution of trichloroethylene; nitrate film burns quickly and explosively, and will not float in trichloroethylene. Both these tests should be conducted only under carefully controlled conditions, in an open, well-ventilated area away from flammable materials. Film identified as nitrate-based should be replaced by safety film and disposed of carefully and quickly.[3]

An ongoing maintenance program for the microform collection should include cleaning, minor repairs, and proper storage and handling. Material should be stored in containers that will protect without harming, that is, acid-free boxes and envelopes, and noncorrosive metal cans and cabinets. Any materials not in high-quality containers should be repackaged.[4] Tape and rubber bands, unless these are free of sulfur, should be removed, as chemical contamination may result; instead, film should be held in place by acid-free paper strips with button-and-string fasteners. All microforms should be handled only by their edges, using lint-free cotton gloves when possible, for example, during inspections; this will not only help to keep them clean, but will guard against contamination by uric acid and salt present on the skin.

Cleaning is an important maintenance technique, particularly where storage conditions are poor—even a small particle of dust can obscure a great deal of a microimage, and dirt is a primary cause of scratches, especially on silver halide film. There are several methods of cleaning microforms, ranging from simple manual procedures to complex mechanized devices. The simplest method is to wipe the item with a soft lint-free cloth or brush; this will remove dust but not grease or fingerprints. For more stubborn dirt, a soft cloth which has been dipped in cleaning solvent is more effective. The mechanized cleaning devices now on the market employ either ionized air or ultrasonic frequencies to remove dirt. Ionized air also reduces static electricity, but, because it is a dry method, will not remove oils or grease. Ultrasonic systems may be either dry or wet; they are extremely costly and are used primarily in the motion picture industry.[5]

Another type of treatment that may be done in-house is splicing to repair tears and breaks in film. Splices should be of the butt-end, heat-weld type, as these are the strongest and least bulky. Cemented splices may also be used, provided the cement contains no chemicals harmful to the film. Pressure-sensitive cellophane tapes should *not* be used, both because of their thickness (they may cause the film to jam in equipment) and because the adhesive may ooze onto other surfaces.

Mold or fungus on silver halide film is the result of excessive temperature and humidity; fungal growths may be removed with a soft cloth which has been dipped in cleaning solvent. Water should not be used to wipe moldy film; the chemical breakdown of the emulsion caused by fungus renders it easily soluble in water, and wiping with water may dissolve the image completely.

Microforms that have been damaged by water must be kept wet until professional help can be obtained; if allowed to dry improperly, the film will stick to itself and the image will be lost. Treatment for water-damage is expensive; it may be less costly to replace items thus damaged than to repair them. In general, outside help and advice should be sought whenever there is doubt as to how to deal with a problem, and in emergencies.[6]

Purchasing reading equipment can be as traumatic as purchasing the microforms themselves. Not only is there a bewildering array of machinery, but specific models also seem to appear and disappear from the marketplace with dizzying speed.

No microform reader should be bought blindly, and there is no better way to test a machine than by using it. Some manufacturers will provide demonstrations or install machines on a trial basis; this is especially true of new models. If not, it may be possible to see a machine in use at another location, and to get the owner's opinion of it at the same time—the grapevine is an excellent means of gathering information. There are also published guides to micrographic equipment.[7]

When shopping for reading equipment, the following factors should be taken into account:

1. Suitability: Is the machine compatible with the microforms to be used with it? Is the screen large enough to display the complete image? Will the lens provided magnify the image to an appropriate and usable size?

2. Physical characteristics: Is the machine suited to the environment in which it will be placed? How much space (including ventilation space) is needed? How will the machine be mounted? How noisy is it? How hot?

3. Image quality: Is the image clear? Is it uniformly sharp over the entire screen? Is the screen uniformly bright, or is there a "hot spot" at the center? Does the level of brightness allow for comfortable use over a long period of time?

4. Operation: Is the machine simple to use? Are instructions clear and easy to follow? Is loading easy, or does it require substantial handling of the microform? Are there any sharp edges that are likely to scratch the microform during use? Are the controls clearly labelled and conveniently located?

5. Maintenance: Is the machine sturdy? Can routine maintenance be performed quickly and easily? What type of service contract is offered? How quickly can repairs be made?

6. Options: It is always wise to investigate optional features before making a purchase. If an option will make the machine more useful, either immediately or in the future, it should be seriously considered.

Once acquired, equipment must be properly cared for; a regular cleaning and maintenance schedule should be set up immediately, following the manufacturer's recommendations. Screen, lenses, and glass flats should be cleaned daily, and dust jackets should be placed on machines when they are not in use. Tools needed for cleaning machinery include window cleaning fluid and a soft cloth for washing, and a soft brush for dusting.[8]

How the microform collection is organized and where it is located will depend on the needs of the individual institution; whatever arrangements are decided upon, appropriate environmental conditions should be provided. Microforms should be stored at a temperature not exceeding 70 °F (21 °C) and with relative humidity between 40 percent and 60 percent; temperature in the use area should be below 80 °F (27 °C). Neither temperature nor humidity should be allowed to fluctuate more than five degrees. High temperature will cause film to buckle, while high humidity encourages the growth of mold and blemishes and causes stickiness. Low humidity or temperature causes brittleness, curling, and an increase in static electricity which in turn will cause more dirt and dust to adhere to the microform.

Fluctuation of temperature or humidity can also result in brittleness, especially in older microforms.

In addition to temperature and humidity controls, the microform area should be equipped with an air filtration system to remove dust and harmful chemicals. If the area is not fireproof, fire-resistant metal storage cabinets should be used, and their contents shielded from sprinkler systems. Microforms should be stored at least 6 inches above floor level to avoid possible damage in case of flooding.

Once the advantages and limitations of microforms are understood, they can be used to good effect. Although they are not appropriate for all purposes, if they are properly selected and cared for, microforms can form an integral part of the library collection.

NOTES

1. Another means of acquiring microforms is to produce them. Anyone interested in setting up a preservation microfilming program should first consult the literature, particularly the following: Don M. Avedon, "Selecting a Service Bureau," *Journal of Micrographics* 10:1 (September/October 1976): 3–8; and Albert H. Leisinger, *Microphotography for Archives* (Washington, D.C.: International Council on Archives, 1968).

2. From a statement by James R. Rhoads in "Dialogue on Standards: Archival Permanence," *Journal of Micrographics* 9:4 (March 1976): 193–94. When this statement was made, Mr. Rhoads was Archivist of the United States.

3. For a more thorough description of the inspection process, see Allen B. Veaner, *The Evaluation of Micropublications: A Handbook for Librarians* (Chicago: American Library Association, 1971).

4. Acid-free microform containers are available from several firms that sell archival supplies. See listing in Appendix.

5. The definitive work to date in this area is Nancy H. Knight, "The Cleaning of Microforms," *Library Technology Reports* 14:3 (May/June 1978): 217–40.

6. Expert advice can be obtained from the Eastman Kodak Company, 343 State Street, Rochester, N.Y. 14650 (tel. 716-325-2000), or from its local branches.

7. Detailed technical information about all types of micrographic equipment can be found in Hubbard Ballou, ed., *Guide to Micrographic Equipment* (Silver Spring, Md.: National Micrographics Association, 1979). This work describes but does not evaluate equipment; it is updated every few years. Two serial publications include both descriptions and evaluations: (1) *Library Technology Reports* (Chicago: American Library Association). Monthly; cumulations issued on microfiche as *Sourcebook of Library Technology*, and (2) *Micrographics Equipment Review* (Westport, Conn.: Microform Review). Semiannual. The National Reprographic Centre for Documentation (NRCd) has published a number of critical reviews of equipment; these are available from NRCd, the Hatfield Polytechnic, Endymion Road Annexe, Hatfield, Herts., England.

8. Kits containing tools and supplies for routine maintenance are available from University Microfilms International (for the equipment which it produces) and Kinetronics, Inc., of Lake Bluff, Ill.

SUGGESTED READING

In addition to the works cited in the notes, the following books will be helpful to anyone seeking more information about microforms:

Avedon, Don M., ed. *Glossary of Micrographics.* Silver Spring, Md.: National Micrographics Association, 1980.

Diaz, Albert James, ed. *Microforms in Libraries; A Reader.* Westport, Conn.: Microform Review, 1975.

Introduction to Micrographics. Silver Spring, Md.: National Micrographics Association, 1980.

Rice, E. Stevens, and Heinz Dettling. *Fiche and Reel.* 4th ed. Ann Arbor, Mich.: University Microfilms International, 1980.

7

Motion Picture Film

EILEEN BOWSER

HISTORY

The first public showings of motion picture films took place in 1895. The photographic images were recorded on a nitro-cellulose base. Its hazards as a highly flammable material were realized at an early stage in a series of disastrous fires, but nitrate continued in commercial use until 1951. Attempts to manufacture a nonflammable safety stock were made from 1909 onward, perhaps even earlier, without much success. The chief problem was the rapid evaporation of the plasticizers used to keep the film flexible, resulting in shrinkage and brittleness. Cost factors, too, played a part. Eastman Kodak began to manufacture a safety film in 22mm in 1912 for the Edison Home Kinetoscope, and later on for the 28mm nontheatrical projection machine made by Pathé Frères in France. In 1918, Alexander F. Victor proposed to the Society of Motion Picture Engineers that a standard nonflammable film be made mandatory for all nontheatrical use and this was eventually accepted. Further developments in safety stock manufacture took place outside the theatrical cinema. In 1923, Kodak introduced 16mm acetate stock, followed by Pathé's 9.5mm in Europe. During the thirties and forties the plasticizers were improved and the base materials changed to acetate propionate and butyrate. Duplicating stocks used for negatives and fine-grain masters continued to be made with the nitrate base and 35mm nitrate projection prints remained the standard for theatrical use.

In 1948, Kodak developed triacetate, which has all the best qualities of nitrate film plus nonflammability and an extremely long shelf life. For the first time motion pictures could be preserved archivally by being duplicated on the new stock. Production of nitrate stock by Eastman Kodak ceased altogether in 1951. Propionate and butyrate stock continued in use for the narrower nontheatrical gauges. It was only in late 1980 that all 16mm Kodachrome material came to be manufactured on triacetate, and some super-

8mm continues to be produced on acetate propionate at the present time. The most recent development is the production of several Eastman Kodak films on Estar (polyester) base, an extremely tough stock resistant to tears and shrinkage. It is used at present primarily for the narrow nontheatrical gauges.

It may not be automatically assumed that all narrow-gauge films are on safety stock. It is extremely rare that they are not, but recently some nitrate 28mm film was discovered. Film is manufactured in wide rolls and then slit to the desired width, which means that nitrate narrow gauges are theoretically possible, but only for film stocks manufactured before 1951. As a rule, the words *nitrate* or *safety* will be found printed on the edge of the film outside of the perforations. However, when duplicate prints and negatives are made, the word will print through and might be misleading.

Although the majority of motion pictures were produced in black and white until the last couple of decades, color was available from the earliest days of the medium. Color was applied to individual prints by hand-painting each frame, by stencilling, and by tinting and toning. Several color processes were developed in the first and second decade of the century, as Kinemacolor and Prizma Color, but the dominant process from the twenties onward was Technicolor, available at first as a two-color system. Full color (three-color) Technicolor was developed in the early thirties, and from 1934 to 1953 this process was preeminent, although other systems were available from time to time. It is a subtractive process, whereas earlier ones were additive. For a large part of this period, it was necessary to use the special Technicolor camera, which divided the images into their component colors during filming. We cannot take the space here to explain the techniques of the system and its various historical developments, but we would like to say a word about the famed nonfading Technicolor imbibition (IB) prints. The original three separation negatives were in black and white and could not fade. From them, three matrices were made, to which magenta, cyan, and yellow dyes were applied. From these, the full-color IB prints were produced, which do not appear to have faded significantly since the day they were struck. Although black-and-white separation negatives or masters are still made to protect valuable color films, it is no longer possible to make Technicolor IB prints. In recent years, the Technicolor Laboratories dismantled their equipment. At the same time China set up new Technicolor laboratories in Peking, which remains the one place in the world where such prints can still be made. The words "color by Technicolor" on a print do not any longer refer to this process. An IB print has a gray sound track and all color is confined to the picture area.

The current Eastmancolor process and its equivalents came in during the early fifties and soon became the dominant system. It is no longer necessary to use a special camera, because the colors are built into the various dye layers of the film stock. It is cheaper and more practical, and some film-makers consider the process to be more sensitive and subtle in color values. Unfortunately, the dyes are not as stable. In the early years of the process, they were particularly unstable, as may be seen in the many totally "maroon" prints that survive from this period. Fortunately, the negative stock appears to have been longer-lasting than the print stock. The dyes have been somewhat improved over the years, but color fading is still inevitable. Most recently, Eastman Kodak brought out a special "low-fade" stock (known as LF) for projection prints, used chiefly for nontheatrical exhibition. Commercial film production has made very little use of it because theatrical prints are expected to wear out through constant use within a year or two, before the colors have faded. LF stock is very important for libraries because they keep their prints in use for much longer. It is to be hoped that the stock manufacturers will gradually phase out all of the fast-fading color films, but for the present LF must be specially ordered. Fortunately, some 16mm stocks such as Kodachrome and Anscocolor have been "low-fade" for some time now. Nevertheless, any color film based on organic dye layers will fade in time.

There were many experiments with synchronized sound throughout the silent period, but none were found commercially viable until the mid-twenties, with the development of sound on the film itself, photographically recorded through light impulses. Photographed or optical sound is of two types: variable density, a constant-width strip whose density varies from dark to light in response to the sound values recorded; and variable-area, in which the width of the strip varies with volume and frequency. The latter type will be found most frequently in commercial use. Printing a variable-area negative sound track on print stock will result in a distortion which must be compensated for in the process. A magnetic sound track is a single strip of metallic oxide coated along the edge of the film on which sound may be recorded by running it past a magnetic recording head. The preservation and care of magnetic tapes is quite different from that of photographic recordings, and will not be discussed here because it belongs more properly to chapter 8.

DETERIORATION

Films consist of a base (nitrate, acetyl-cellulose, or polyester) and an adhesive layer (gelatin) and the emulsion layer, in the case of black-and-white films consisting of a suspension of particles of silver halogens. Modern color films have several layers. A varnish layer is sometimes added as a protective covering. Few librarians will encounter nitrate movie film and it will not be possible to follow the special regulations for handling and storing this material in most library practice. It is recommended that valuable nitrate materials be turned over to a properly equipped and experienced film archive. However, nitrate may turn up in archival collections or may be brought in by members of the public, and therefore it is necessary to recognize the stages of deterioration. Nitrate film is inherently unstable. In its most severely deteriorated stages, it is liable to spontaneous combustion at temperatures equivalent to those of a very hot summer day, or in the sun-warmed windows of an automobile. The early stages are discoloration, then the giving off of an acrid odor, and stickiness. Under these conditions, it may still be possible to preserve the motion picture by copying it on triacetate stock. In later stages, the film begins to bubble or turns to powder. If the severely deteriorated sections are cut out, it may still be possible to save some of it, but otherwise it will be necessary to destroy it at this stage. It should be immersed in water for temporary safety, and then turned over to a salvage company for disposal. A local fire department may be able to help if there is not enough material for it to be worthwhile for a salvage company to send a truck. When nitrate film is burned, it gives off dangerous fumes. It may not be legally sent through the mail and when shipped by freight it must be clearly labelled as flammable material and packed in suitable containers. A single frame of nitrate may be burned as a test, but it should be done in the open air. Nitrate should never be stored in buildings where people live or work and when it must be held temporarily, it must be kept in a cool, dry place away from any heating element.

Acetate or safety stocks do not present any fire hazard. However, they will become brittle in too dry a climate, or the emulsion layer will separate from the base in too moist an atmosphere. They may shrink, resulting in distortions of image and sound, and perforations that no longer fit on motion picture equipment. Bacteria and fungi may attack the gelatin layer in moist conditions, and modern air pollutants may damage the film as well. Some acetate stocks of the period before the fifties have shown a tendency to deteriorate, sometimes more rapidly than nitrate. They first release acetic acid with a strong and unpleasant odor. This is followed by a softening of the emulsion and a breaking of the bond between base and emulsion, finally fusing into a sticky mass. Recent research on the causes of this deterioration points to excessively warm and humid storage conditions, but the reasons for the deterioration of some acetate films and the long life of others have not yet been fully established, nor do we know if the release of acetic acid might be harmful to nearby films in storage. As in the case of nitrate deterioration, once it begins it cannot be halted, and the only way to preserve such films is to duplicate them on triacetate stock. The originals must be discarded when no longer usable, or in the case of nitrate, when they become dangerous to store. The problem of fading in modern color films has already been mentioned. The long life of all kinds of films—nitrate, acetate, polyester, black-and-white or color—depends in the first place on careful processing and the thorough washing off of all chemicals. It is possible to ask the laboratory for a special "archival wash." In the second place, it depends on correct storage conditions and handling, described below.

PROLONGING THE LIFE OF FILM

STORAGE

In the storing of black-and-white safety film, the most important condition is constancy: as with all library materials there should be as little fluctuation in the temperature and humidity as possible. The temperature should never be higher than 70 °F (21 °C) and the relative humidity no higher than 60 percent, no lower than 50 percent. Too low a humidity will result in brittleness. However, at lower temperatures, the relative humidity must be lowered accordingly. A temperature of 50 °F (10 °C), which is recommended for archival storage of valuable black-and-white materials, calls for a relative humidity of about 50 percent. To slow down the fading of modern color film, lower temperatures and relative humidity are needed. Temperatures of a few degrees below freezing are said to keep colors relatively unchanged for hundreds of thousands of years, according to artificial aging tests made by scientists in the Soviet Union and by Eastman Kodak. The low humidity called for in such extreme temperatures, about 30 percent, is extremely difficult and expensive to establish and maintain. Only a few of the world's film archives have so far been able to construct and maintain true deep-freeze vaults for their color holdings, and research is still going on to determine any possible deleterious effects of taking films in and out of such conditions. It is at least recommended by the Preservation Commission of FIAF (Federation Internationale des Archives du Film) to have slow conditioning chambers for that purpose. Kodak's most recent tests of its LF stock forecast a life of hundreds of years without noticeable fading when it is stored only at 45 °F (7 °C) and 40–50 percent RH, and for most collections this would be considered sufficient longevity. As a general rule, the colder the temperatures, the slower the colors will fade. For smaller collections of color film, new research is exploring the possibility of sealing films in ordinary freezer bags, which would maintain the same humidity conditions through extreme changes of temperature. Such films would first have to be brought to the correct humidity conditions before sealing, but they could then be stored in an ordinary frozen food locker. The sealing would have to be perfect, and would have to be repeated each time the film was brought out of storage.

There is no need to store projection prints that are in active use at low temperatures, as they will wear out before deterioration begins. It is generally recommended, however, that a circulation collection be kept under cli-

Figure 7.1. Film Storage Racks, the Most Economical and Flexible Film Storage System for Libraries. Photograph courtesy of RTI, Research Technology International, Lincolnwood, Illinois.

matic conditions equivalent to those recommended for book storage, and at the very least, in an air-conditioned room.

Films should be stored on cores. Very large and heavy reels, which would include most 35mm films, should be stored flat. The weight of films resting on edge in long-term storage will result in warping and buckling, which will become evident in focus problems when projected. The container in which the film is stored should not be warped, dented, or rusted because this will contribute to film damage or deterioration. An active circulating collection in 16mm or narrower gauges will normally be stored on reels and in shipping containers. They may be safely stored on edge, like books on the shelf, as long as the reels are not of great size, because the pressure is not great enough to damage them.

FILMS IN USE

Librarians are generally more concerned with prolonging the life of their prints than in problems of archival storage. All films wear out in use. Even negatives will wear out when they have been run through printing machines too many times. No negatives or masters should ever be projected. It may be remembered that in the history of film preservation it has very often occurred that a worn projection copy is the only surviving material. Conscientious librarians should make every effort to ascertain whether good-quality protection materials exist, preferably in a qualified film archive, before permitting the destruction of what might be a unique copy of a valuable motion picture through use. Film companies go out of business and distribution rights come to an end. It may sometimes be practical to buy an extra print, to store away and use only for special purposes, against the day when it is discovered that no more prints can be manufactured from the original materials. This practice is especially valid when purchasing films from independent filmmakers, who frequently cannot afford proper protection of their work and often project their own originals.

Color prints should always be ordered on LF stock, to guard against rapid fading. Some librarians also prefer to order prints made on polyester stock, which is strong enough to survive all kinds of misuse by the nonprofessional projectionist. A third step that may be taken to prolong the life of a projection print is to give it 3M's Photogard treatment, a coating that seals off both the emulsion and the base with a scratchproof and waterproof plastic. It may not be removed. There are many other coating treatments that will help to reduce scratches and to restore flexibility, but only the Photogard treatment gives this protection. However, these steps should be weighed against the cost of replacement prints or replacement footage, and the possible effect on the quality of the image. It would be advisable to do some testing of the effects before following these procedures, or to seek the experiences of other libraries. For archival materials, no treatments of any kind are to be recommended if the manufacturer is unwilling to disclose the constituent chemicals, because the long-term effects are unknown. Some objections have been made to polyester stock because cement splices cannot be used on them, and the tape used in splicing them has a tendency to pick up dirt from projection machines that have not been properly cleaned before each use. Estar (polyester) film scratches more easily, but the application of Photogard would overcome that disadvantage. Because the stock is so resistant to tears, fewer splices would be needed.

As soon as a new print has been received, or after it has received a treatment, it should be inspected for the quality of image and sound. A projection room of adequate size is recommended for this inspection because it is quite difficult to judge quality on a table viewing machine. At this stage, if the film is not of expected quality, it should be rejected and sent back to the manufacturer. It is particularly important to clean the projection machine before each reel is shown, because new prints tend to be soft, or "green," for the first few months and may be more easily scratched by dirt particles. Further, such prints move with resistance through the projector and it is easy to tear them. They should come from the laboratory already edge-waxed to prevent this from happening, but sometimes this step is missed. The print should then be sent out to a laboratory for edge-waxing before its first projection. In an emergency, sometimes a little bit of ordinary spray-can furniture polish is sprayed very lightly on the edges while the film is still wound on its core, and any excess wiped away. This practice is questionable, however, and any time it is used the print should be thoroughly cleaned afterward.

Whenever a film is handled, white gloves should be worn to avoid getting the dirt and oil of the human skin on the film. Special cheap white gloves are made for the purpose, inexpensive enough to be thrown away as soon as they get too dirty. The exception to this rule would be when examining the edges of a film for torn perforations on a rewind machine, because the fabric may catch and increase a tear. In this case, great care must be taken to touch only the edges and not the picture or sound area.

Circulating prints must be inspected after every use to determine what damage if any has occurred, what repairs are needed, and if necessary, to attribute the expense of replacement footage to the user who caused the damage. Circulating prints may be examined by automatic electronic inspection machines, which will stop for each torn perforation or broken splice so that repairs can be made, and which may also perform the function of cleaning the films. These machines are not adequate for archival inspection. A more thorough examination should be scheduled for circulating prints at regular intervals to determine the extent of scratches, dirt, and color fading. This inspection may be done on viewing tables or in the projection room.

Films should never be taped down on the inside to the core or the reel. This practice may cause tears as the film runs to the end, and may add gummy substances as the loose tape passes through the gate, contributing to dirt and scratches on the subsequent reel of film. Conversely, the film should always be firmly taped down with masking tape, available in correct sizes from film suppliers, on the outside of the reel whenever it is being moved about, or bound with a reel band. This will keep the film tightly wound and avoid accidents such as crinkling and bending. In addition, a closely fitted can selected for the size of the reel will help avoid damage in handling. Bent or warped cans should be discarded.

Damage and wear usually occur first at the beginnings and ends of film. The use of very long head and tail leader will protect them, and this should be replaced as it wears out or tears. Color-coded leaders give an instant guide as to whether the film is heads or tails out. Such leader can also be ordered with the name of the institution that owns the print already printed on it. The trade name Protect-a-Print is a roughly textured leader which will help clean the projector of loose dirt as the film passes through it, for use in those situations where nonprofessional projectionists are apt to neglect regular cleaning procedures. When splicing on leader, especially that with one-sided perforations, be sure that it goes on in the right direction, the same as the way in which the film will be projected.

In selecting any kind of equipment for film handling and projection, avoid:

1. Equipment that permits film to be wound too tightly or at too great a speed, to avoid "cinching" marks and scratches

2. Equipment that permits the film to be unevenly wound, to avoid edge damage

3. Film cleaning machines that permit dust and dirt that may scratch subsequent films to build up on the surfaces

4. Rewind equipment that has sharp or rough projections which may scratch a film when it momentarily runs out on the table

The safest equipment uses a continuous movement of the film, the fewest necessary sprocket mechanisms to move it along, and slow start-up and stop devices.

Projector lamps gradually lose brilliance. The light should be measured and bulbs replaced periodically, to ensure the accuracy of judgments about print quality. All equipment should receive regular maintenance and the schedules should be rigorously adhered to once established. The manufacturer should be asked for his recommendations for service. Although a lot of foreign-built equipment is excellent, one would be well-advised to ascertain the degree that service and spare parts will be available before deciding to purchase it. It will also be necessary that the staff operating the equipment be properly instructed. Film may be damaged by operating the equipment at too high a speed, by improper threading, by failing to read the instructions, and (the commonest fault of all) by failure to clean the machine after every use.

REPAIRS AND RESTORATION

The most frequent repairs needed are the mending of perforation tears and splicing, and any library should be able to do these in-house. Films are pulled through projection machines by their perforations and the constant strain eventually weakens and tears them. Torn perforations may be repaired with perforated polyester splicing tape, but extensively damaged footage may not be worth the labor. Many suppliers will sell replacement footage, or will give a price reduction on a new print when damaged prints are returned. The continued projection of films with slightly torn perforations will soon result in larger damaged sections, rips, and tears. Even new prints will have splices where leader has been added or reels combined. Additional splices will be needed to repair breaks as they occur.

The historic type of splice, and still the most common one, is the overlapping cement-bonded splice. The emulsion is scraped off to give a consistent thickness to the repair. This method has the disadvantage that frames are lost, and the loss is multiplied whenever a splice has to be remade. With too many splices, the picture becomes jumpy and blips appear in the sound track. The more modern way to splice is to make the abutted polyester tape splice. Mylar tape has a pressure-sensitive adhesive. The recommended type of tape splicer is the frame-line to frame-line, using self-perforating tape. With abutted tape splicers, the splicing task is faster than with a cement splicer, and no frames need be lost, no matter how often the splice may have to be remade. The new tough polyester-based stock requires a tape splice as the old-fashioned cement splice will not adhere. Another possibility for polyester film is a hot-splicer which ultrasonically fuses the two ends of the stock, but the equipment is quite expensive. In making splices, attention must be given to perfect alignment. A slight edge sticking out will cause the film to tear in the projection machine, and misframes can be very disturbing to viewers. Any splice oozing a gummy substance should be immediately replaced, because it will pick up dirt or adhere to the next layer of film. No variety of adhesive tape not specifically designed for use with film should ever be used, nor pins or any other kind of fastener. Broken ends may be temporarily overlapped in winding and marked with an inserted bit of paper until the repair can be made, which must be done before another projection.

Worn, dirty, scratched, and brittle film may be restored by sending it out to the film service laboratory for cleaning, buffing, lubricating, and rejuvenation, which restores plasticity. Some of these processes may be done in the library, but they usually require equipment that has to be vented to the outside, and chemicals that have to be used in well-ventilated areas. Unless the collection is a very large and active one, it may not be worth the expense of the equipment, the space it takes up, and the professional training of the staff. However, very light cleaning may be done while running the film through the rewinding equipment. One should avoid any paper or cloth products that might scratch or catch on torn perforations, and any heavy pressure. There are products designed to lubricate as well as clean. However, any archival film material should be cleaned or treated only by professionals.

DUPLICATION

Because prints are inevitably worn out in projection and are subject to various kinds of deterioration to a greater or lesser degree even in storage, the ultimate protection is the making of duplicate copies in the laboratory. For nitrate films and for certain kinds of early acetate, it is absolutely necessary for the survival of the motion pictures. Laboratory work is highly specialized. Every duplication means a certain fall-off in sound and image quality from the original, although expert work and special care will be able to reduce this to a minimum that will not be detectable by the average viewer. The more stages of duplication that take place and the farther the copy is removed from the original by various duplications, the more the loss in quality becomes visible.

Laboratories with the safety conditions and the expertise to handle nitrate films have become very rare and will normally be found only in the vicinity of a few major cities. The technology for making high-quality black-and-white materials is rapidly disappearing from commercial laboratories as well because almost all motion pictures are now produced in color. Some of the biggest commercial laboratories have discontinued all black-and-white printing. Nevertheless, there are still some qualified specialists in a few laboratories, often very small ones, and chiefly restricted to the vicinity of the east and west coasts, who are capable of doing black-and-white printing. Optical sound tracks are liable to be distorted during the duplicating procedure, and this distortion is increased when doing reduction printing from a 35mm negative to a 16mm print. The re-recording of sound tracks by a specialist sound laboratory is to be recommended. Good color laboratories are not difficult to find, although it is sometimes necessary to make several answer prints before getting good color reproduction. Once the timing of either black-and-white or color films is correctly done, records are usually kept in the negative cans and at the laboratory for future printing. (Timing cards have a high acid content, and it is preferable to fasten an envelope on the *outside* of the can in which they may be stored.) The ultimate protection against color fading is the making of black-and-white separation negatives, from which a color reversal internegative (CRI) is made, from which, in turn, projection prints are struck. Not only is this a very costly process, but the required storage space is multiplied as well. It is beyond the reach of most film archives dedicated to film preservation, which is the reason they have selected the course of cold storage for the present time for the bulk of their color holdings. Important commercial productions are still frequently protected by the making of separations, but it is by no means done for all of them. The making of separations should be given consideration, however, for any very important archival color material held by the library. The film archives continue to encourage research for a simpler and less costly procedure for achieving color separation, one that would result in high quality, permanence, and less need for storage space, and that would avoid the still-present possibility of differential shrinkage of the separations. Librarians with color archival materials would do well to keep abreast of any developments in the field.

The chief problems encountered with duplication of the image are contrast and density problems, graininess, and unsteadiness of the image. For color film, there is also the problem of accurate reproduction of the color values. Poor duplication may result in washed-out or too-dark prints in which details are lost, or in jiggly images, or in focus problems. There are a variety of techniques known to a good lab technician for overcoming these problems, as well as methods of reducing the evidence of scratches in the original materials. There are trade-offs with each of these techniques which must be evaluated. Step-printing, done frame by frame, is usually more desirable than the faster method of continuous printing. In judging the results, the condition of the original materials being copied has to be kept in mind, and viewing conditions must be kept constant. The untrained evaluator should feel free to get the opinion of another specialist, and should reject poorly done work.

Librarians concerned with obtaining good quality duplication of valuable archival materials might seek the advice of the film archive in the nearest city for the names of qualified specialist laboratories. If the motion picture may fairly be considered of national rather than regional interest, it may be that the film archive will be able to take over the work of copying it, as long as it is permitted to retain the preservation copies that it manufactures, and in some cases it may be willing to return new projection copies. In the United States, the major large film archives are in the Library of Congress, the National Archives, and the American Film Institute in Washington, D.C.; in the Museum of Modern Art in New York City; in the International Museum of Photography in Rochester, New York; and in the UCLA Film Archives in Los Angeles. There are numerous smaller archives which may also be able to give expert advice. Film archivists representing the above-named institutions meet regularly in the Film Archives Advisory Committee and exchange information. They try to avoid duplication of effort in the preservation of film, which is a very costly and time-consuming task, and pursue avenues of research that may lead to more satisfactory methods of film preservation.

Videotape is unstable and will not serve as a preservation medium (see Chapter 7). However, videotape reference copies can be made to protect valuable film originals which will then not be projected but reserved for future duplication. The video image seriously distorts the film image, and therefore videotape copies are not adequate for serious film study or for a genuine appreciation of the medium. However, when the need for a reference copy is only to observe the film's content, videotape copies may be found satisfactory and are much cheaper than making film copies. The videotaping of motion picture films should be carefully overseen to ensure that valuable archival materials are not damaged during the process.

SAMPLE GUIDELINES

These guidelines might be sent out with a film for projection by nonprofessionals.

FILM IS A FRAGILE MEDIUM. TO AVOID DAMAGE TO THIS PRINT, PLEASE FOLLOW THESE PROCEDURES:

1. Clean the projector thoroughly before every showing with a clean, lint-free cloth, paying special attention to the gate. Very slight accumulations of dirt and debris will scratch the film.

2. Check that all reels are correctly wound heads out, ready for projection. Never run a sound film on an old projector made only for silent films.

3. The take-up reel must be of the same size as the film reel, and no warped or bent reels should be used.

4. Check carefully that the film has been correctly threaded and that adequate loop has been provided, before beginning projection. Many projectors have a knob that permits manual operation of the film through the film path, which provides a good way to check the threading. Threading instructions are found on the projector itself, or are provided in the booklet that comes with the machine. Read them carefully.

5. Start the film on the leader, not on the film itself. Turn on the motor and test the light while the film is still showing only its leader.

6. Monitor the film frequently during the projection to be sure that no damage is being incurred. Never touch the picture or sound area with bare fingers, which will leave an oily deposit. Always stop the projector instantly if you detect any problem and do not continue the projection until the problem has been resolved.

7. Do not rewind the film after use unless absolutely necessary to recover your own takeup reel. It will be inspected and rewound after you return it.

8. Tape the outside end of the film firmly down on the roll of film before putting it back in its container. If an end comes loose while the film is being moved about, the tight wind will become loose and edge damage may occur, and the loose end is apt to be bent, creased or torn.

9. Always return the film in the same container in which it came and do not change or obliterate the identification markings on the container.

SUGGESTED READING

American National Standards Institute. *American National Standard Practice for Storage of Processed Safety Photographic Film* (PH1.43-1979). New York: ANSI, 1979.

ANSI produces several standards relative to motion picture film. Lists of their publications and updated versions of their standards should be requested.

Bowser, Eileen, and John Kuiper, eds. *A Handbook for Film Archives*. Brussels: Federation Internationale des Archives du Film, 1980.

Based on the experience of FIAF member archives, primarily intended for the new or developing film archive. It contains chapters on acquisition, selection, preservation, cataloguing, documentation, copyright, film culture, access to the collection, and practical work. The chapters on preservation and practical work will be particularly useful to the librarian in connection with the care and handling of film material.

Eastman Kodak, Rochester, N.Y.

Kodak issues many practical publications on the care of the film it manufactures, free or at a modest cost, and a full list of them should be requested. Among the most practical guides are those in the series, "Film Notes for the Reel People":

H-50-1: *Splicing for the Professional*. 1976.
H-50-2: *Film Handling*. 1976.
H-50-3: *Projection Practices and Techniques*. 1977.

Harrison, Helen P. *Film Library Techniques: Principles of Administration*. New York: Hastings House, 1973.

A comprehensive manual on film librarianship with chapters on "Film Handling and Retrieval" and "Storage and Preservation."

Motion Picture, TV and Theater Directory Hand Guide. Tarrytown, N.Y.: Motion Picture Enterprises Publications, Inc. Published semi-annually.

Lists dealers, suppliers, manufacturers, and laboratories throughout the country.

Rehrauer, George. *The Film User's Handbook*. New York: R. R. Bowker, 1975.

The major source for information about film libraries. Chapter 6 contains a section on "Film Care and Maintenance," pp. 118-124, with much practical information. However, the figures given for temperature and relative humidity for storage are not reliable. The RH factors are generally far too low and will cause brittleness.

Sargent, Ralph N. *Preserving the Moving Image*. Washington, D.C.: Corporation for Public Broadcasting, 1974.

A survey of opinion on conditions in the field and prospects for new image technologies, in very technical language. It also contains some background in the art of moving image preservation.

Sloan, William. "Projections," *Film Library Quarterly* 12:4 (1979).

A few comments by the then-head of the Film Library, Donnell Library of the New York Public Library, on the way to prolong the life of prints with polyester stock and 3M's Photogard coating.

Society of Motion Picture and Television Engineers. *Journal of the SMPTE*, New York.

This journal contains hundreds of scientific articles relating to the care and preservation of motion picture film and the latest developments in the field. The index should be regularly consulted.

UNESCO. *Recommendations for the Safeguarding and Preservation of Moving Images*, adopted by the General Conference at its 21st Session, Belgrade, 27 October 1980.

A declaration of major importance to the field as a whole, it states the basic principles and the obligations of the member states toward their moving image cultural heritage. UNESCO's interest in this field will probably be followed up by useful publications and lists should be consulted in the future.

Volkmann, Herbert. *Film Preservation. A report of the FIAF Preservation Commission*. London: The British Film Institute, 1965.

A manual based on the experiences of FIAF archives and the research of its Preservation Commission. This will be reprinted as one chapter in a volume to include the preservation and restoration of color and sound in films, and the preservation of videotapes, in the very near future. For information, write FIAF Secretariat, Coudenberg 70, 1000 Brussels, Belgium.

Williamson, Peter L. "Archival Aspects of Early Safety Film Bases," an unpublished paper by the Technical Coordinator, Film Department, Museum of Modern Art, New York, 1981.

Information about early acetate stocks presently unavailable in a published form, with notes about experiences of acetate deterioration in the MOMA film collection. Of interest chiefly for collections of old safety film.

8

Videotape

SUSAN G. SWARTZBURG AND
DEIRDRE BOYLE

HISTORY AND DEVELOPMENT OF VIDEOTAPE

Videotape is an all-electronic medium: tape holds a magnetic charge along a field of ionized metal-backed plastic. Unlike film, which is a series of still photographs that are evident to the naked eye, videotape reveals nothing to the naked eye. It must be scanned electronically and its signal translated into shades of light and dark on the television screen.

In 1951 Bing Crosby Enterprises developed a black-and-white video recording system on magnetic tape; it used one-inch-wide tape, twelve heads, and operated at 100 IPS (inches per second). In 1956, the Ampex Corporation presented the standard that would be used by the broadcasting industry for nearly twenty years—two-inch Quadruplex videotape. Because it was recorded and played back by means of four separate heads, it was commonly referred to as "quad." In 1959, Toshiba demonstrated helical-scan video recording in Japan—this was two-inch-wide tape running at 15 IPS. Because the helical tape runs on a slant against the moving recording heads, the same amount of information on a two-inch tape can be compressed onto a much narrower tape; the narrower the tape, the lower its cost.

By 1968, the first half-inch video system with a camera was sold in the United States—Sony's Portapak. It gave rise to a new demand for video productions outside the broadcast industry. Sony and its competitors aimed their equipment at the "AV market"—schools, libraries, industry, and other institutions. While this was happening, video practitioners realized a number of new uses for this portable production medium that went far beyond its traditional broadcast uses. Sparked by the growth of the cable industry and public access channels in the early seventies, a "video movement" often known as "guerrilla television" or "grass roots video" led to new kinds of programming which have influenced the broadcast, cable, and information industries to this day.

In 1972 Sony introduced the three-quarter-inch cassette format, known as U-Matic. This was quickly accepted by other manufacturers as a new standard for the educational and industrial market. Unlike the open-reel helical-scan formats, U-Matic housing was contained in self-loading plastic cases. This meant less wear and tear on the tape and greater ease in inserting the tape in recording and playback modes. The technology also improved on the signal quality and on the picture stability of the narrower tape. Within two years of its appearance, the three-quarter-inch U-Matic cassette system had become standardized and interchangeable. By the late seventies, the broadcast industry had adopted it as a format which measured up to the industry's tougher technical standards.

In 1975 Sony introduced the first half-inch cassette system—Betamax. Sony's competitor, Matsushita, soon introduced a competing and noninterchangeable format of its own, VHS (Video Home System). Although there are differences in the technical operations of the Beta and VHS formats, competition has hinged on the differing capacities for length of recording. Most of the market has gone to VHS, which offers six hours of recording time versus Beta's five.

Any variety of configurations can be found in a library's video collection. The three-quarter-inch U-Matic cassette is still an institutional standard, although the rise in consumer equipment on either VHS or Beta has meant that libraries that principally circulate tapes to individual borrowers are increasingly concentrating on the half-inch cassette format. Many libraries that became involved in video production and/or collection beginning in the early days of the Portapaks still have half-inch open-reel tapes. Some institutions still produce on this equipment, although it is more and more a dying production format.

CARE, STORAGE, AND HANDLING

Videotape is made by a number of manufacturers, such as Sony, 3M, TDK, Maxell, and Memorex, among others. There are no definitive data as yet on the quality of the tapes now being produced. Some librarians report obvious distinctions, with Sony and 3M rated high. Where possible, video librarians have negotiated with producers and distributors, specifying what tape stock is to be used for the programs they purchase. The quality of the tape can be a serious consideration for its life as well as its sound and image quality.

The average videotape has a circulating life of about two years. Few problems have been noted thus far with tapes that circulate frequently; both image and object hold up well. Damage generally occurs due to user negligence rather than to a deterioration in the image or from its housing. Many patrons do not know how to correctly operate a player or will play a tape without cleaning the machine's heads: as a result, damage can occur.

As with circulating slide and film collections, which have been discussed in previous chapters, it is a good idea for the library to enclose instructions on the care and use of videotapes with each tape circulated. Such instructions might include:

1. Please keep this cassette in a cool place when not in use. Heat will destroy this tape.
2. Please clean the heads on your equipment before playing this cassette.
3. Please keep cassettes away from possible sources of electromagnetic fields (for example, microwave ovens, color television sets, etc.).
4. If you have any difficulties in viewing this program, please bring it to the librarian's attention when you return it.

Such advice will not only inform the patron of good cassette practice, but will also communicate the library's concern for its property and thus encourage better patron care.

If there is sufficient staff, it may be advisable to ask patrons not to rewind the tape after use. It can then be routinely inspected as it is rewound by a library staff member upon its return. Tape should always be rewound promptly and at a constant speed; undertaking this operation in the library will guarantee this. In a one-person library video operation, this procedure may not be possible, but all returned tapes should receive at least a cursory inspection to see that the tape is not broken or jammed before it is returned to the shelf to await the next user.

Videotape in low use or in archival collections should be rewound annually. Without this periodic rewinding, there is a risk of print-through—a layer-to-layer signal transfer problem where "magnetized ferric oxide particles on one layer of recorded tape stored on a wound reel are subjected to the magnetic field produced by the particles on an adjacent layer."[1] In other words, the image and/or sound will blur and merge together. Print-through can also be caused by other factors, such as the intrinsic quality or thickness of the tape. This is a common danger for tapes produced between 1971 and 1975.

In addition, plastic magnetic tape is subject to a phenomenon called cold flow, caused by the various unequal stresses and strains that are wound into it while being played. These strains tend to equalize themselves when the tape is in storage and the changes can be virtually eliminated by rewinding on an annual basis. If the tapes cannot be rewound, they should at least be inspected for cinching, buckling, or other anomalies. It is essential to keep records for all videotapes in an archival collection, indicating which have been rewound and the date of last rewinding.

It is estimated that videotapes produced since 1971 have a tape life of twenty years. Although a number of libraries have tapes dating back to 1968 that are still in good condition, others note deterioration in tapes produced as recently as 1978. A critical factor in the preservation of videotapes is their storage.

While researchers do not know how to preserve videotape indefinitely, it is clear that temperature and humidity play a critical role. Basically, storage conditions that are appropriate for film are appropriate for videotapes. If a library is to maintain a videotape collection, air conditioning is imperative. Extreme heat and fluctuations in temperature and humidity will quickly trigger intrinsic deterioration because videotape is extremely sensitive. Such fluctuations will also trigger the cold flow phenomenon. Although videotapes can be stored in cool conditions, the acceptable temperature for housing library collections, 68 °F (20 °C) and 55 percent RH are acceptable conditions for storing videotape.

The strategic placement of fans and dehumidifiers can curtail the damage caused by heat and humidity if the library does not have climate-controlled conditions. However, with heavily circulating collections, the library has no control over the environment in which the borrowed videotape is to be kept while out with the patron. An average life of a circulating videotape is estimated at one hundred passes—or viewings. When a tape gives an unacceptable signal and can no longer be viewed, it is generally caused by a drop-out or by a loss of RF (radio frequency) activity. Drop-out, according to Sargent, is "an impairment or complete loss of video information caused by a significant loss in the level of the recorded signal. It normally appears as the black or white horizontal line in the picture."[2] RF activity is the strength of the recorded signal: loss of RF activity is analogous to fading of an optical image. Videotapes in circulation, like popular paperback books, are more likely to wear out from patron use before they disintegrate from intrinsic flaws caused by environmental factors.

When not in use, videotapes should be shelved upright on metal shelves that are grounded to eliminate any problem of demagnetizing the tape by exposure to an electromagnetic field. Since videotapes and playback equipment are susceptible to contamination by dust and dirt, scrupulous housekeeping practices should be enforced in the area where they are housed.

Videotape record and playback heads should frequently be cleaned on in-house equipment. Commercial tape head cleaners are available in cassette forms, but many purists prefer to clean them manually using either a spray cleaner or swabs and an alcohol solution.

Videotapes and their containers are especially susceptible to fire. Fire protection in storage areas is most important. Tape reels, cassette cases, and storage containers should be made of fire-resistant materials. Under no circumstances should smoking be permitted in tape handling areas. Apart from the danger of setting a fire, tobacco and ashes—as well as the particulate matter in smoke—can also damage the videotape and cause drop-out. Borrowers should be reminded of this as well. If water extinguishers are used when a fire occurs, the videotape must be carefully air-dried within twenty-four hours. It is advisable to contact the manufacturer to see if air-drying alone is sufficient.

Librarians report a high reliability of videotape, even when it is frequently circulated. The most typical breakdowns occur when the tape comes away from its core or when the leader breaks. Both can be repaired easily in-house by a trained technician or the video librarian. When tapes break in the middle of a program, many believe that it is preferable to replace the tape with a new copy rather than attempt to patch it. Some librarians are reluctant to splice a tape break in the program itself, whether for fear of altering the sync signal and thus impairing the program, or for fear the splice will cause some damage to the heads on the patron's home equipment. Others are less worried, and some video librarians apply a pre-cut splice on the break and then cover it with a developer, to minimize any sync problems. Following good conservation practice, it is best for untrained personnel in small collections not to attempt such a repair. Large, well-staffed collections will have trained technicians who can undertake such repairs.

Sargent cites the following rules for handling tape in active work areas:

1. Tapes should not be touched with the fingers. The use of lint-free gloves is recommended where an unusual amount of handling occurs.

2. Working areas should be devoid of all substances that can adhere to the tape and cause dust and lint to collect. (Such dust is caused largely by static electricity, and static eliminators are available to minimize this.) Substances that can cause problems include cigarette ashes, food, drinks, and waxes.

3. No eating or smoking should be permitted in tape storage areas. Food particles can be much more harmful than smoke particles.

4. Tapes should be handled in a careful manner, not pulled, yanked, squeezed, or scratched. They should be protected against heat changes and fire hazard during transportation.

5. Tapes, reels, or cassettes should not be thrown or dropped, when either empty or full.

Many libraries negotiate with videotape distributors for the right to make duplicates. Thus they keep a "master" under quasi-archival conditions and can strike a copy when needed for circulation. When the circulating copy has worn out, it can be replaced with another copy from the master. The ability to make copies from masters is one of the advantages videotape has over film. If a library has the right to copy a tape, circulating copies can be transferred from one format to another (for example, from three-quarter-inch U-Matic to half-inch Beta).

Some distributors also lease a tape for its life. Libraries can then replace a title at a reduced rate when it wears out. The terms of such leases vary from distributor to distributor, but for high-use collections, especially those short on staff and duplication equipment, this may be the best arrangement.

Videotapes can be pirated far more easily than films, and pirated videotapes are readily available today. Such copies are usually of inferior quality, so when the librarian is offered a real bargain—"caveat emptor." As with everything else, it is best to deal with established and reputable dealers.

ARCHIVAL CONSIDERATIONS

As Eileen Bowser has noted in the preceding chapter, videotape is unstable and cannot serve as a preservation medium. No videotape presently manufactured is of archival quality. Videotape is a popular entertainment and creative medium, and libraries and individuals are using it to document events for which a permanent record is desired: community events, oral/visual histories, even a person's last will and testament.

Video as a medium to record the moving image has only been with us for about twenty-five years. As has already been noted, videotape was originally popular for its immediacy and little thought was given at first to its preservation by the broadcast industry. Much programming was lost or destroyed before archival efforts were undertaken to preserve this material. At present the videotapes owned by institutions such as the Vanderbilt Television News Archive, the Museum of Broadcasting, and the Museum of Modern Art are housed in cold storage, humidity-controlled vaults. Evidence to date indicates that cold storage is best to retard the deterioration of videotapes, as well as of motion picture film.

During the past decade many libraries have produced their own unique videotapes, which record events or images that are meant to be preserved. Like other media discussed in this volume, the material recorded on videotape documents our cultural and artistic heritage. Few organizations or institutions can attempt to save this material *in the original* (in vaults such as those located in the New Jersey Palisades), but one of the advantages of videotape is that it can be easily reproduced. As librarians deal with new media, they should not be locked into optimum requirements for reproduction that may not be applicable to the new media. A community can preserve its history on videotape and an individual can preserve major life events *if* the videotape is properly cared for and reproduced before deterioration begins.

Videotape is a medium that offers a new and convenient way of viewing the world around us. Some libraries are concerned with it as a delivery medium for entertainment programs, circulating feature films to their patrons on tape. Other libraries have video collections that only include programs originally produced on tape. Videotape is a format for art and information, like each of the media discussed in this volume. The codex format is two thousand years old; the videotape format is a little over twenty-five years old. Its place in our cultural history is constantly being redefined. Its preservation and its use as a medium for preservation of the visual record call for more exploration.

NOTES

1. Ralph Sargent, *Preserving the Moving Image* (Washington, D.C.: Corporation for Public Broadcasting, 1974), p. 135.
2. Sargent, p. 133.

SUGGESTED READING

There is little, other than the work quoted above, in the published literature that is appropriate reading for the nontechnical specialist on this evolving medium. A copy of the Sargent volume belongs in every library with a film and videotape collection. Its Section 3, "Videotape," pp. 129–49, remains the most informed nontechnical material available. The best way to keep abreast of changing technology is to read and clip the business pages of newspapers such as the *Wall Street Journal* and the *New York Times* and the technology magazines such as *Videography* and *Educational & Industrial TV.*

9

Sound Recordings

JERRY McWILLIAMS

The preservation of sound recordings has become a topic of interest among librarians and archivists. For many years recordings were considered a recreational medium. However, as people have become aware of the part that sound recordings have played, and play today, in our cultural, economic, and political life; as collections of sound recordings have grown in size and value; and as librarians, archivists, and collectors have become aware of the need to preserve library and archival materials in general, attention is now directed to the care and preservation of sound recordings.

While sound recordings have been produced in a wide variety of sizes, shapes, and technologies, almost all have been manufactured from organically derived substances. This origin, shared with printed materials, to some extent simplifies preservation requirements. For most kinds of sound recordings, special environmental control and shelving are not required, provided that conditions that are good for books exist. On the other hand, most deterioration of sound recordings occurs during playback, a feature of the storage/use cycle for which there is no equivalent for printed materials. It is at this stage that good equipment can have significant impact on the quality and effective life of sound recordings.

Before considering the storage and playback of sound recordings in detail, it may be useful to review the types of recordings most likely to be found in libraries and archives. The most common type is the familiar long-playing, microgroove polyvinyl chloride disk. The long-playing disk began to be manufactured in the early 1950s and by the 1960s was ubiquitous. Because of its longer playing time, relative sturdiness, and improved fidelity, it soon replaced the shellac disk. Long-playing disks have been made in several sizes, including 7 ", 10 " and 12 ". Most were intended for playback at 33-1/3 RPM (revolutions per minute) although some, such as the so-called spoken word recordings, must be played back at 16-2/3 RPM.

In collections that include popular music, the 7 " large-diameter spindle, microgroove 45 RPM disk will be found. Such disks were called "Extended-

Play" by RCA, who first manufactured them, and were introduced in the 1950s. They are still made today. Many were pressed from polyvinyl chloride although some were produced by an extrusion technology using polystyrene.

Shellac disks appeared around the turn of the century and after a commercial battle with cylinder recordings emerged triumphant in the late 1920s. The shellac disk was the principal commercial recording medium of the 1930s and 1940s. Because shellac disks were made over a long period, size and playing speed are less standardized than for vinyl disks. Most, however, were 10″ to 12″ in diameter and designed for playback at 78 RPM.

In the noncommercial sphere, the instantaneous recording was important in the 1930s and 1940s. An instantaneous recording is a disk in which the grooves are cut in a cellulose acetate or cellulose nitrate medium which in turn has been laid down upon an aluminum or glass platter. Instantaneous recordings were made of events such as radio shows and speeches and also found widespread use in home recording. They were never intended for commercial production. These disks were produced in various sizes from 7″ to 20″. Most were recorded at 78 RPM.

Collections of early sound recordings will often include cylinders. The first sound recording was a type of cylinder recording. Cylinder recordings gained in popularity after 1900. Their technological development peaked in the early 1920s but by the end of that decade production had been stopped. Cylinders were issued in different sizes ranging from 1-5/16″ to 5″ in diameter and were made from wax compounded with other substances. As with shellac, actual composition varied considerably from manufacturer to manufacturer over the years.

Most collections of sound recordings will include some form of tape recording. Reel-to-reel tape recording was introduced in the United States at the end of World War II. It quickly became the standard in the recording industry because of its ease of editing. Low-priced units became available in the mid-1950s. Perhaps because of its relatively late introduction, reel-to-reel tape formats and speeds have been well standardized. Professional work has been done largely on 10-1/2″ reels at 15 or 30 IPS (inches per second) tape speed. Noncommercial recording has usually been done at 3-3/4 IPS or 7-1/2 IPS on 5″ and 7″ reels. Until the development of multitrack recording in the 1960s, reel-to-reel recordings were made largely on tape 1/4″ in width. Format has varied from full track (where one channel of sound occupies the entire width of the tape) to half-track and quarter-track (four channels on the tape). The magnetic coating of recording tape (the material that contains the sonic information) has been deposited on two types of base: Mylar and cellulose acetate.

The tape cassette was introduced in the 1960s and has become popular because its equipment is compact, portable, more convenient to use than reel-to-reel, and generally less expensive. It has found wide application in

oral history and field recording. Most audio tape cassettes follow the
"Compact Cassette" format established by Philips. This uses 1/8 " wide
tape operating at 1-7/8 IPS.

In addition to the types of sound recordings mentioned above, collections
may include wax disks, metal disks, wire recordings, tape recordings on
paper-base tape, old disk recordings in unusual formats, 1/2 ", 1 ", and 2 "
multitrack professional tape masters, Dictaphone belts, and, today, digi-
tally encoded tapes and disks. It is beyond the scope of this article to deal
with these materials.

STORAGE OF SOUND RECORDINGS

The provision of good shelf conditions for sound recordings is not difficult when the recordings have good internal stability. As has already been
mentioned, today long-playing records are pressed from a vinyl chloride
compound, the main ingredients of which have not changed greatly over the
last thirty years. They include vinyl chloride (the base), vinyl acetate (a plas-
ticizer), lampblack (to make disks black), and various stabilizers, fillers,
and destaticizing agents. Since vinyl chloride is unstable at the high temperatures involved in pressing disks, a stabilizer is added. Significantly, some
stabilizer remains in the vinyl when pressing is completed and the disk has
cooled. It is this residual which retards the destructive oxidation-reduction
reactions continuously taking place when the disk is on the shelf. The degree
of retardation is great. A study conducted for the Library of Congress by
A. G. Pickett and M. M. Lemcoe concluded that vinyl LPs, stored under
correct conditions, are safe for at least one hundred years.

Tapes made of Mylar (or polyester) backing, particularly those of 1.5 mil
thickness, are similarly stable. Sound archives routinely use such tape to
make master copies of recordings existing on unstable media. Mylar tapes
are included in time capsules. In fact, there appear to be no definitely established limits to how long Mylar tape will last.

Shellac disks made from good quality shellac compound are also stable.
Properly formulated shellac cures as it ages—a cross-polymerization occurs
which guarantees good long-term life. Unfortunately, the composition of
shellac compounds varied over the years, especially during World Wars I
and II when shellac supplies were interrupted. As a result, it is not wise to
generalize about the inherent stability of 78s, although it is probably safe to
say that most 78s made during the interwar years are stable.

Although most sound recordings are inherently stable, appropriate storage conditions will prolong their life. Sound recordings should be posi-
tioned on the shelf so that they are not subject to physical stress. This is a
widely known fact but bears repetition for, well known as it is, it is often ig-
nored. Disks should be shelved vertically at all times. They should not be
tightly packed. If disks are allowed to slant or are stacked horizontally,

warping may result and this cannot always be corrected. Standard metal library shelving may be used for disk storage. Vertical subdivisions should be provided every twenty disks to help prevent slanting. If more than a few disks are to be temporarily removed, a book or other object may be inserted to keep the other recordings on the shelf in a vertical position.

Similarly, reel-to-reel tapes should be shelved vertically. This reduces the likelihood of distorting the reel shape. Individual reels of tape are usually packaged in a cardboard box. These may be arranged on the shelf just as disks are. Tape cassettes are distributed in small plastic boxes. These make excellent storage containers and may be arranged on the shelf in the most convenient way.

Horizontal shelving can be employed in some circumstances. For example, 45s may be grouped into drawers of about fifteen disks each. Because 45s are lightweight, this small number stacked horizontally will not create stress.

It is important to keep collections of sound recordings within certain limits of temperature and humidity. There are several reasons for this. Adequately low temperatures ensure that the rate of deterioration caused by oxidation-reduction reactions taking place in the sound recordings is minimized. The rate of these reactions follows Arrhenius's equation, by which the reaction rate is geometrically proportional to increases in temperature. Also, low temperatures, and especially low humidity, prevent the development of fungus. When fungus grows on disk surfaces, it causes pitting. Fungus may also grow on the site of tape splices. High temperatures are undesirable not only because they accelerate oxidation-reduction reactions but because they allow the relaxation of microscopic stresses in long-playing disks. Microscopic stresses are normally present in LPs. When they are relaxed, warping may occur. Extremely low temperatures are also harmful. Shellac and vinyl become brittle below 0 °F (-18 °C).

More damaging to sound recordings than any one extreme of temperature is thermal and hygroscopic fluctuation. This fluctuation—typically caused by heating/air conditioning being switched on in mornings and off in the evenings or by natural diurnal temperature changes within a building—causes expansion and contraction. This weakens the structure of the recordings. In disks it may cause warping, in tapes the loss of oxide coating, in both distortion of sonic content. Tape is particularly sensitive to such fluctuations.

For optimum protection, disks may be maintained at 70 °F (21 °C) and 50 percent RH (relative humidity) year-round, with a permissible deviation of plus or minus 10 percent from these values. Some variation in temperature and humidity is, of course, inevitable and in certain climates good environmental conditions may be expensive or even impossible to maintain. It is important, however, to minimize fluctuations as much as possible and to avoid extremes. For disks, the maximum safe upper temperature is 80 °F

(26 °C). Temperatures lower than 70 °F (21 °C), which theoretically preferable, will not have a major impact on the shelf life of the disk but will benefit the paper products in which disks are usually packaged.

Tapes should be kept under similar conditions but because of their greater sensitivity to cycling, temperature should vary by no more than 5 °F (3 °C), and humidity by no more than 10 percent RH. Maximum recommended ambient temperature for tapes is 70 °F (21 °C).

In order to help maintain these conditions some obvious points should not be overlooked. For example, shelving should not be located near windows, outer walls, heating/air conditioning outlets, or where sunlight will fall upon it—these are areas where fluctuations in temperature and humidity will be greatest. Also, no collection of sound recordings should be housed in an attic or poorly ventilated upper story where high temperatures are often found. If it is properly sealed against moisture and protected from flooding, a basement is often a good place to store sound recordings.

Sound recordings should be stored in a clean, dust-free environment. Both tapes and disks can be damaged by dust and other airborne contaminants. Particles settling on groove walls may create permanent ticks and pops when disks are played. Small dust particles trapped between layers of tape can cause drop-out (the temporary loss of signal from a tape during playback). A convenient, although expensive method of storage is to shelve sound recordings in cabinets with snugly fitting doors. If, however, they are to be housed in an open area of the library or archives, the environment should be vacuumed regularly. More importantly, air conditioning should include filtering equipment to remove as much dust as possible. These are measures that benefit all library materials.

Packaging is another protection against dust. Original packaging supplied with LPs, including inner liners and cardboard dust jackets or boxes, can usually be retained if the inner liners are of polyethylene. These are preferable to paper liners which, in humid environments, can allow fungus to develop. Supplementary polyethylene liners are widely available and can easily be substituted for paper liners. The plastic or cellophane shrink-wrapping in which LPs are commonly sold should be removed immediately after purchase. It is highly sensitive to fluctuations in temperature and can cause warping if left on the dust jackets. Reel-to-reel tapes are customarily packaged in a plastic bag within a cardboard container. This offers good protection against dust and humidity. The plastic boxes in which cassette tapes are supplied offer excellent dust protection and should be retained.

While it may be of historical interest, original packaging for 78s is not generally suitable for storage. This is particularly true for the leaved albums in which multi-disk sets were sold. These have a tendency to break disks unless they are handled very carefully. A better alternative is to package all 78s individually in acid-free paper or foil-lined paper envelopes. This is the way 78s are stored in most archives. Appropriate envelopes are available from several archival supply houses, which are listed in the Appendix. Instantaneous recordings must never be stored in polyethylene liners. Under certain conditions, the nitrate/acetate materials will bond with the polyethylene and be stripped from the underlying platter when the disk is removed from the liner.

While tapes and disks have similar storage requirements, there are two problems unique to tape: winding tension and accidental erasure. When a reel-to-reel tape deck is in record or playback mode, tape tension is normally maintained at about 2–3 ounces for a 1/4 " tape. Tape is designed to be stored on reels at this tension; given favorable environmental conditions, it will not deform. When tape decks operate in fast-forward or rewind modes, however, tape tension fluctuates, often exceeding the low-speed level. This means that if one side of a tape is played and the tape rewound, the tape will be stored under uneven, and probably excessive, winding tension. This will cause dimensional distortion in the tape and eventually can lead to loss of oxide coating. For this reason, reel-to-reel tape should always be stored in a played, or "tails-out" state. While maintaining this procedure can be time-consuming and inconvenient, it is the only correct way to store tape.

Concern is often expressed over the possibility of erasure of tape recordings from accidental exposure to magnetic fields. While it is true that a strong magnetic field brought into contact with a tape recording can cause erasure, in practice this almost never occurs as the result of an accident. This is because the strength of a magnetic field decreases geometrically as the distance from the source increases. Provided that tapes are not played directly against the source of a magnetic field, such as a transformer or electric motor, there is almost no chance of accidental erasure. There is no evidence to suggest that storing tapes on metal shelves in any way affects sound quality. One source of potential erasure that should not be overlooked is the electronic theft detector at library exits. Tapes should be passed well around detectors rather than through them.

So far, we have discussed the storage of sound recordings with good preservation characteristics. Many collections, however, will contain recordings that are either inherently unstable or, if stable, not suitable for long-term retention for other reasons. Such recordings include wax disks, cylinders, laminated disks, wire recordings, instantaneous recordings, tape recordings on acetate or paper base, polystyrene 45s, disk recordings on unusual surfaces, and C120 and C180 tape cassettes.

The basic philosophy when dealing with any recording in an unstable medium is to determine the importance of the recording and, if important, to dub it to 1.5 mil Mylar tape. In this way, at least the sonic content of the recording is preserved. Originals should be retained as they are often of significant historical interest.

Disks made of any material other than vinyl or shellac should be dubbed. Instantaneous recordings are a prime example. The acetate/nitrate coatings are chemically unstable and will eventually disintegrate along with the sonic content of the disk. The coatings have a tendency to separate from the underlying platter, as has been mentioned before. The plasticizers within the coating will often separate from the coating, creating an oily mess on the disk surface. Originals, when cleaned, may be stored in individual acid-free envelopes.

Unfortunately, the fact that a disk is made from "shellac" does not ensure that it is stable. As has already been mentioned, the composition of shellac disks varies considerably. Some may be susceptible to hygroscopic fluctuation. Laminated disks, in which a paper core is sandwiched between shellac surfaces, are an example. Columbia was a major producer of the laminated disk and their recordings should be dubbed. The originals may be shelved with other shellacs, but special care should be exercised to see that they do not get wet.

The stability of cylinder recordings varies from one type to another. Edison Blue Amberol cylinders, perhaps the highest quality cylinder recordings made, are apparently quite stable, while cylinders of other manufacturers may contain materials which make them susceptible to variations in humidity. It is a good idea to dub all cylinder recordings, not only for reasons of preservation, but because it is inconvenient and undesirable for users to play them directly. Storage of originals poses something of a problem. Sound archives have been forced to develop their own solutions. However, any arrangement is suitable that allows the cylinders to remain on end, well ventilated (air should be able to circulate around them), free of stress, and protected from dust. Thermal and hygroscopic fluctuations should be kept to an absolute minimum.

Many tape recordings from the 1950s will be found on acetate-base tape. Cellulose acetate is unstable. It will eventually crumble, destroying the sound recording, or cause patches of the magnetic coating to fall off, destroying areas of the recording. Acetate-base tapes may hold up well for years but eventually they will self-destruct. All such tapes must be dubbed to 1.5 mil Mylar-base tape. If tapes are in original manufacturers' containers, information on the tape base will often be printed on the container. When there is doubt or the tapes are known to date from the 1950s, it is safest to dub.

There are other types of tape recordings, even if they are produced on Mylar-base tape, that are not suitable for long-term storage. For example, recordings on .5 mil or 1.0 mil Mylar-base tape, while chemically stable, are produced on such a thin base that a phenomenon called print-through may take place. Print-through occurs when the magnetic domains of one layer of tape "print through" to an adjacent layer, creating an audible shadow, or

low-level copy, of the original. This same danger exists for cassette recordings which are all produced on a thin-base tape. Materials on these tapes
that are required for long-term storage should be dubbed.

PLAYBACK OF SOUND RECORDINGS

Playback conditions, including handling, cleaning, and the type of equipment used and its maintenance, will have a dramatic effect on the life of
sound recordings, especially disks, because it is during playback that most
damage occurs. A long-playing disk, reproduced under optimum conditions, will suffer little, if any, degradation of sound for at least one hundred
playings. In some tests, the figures are more impressive. Mylar tape, especially 1.5 mil, offers similar longevity. On the other hand, one playing
under unfavorable conditions can materially affect the audio quality of a
disk or tape.

Correct playback procedure for disks begins with handling. Disks should
be handled as little as possible in the transfer from packaging to turntable
and back. It is particularly important to avoid touching groove surfaces
with fingers. Oil, which is always present on the skin, when deposited on
grooves will attract and hold dust particles. Oil can also serve as a base upon
which mold will develop. Disks should be held by the fingertips at their
outer diameter. A convenient way to hold disks, and to remove them from
wrappers or dust jackets with one hand, is to support the disk from underneath with fingertips on the center label and the thumb on the outer edge
(see Figure 9.1). The disk can be balanced easily this way, and the other
hand is available to stabilize it if necessary or to help remove the liner.

Frequency of use is an overlooked aspect of disk playback. When a disk is
played, it is subject to stress. Because of the small dimensions of the stylus
tip, force of only one gram from a microgroove cartridge produces an enormous pressure against the groove walls, between 6,000 and 16,000 pounds
per square inch. This pressure exists between two objects in relative motion
and therefore develops friction which, in turn, produces high temperatures
of up to 2,000 °F (1,100 °C) at points of stylus-to-disk contact. However,
this temperature is created for only a fraction of a second. The thermoplastic properties of vinyl are such that it will not be permanently deformed
under these conditions. Nonetheless, significant stress is created. It is for
this reason that no disk should ever be played more than once every twenty-
four hours. This is very important. The twenty-four hour interval allows the
vinyl or shellac to "relax" after its stressing. It has been found that playing
a vinyl disk two times in a row creates the same amount of wear as fifty to
one hundred normal playings spaced sixteen hours apart.

Disk cleaning is another important aspect of disk playback. Cleaning the
disk prior to, during, and after playback is vital to preserve its sound quality. Dust and other particles are always present in the air and will settle on

Figure 9.1. Disk surfaces should not be touched during handling. Support the disk from underneath with the fingertips on the center label and the thumb on the outer edge. The disk can easily be removed from its dust jacket in this manner. Reprinted from *The Preservation and Restoration of Sound Recordings*, by Jerry McWilliams, by permission of the American Association for State and Local History. Copyright © 1979, American Association for State and Local History, 708 Berry Road, Nashville, Tennessee 37204.

the record surface. In fact, a revolving disk creates a vortex that draws air down to the disk and out over its surface, acting as a siphon for dust.

Dust particles resting in groove walls will interfere with playback in two ways. First, when the stylus strikes a dust particle, a loud tick will be heard. The noise detracts from the listening experience. More seriously, the dust particle may be permanently impacted into the groove wall. A microgroove stylus moves at a considerable speed in outer grooves and operates at high pressures and temperatures, conditions sufficient to implant the particle in the vinyl, lodging it there for the life of the disk. If disks are not systematically cleaned with each playing, new ticks will continue to be added to the grooves, resulting in an unpleasantly noisy recording.

In recent years a number of products have come on the market to help clean disks. These range from simple plus-pad brushes, to various sprays and films, to elaborate groove vacuuming systems. Criteria for a good disk cleaner include the following: (1) it should be simple; (2) it should not be expensive to use on a per disk basis; (3) it should not involve the application of any liquid, film, or other substance to the disk; and, (4) it must work.

One problem plaguing disk cleaners in the past was that although they were effective in removing dust from the grooves, it was generally impossible to remove the cleaning pad from the disk surface without redepositing some, if not most, of it. Another problem was that wiping disks with cleaning pads often induced a powerful electrostatic charge on the disk, making cleaning all the more difficult. Finally, a sufficiently soft, fine fiber that could penetrate to the bottom of grooves was not available.

Today these problems are largely solved by the carbon fiber record brush, one of the best overall disk cleaning devices available (see Figure 9.2). The carbon fiber brush was introduced by Decca but other manufacturers now supply it. It consists of many thousands of carbon fiber bristles. These are soft, very narrow, and electrically conductive. They can reach deep into grooves with safety and remove dust. At the same time, they will conduct static charges away from the disk surface. The amount of dust that the carbon fiber brush can remove from an apparently clean disk is remarkable.

Some manufacturers also offer a carbon fiber dust bug (see Figure 9.3). After the disk has been cleaned with the brush, the dust bug can be used to keep the grooves free of dust during playback. The dust bug consists of a base and pivot, an arm, and a carbon fiber brush. The carbon fibers allow the static to be discharged through the arm and a ground wire.

The combination of the two products retails for about $30.00. They are well worth the cost. While these products were designed primarily for use with LPs and 45s, they may also be used with shellac 78s. It would be a good idea to maintain two sets of disk cleaning equipment, one for 78s and the other for microgroove recordings.

Static buildup is a problem which under certain local conditions is annoying. Disks are electrostatically charged if they produce a crackling sound when removed from the turntable. Electrostatic voltage should be removed from disks, not only because it will cause dust to be attracted to the disk surface but also because, if severe enough, it may interfere with the performance of the cartridge. While a destaticizing type of dust bug may curtail static buildup, it is not usually adequate.

The most effective way to discharge disks is through the use of an antistatic pistol. The original antistatic pistol was developed by Zerostat, but others now manufacture the device. It incorporates a quartz element that is alternately stressed and relaxed. This releases a stream of positively and then negatively charged ions. The result is to discharge any electrostatic voltage on the disk. The antistatic pistol is highly effective and it is recommended. As a general policy, all LPs should be destaticized both before and after use. The antistatic pistol is not a rugged device and care must be exercised to see that it is not dropped or otherwise abused.

One of the most interesting disk-care products to become available in recent years is Sound Guard. Sound Guard is not a disk cleaner; rather, it is a disk-protection product. It is a liquid that can be sprayed onto the surfaces of LPs and 45s. The liquid dries, forming a microscopically thin layer of lubricant over the grooves, helping to protect them during repeated playings.

The use of the product has received favorable comment in the audio press. The major thrust of the published test results has been to demonstrate that the high-frequency response of treated LPs is significantly preserved. When high-frequency modulations are eroded by wear, a disk will sound lifeless and dull; it is clearly desirable that this not occur. Reduction in surface noise buildup has also been demonstrated when Sound Guard is used. Application of Sound Guard appears to have no adverse effect on sound quality. However, there are some inherent problems with the use of the product.

First, Sound Guard does not clean or restore disks—it simply protects what it already there. Thus, any dust or other particulate matter on the groove walls will be encapsulated by Sound Guard and may become a permanent feature of the recording. Therefore, Sound Guard should be used only on records that have been scrupulously cleaned. Second, Sound Guard is not applied with equal success by all users. There have been reports that one can easily apply too much Sound Guard, with the result that the preservative will accumulate on the stylus and cause other problems. Finally, the use of any product that creates a permanent, unalterable change in a physical object runs counter to the best preservation practice. Once Sound Guard is applied, it is there for good. The conservative archivist might not wish to use it for this reason, although it is recommended for expendable, circulating collections as a means of extending the life of a sound recording.

Disk cleaning, as important as it is, is only one of the requirements that must be met if disk life is to be preserved. Playback equipment also has a

Figure 9.2. The carbon fibre disk brush is one of the best cleaning devices currently available. The brush is held against a disk for several revolutions then is pulled to the center of the disk and removed. The carbon fibre brush can lift a considerable amount of dust even from an apparently clean disk. Reprinted from *The Preservation and Restoration of Sound Recordings*, by Jerry McWilliams, by permission of the American

Figure 9.3. The carbon fibre dust bug continuously cleans the disk as it is played. Note the static discharge wire emerging from the left side of the dust bug's base. Reprinted from *The Preservation and Restoration of Sound Recordings*, by Jerry McWilliams, by permission of the American Association for State and Local History. Copyright © 1979, American Association for State and Local History, 708 Berry Road, Nashville, Tennessee 37204.

direct bearing on disk life. It must meet and maintain adequate levels of performance if disks are not to be damaged in use. The following elements of the disk-playback chain have an effect on disk life: stylus, cartridge, and tone arm.

Of all the components in the chain, it is the stylus, traveling directly in the groove, that has the greatest impact on groove life. The shape of the stylus, its dimensions, and the force with which it contacts the groove are the principal factors to be considered.

Stylus tip shape was originally spherical and it is this type of stylus that is used for 78s. With the development of the microgroove disk, and the subsequent ability of manufacturers to produce stylus tips of smaller size and more accurately controlled shapes, it was discovered that there were technical advantages to using an elliptical stylus shape. The spherical stylus presents a hemispherical shape to the groove while the elliptical stylus presents an elongated, elliptoid shape. Elliptical styluses are the kind most frequently used today for reproducing LPs.

There is little disagreement that spherical styluses should be used for 78s. There has been disagreement, however, about the effect of the elliptical stylus on groove life. The elliptical stylus presents a smaller surface area to the record groove and therefore exerts greater pressure than a spherical tip tracking at the same force. Although elliptical styluses are by far the more prevalent type available for use with LPs, the spherical-tip stylus remains available from a limited number of manufacturers.

In a classic investigation published in 1968, J. G. Woodward applied scanning electron microscope techniques to the study of disk surfaces. Photographs taken by Woodward show that in repeated playings the spherical tip produces less wear on the groove wall than an elliptical-tip stylus tracking at the same force. Several leading American sound archivists have stated that the spherical tip produces less wear. Although the spherical tip will produce more wear on the groove wall with the initial playing, wear thereafter is minimal. The elliptical tip continues to wear with each playing. The use of spherical-tip styluses in two of the nation's largest sound archives lends a considerable measure of professional support to this choice. Nonetheless, opinion on the matter remains divided among authorities. Those seeking to employ spherical-tip microgroove styluses will find that only a few cartridges are designed to accommodate them and that they are relatively expensive.

While the dimensions of styluses for microgroove recordings are fairly standard (.5 to .7 mil for spherical and .3 × .8 mil for elliptical), a considerable range of stylus diameters may be necessary for optimum playback of 78s. This is due to the lack of standardization among early record manufacturers. However, for most 78s made from the 1920s on, a 2.5 mil spherical-tip stylus will be adequate. The correct stylus diameter will produce the best fidelity, minimize scratch and hiss, and cause least wear to the disk. When the question of correct stylus diameter arises, determination is best left to an experienced sound recording technician.

Playback styluses of all types require regular maintenance if they are to operate effectively and not damage disks. The two main areas of maintenance are stylus cleaning and wear inspection. As the stylus travels through miles of grooves, it will accumulate dirt on the tip. The dirt may consist of grease or oil, vinyl or shellac particles, dust, or a combination of all of these. A buildup of dirt will occur even on disks that have been thoroughly cleaned prior to and during playback. This accumulation is undesirable from several standpoints. First, it will affect stylus performance. When the stylus is encrusted with dirt, it cannot make proper contact with groove surfaces, nor can it respond accurately to groove modulations. Second, the accumulation of dirt may cause abrasive damage to groove surfaces, particularly on microgroove recordings. Dirt buildup may easily be observed by examining an uncleaned stylus with a 10X or 20X jeweler's eyepiece. The stylus will appear clear of particulate matter to the naked eye, but when examined with the eyepiece, the stylus tip will be seen to be covered by a variety of materials.

The stylus should be brushed lightly with a soft camel's hair brush before each playing. Care must be taken during this operation not to damage the delicate stylus cantilever (the thin metal armature on which the stylus is mounted). The stylus should be brushed with a gentle stroke from the back of the cartridge forward. No pressure should be exerted upon the cantilever. Several strokes are all that are necessary.

In addition to brushing, the stylus should be cleaned with a solvent. Dishwasher solution is ideal for this purpose. A drop or two of liquid is usually sufficient. The solvent may be placed on a camel's hair brush or on a stylus-cleaning pad, or the brush supplied by the cartridge manufacturer. A gentle stroking motion is used. It is important not to allow any excess liquid to remain on the cantilever or to flow back into the cartridge as it will almost certainly ruin the cartridge. Cleaning the stylus with a solvent should be performed once a week under normal use. Do not use pure alcohol or other undiluted organic solvents to clean the stylus. These can cause the cement bonding the stylus to the cantilever to dissolve, allowing the stylus to rattle in the cantilever or simply to fall off. A jeweler's eyepiece can be used to check how thoroughly the stylus has been cleaned. Some disks will have dirtier grooves than others. In such instances, it may be necessary to clean the stylus after each playing.

The stylus should be periodically inspected for wear. Although made of diamond, it is gradually worn by use. At a certain point, severe damage to grooves will occur. Therefore, it is essential that disks are never played with a worn stylus. A record should be kept of the number of hours of use logged on the stylus. Cumulative hours can then be compared with the manufacturer's suggested stylus life. When hours of use begin to approach that figure, the stylus should be inspected in a properly set up stylus microscope to determine the extent of wear. Although it has been suggested that it is possible to check stylus wear using a jeweler's eyepiece, in practice this is difficult to do. A microscope is required. Any dealer in high-quality audio equipment should have a stylus microscope. Unfortunately, not all do, nor do those who do necessarily know how to interpret what they see. When a collection is worth preserving, it is a good idea to replace each stylus after five hundred hours of use, even though it may not yet be badly worn. This simplifies the inspection problem.

A convenient way to keep track of stylus wear is through the use of a stylus timer. These are available from several companies and retail for about $15.00. They are generally accurate to within twenty-five hours per thousand hours of stylus use, an adequate figure.

The type of cartridge selected for playback will not normally have a significant effect on disk life, providing that it can track at two grams or less. Tracking force is the pressure upon the stylus necessary for the cartridge to accurately follow groove modulations with an allowance for some degree of disk warp. Most modern cartridges are capable of tracking at two grams or less. In theory, the lower the tracking force, the less disk wear will occur for a given cartridge. If tracking force is too low for the cartridge, however, the stylus will bounce in the groove, which also causes wear.

The tone arm positions the cartridge and stylus over the disk grooves; thus it plays a major role in disk preservation. The tone arm must provide the correct tracking force for the stylus, allow it to move freely in both horizontal and vertical tracking angles (angles at which the stylus intersects the groove), and provide compensation for skating force, which tends to draw the cartridge toward the center of the disk.

Tone arms come in two forms, those that are an integral part of a turntable and those that are separate units. Separate units are more expensive and are sometimes difficult to install, but they usually offer superior performance.

Most tone arms, whether integrated or separate, will have a tracking-force control with some kind of indicator to facilitate adjustment. Tracking force should be set to the cartridge manufacturer's recommendation. This is usually specified as a range. Experiment can be made within this range to determine the point at which the cartridge sounds best. The tracking-force gauges on tone arms are not necessarily reliable. A stylus tracking-force scale should be kept on hand to verify readings on the tone arm. These are available for about $5.00 and should be considered essential equipment.

The determination of the proper tracking geometry of tone arms is a complex problem; most librarians and archivists would prefer not to deal with it. Although technical information has been published on how to adjust optimum horizontal tracking angle for tone arms, the practical problems in-

volved in carrying out the theoretical descriptions are nearly insurmount-
able. With integrated tone arms, some of the problems have been resolved
by the manufacturer. Even so, a number of variables, such as stylus overhang, tone-arm height, and the angle at which the cartridge is mounted in
the headshell, will affect performance and disk wear. As a practical matter,
manufacturers' installation and mounting instructions should be carefully
followed. This will ensure that horizontal and vertical tracking angles are
within reasonable bounds.

Many tone arms, both integrated and separate, now possess anti-skating
compensation. This is usually adjustable by means of a dial calibrated to
provide correct compensation for a given tracking force. Such a dial should
be carefully set. If it is not, uneven groove wear will occur.

In public and academic libraries where patrons are given direct access to
disks and playback equipment, it is impossible to maintain ideal disk playback conditions. Disk cleaning equipment may not be used properly, if used
at all; brushes and dust bugs will probably disappear, making it uneconomi-
cal to provide them in the first place; playback equipment may be abused so
that it damages the disks; and, of course, where disks are circulated to the
public, no control at all can be exercised over playback conditions. How can
disks best be preserved in such circumstances?

The long-term outlook for these disks is not good but measures can be
taken to extend their life somewhat. Treatment of LPs and 45s with Sound
Guard is one possibility. The unit cost of application is not great, and when
properly applied Sound Guard should offer a significant extension of the
life of the disk.

It is a useful practice in any collection of sound recordings to place a
small, pencilled tick mark on the dust jacket of a disk each time it is circulated or played. When the disk has been used ten times, several options can
be considered. A backup copy of the disk can be purchased so that when the
audio quality of the first copy deteriorates to the point where it can no
longer be used, a second copy is available. Purchasing a backup copy ahead
of time is prudent because once disks leave the market, they often are not
reissued and are difficult or impossible to obtain.

Alternately, the disk can be taped while audio quality is still good and
patrons can be given the tape to play. However, this approach may run
counter to the Copyright Law of 1976 which states that a library or archive
may make a tape copy of a deteriorating sound recording only when a copy
is not available through standard commercial sources. Thus, before taping
is undertaken, a search should be made through the catalogue of standard
suppliers and a record kept of the search. Taping, while expensive in time
and material, is the ideal way to deal with the disk use problem.

One of the principal advantages of tape over disk is its comparative freedom from use-associated problems. For example, under normal conditions,

tape will never require cleaning during recording or playback. If it is used in a clean environment, it is unlikely that it will ever accumulate enough dust to interfere with sonic quality, regardless of frequency of use. Also, tape undergoes less deterioration of sound quality with repeated playings than do disks.

While tape has these advantages, it is not without drawbacks. It is more awkward to use than disks, as it requires winding and threading and has some special handling needs that must be observed if sonic quality is not to be diminished. In addition, tape equipment must be periodically cleaned, demagnetized, and aligned if optimum performance is to be attained and tapes not damaged.

As with any type of sound recording, handling of tape should be kept to a minimum. Excessive handling will result in the deposit of grease and oils on the tape surface. Dust particles will then tend to accumulate on these areas, increasing the possibility of drop-out.

Unless tape is being edited or otherwise specially processed, most handling will occur when the tape is threaded into the machine. Handling problems at this stage can be largely eliminated by the use of leader tape. A leader tape is a short piece (about six feet) of nonmagnetic tape attached to the beginning and the end of the tape. It serves a number of functions. First, it ensures that only the leader is handled during threading. This keeps the tape itself clean and prevents the ends from becoming frayed with repeated use. Second, it prevents the main tape from being damaged if the tape machine is not stopped in time in fast-forward or rewind modes. When the end of the reel is reached in high-speed wind or rewind, the tape will be whipped around the tape guides. When leader is used, the tape will not be subject to that stress.

Leader tape should be attached to the beginning and end of all reels that lack it. Many tapes will already have leader attached, particularly audiophile-quality tapes of recent manufacture. In such instances, the leader is often Mylar or some other plastic. Paper leader may also be used. Leader tape is available from suppliers of professional recording tape and is attached using normal splicing techniques. The necessity of leader tape and other special handling procedures is eliminated in the cassette format.

A major problem with the magnetic-tape medium is the print-through phenomenon. The degree of print-through is a function of several variables, including temperature. Because elevated temperatures may occur on the top of or inside tape decks under conditions of prolonged use, tapes should not be left on tape machines any longer than necessary. Their prompt removal after use will reduce temperature-induced print-through.

Modern Mylar-base tapes should not present handling problems once they are on the tape machine. When tape machines are operating properly, breakage or other damage to tape will not occur. Inferior tape decks, however, may cause tape breakage or spillage. Such equipment should not be used in libraries. Older acetate-base tapes may begin to crack or break when played due to deterioration. The best that can be done for these tapes is to splice them and dub them to a Mylar-base tape.

From time to time, tape editing is desirable. Editing can be used to remove unwanted portions of a tape or otherwise rearrange the sequence of recorded materials. Editing and splicing should be carefully performed, or winding problems will develop.

Splicing should be done on an aluminum splicing block. These are available from professional recording equipment suppliers. Consumer-grade splicing kits are not suitable for serious work. Professional splicing tape should be used. Under no circumstances should regular Scotch tape be used. The adhesive from Scotch tape will spread, causing adjacent layers of tape to stick together. The use of any iron or steel equipment in contact with the tape during editing or splicing should be avoided. If such equipment is required, it must be demagnetized prior to use to avoid damaging the magnetic information on the tape.

Tape equipment needs periodic maintenance to achieve maximum playback quality and to minimize deterioration of sonic quality. Such maintenance includes cleaning, demagnetization, and replacement of pinch rollers. Other areas requiring attention are alignment of magnetic heads, adjustment to tape tension, replacement of worn heads, and adjustment of bias and equalization. The latter operations are normally performed by a service technician.

When tapes are played, abrasion causes small amounts of the magnetic coating to come off. The coating is deposited in a thin layer on the surfaces that come into contact with the tape. Sometimes it can be seen as a reddish-brown powder or, with modern tapes, the residue may be gray or white. Although it is often difficult to detect with the naked eye, it is there nonetheless. It will cause uneven tape motion and drop-out. If enough accumulates on the magnetic heads, it may cause partial loss of signal.

In order to control the deposits of magnetic coating, tape machines should be cleaned after every eight hours of use. Parts to be cleaned are (1) magnetic heads, (2) the capstan (the revolving metal shaft that drives the tape), (3) the pinch roller (the rubber wheel that presses the tape against the capstan), (4) tape guides and lifters (the metal parts that direct the tape across the heads and lift it from the heads during high-speed transport), (5) scrape-and-flutter filters (the round metal rollers over which the tape passes), and (6) the tape tension arms.

These parts may be cleaned using Q-tips and denatured alcohol or Freon TF. Cleaning kits are available from many manufacturers, although they are more expensive in the long run. All metal surfaces with which the tape comes in contact should be swabbed. Particular attention should be given to the magnetic heads. These must be kept scrupulously clean if good performance is to be obtained. Cleaning should be a standard operating procedure in all libraries and archives. To clean the rubber pinch roller, use one of the specially formulated rubber cleaners available for the purpose rather than alcohol. The pinch roller does not need to be cleaned as often as the tape heads. For cassette equipment, special cleaning cassettes can be inserted into the deck and played as a tape would be played. These give satisfactory results.

Tape heads, as well as metal parts that the tape contacts, are subject to magnetization. Magnetization of these parts imposes a threat to the sonic integrity of the tape. If severe enough, magnetization will cause partial erasure. For that reason, demagnetization is a standard part of tape-machine maintenance. Demagnetization is accomplished by the use of a device that produces a magnetic field capable of neutralizing magnetic polarity on the metal parts of the tape deck. When energized, the demagnetizer is slowly brought into proximity with each metal part and then withdrawn. This operation creates a random alignment of magnetic polarities. Demagnetizers are available from suppliers who carry head-cleaning kits or from professional recording equipment suppliers. Tape recorder manufacturers' recommendations for frequency of demagnetization should be carefully observed. Demagnetization is customarily performed every forty hours of operation. Special battery-powered demagnetizer cassettes are available for use with cassette equipment. For cassette decks, as well as reel-to-reel, demagnetization is an essential part of maintenance.

The effect of improper tape tension on the storage life of magnetic tapes has already been discussed. Usually one can tell by visual inspection whether winding tension is within acceptable limits. Correct tension will produce a smooth, even wind in play or record mode, with no ridges or other irregularities. If incorrect tension is suspected, the problem should be remedied by a service technician.

Improper head alignment is another problem that can be corrected by a technician. Magnetic heads should be aligned in perpendicular relation to the tape for accurate recording and playback. Alignment takes place along several axes, and screwdriver adjustments are provided on most head assemblies for this purpose. Alignment is set at the factory and should not require readjustment unless the heads have been changed or the tape machine subjected to physical shock. However, when tape machines are serviced it is a good idea to have the alignment checked. Incorrect alignment will cause reduced output and distortion.

RESTORATION OF SOUND RECORDINGS

The restoration of sound recordings is a problem quite apart from their preservation. Damage to sound recordings, including warping, accumulation of heavy deposits of dirt and other detritus, and breakage, can in many cases be corrected by applying such techniques as hot pressing, washing, etc. Deterioration of recordings, typically the development of surface noise, can also be compensated for by using filtering, dynamic range expansion, and digital processing. A discussion of restoration techniques is beyond the scope of this chapter. Most restoration techniques should only be undertaken by an experienced technician.

SUMMARY

Most types of sound recordings will remain in an excellent state when they are maintained in conditions suitable for the preservation of books. Some, on inherently unstable media, require dubbing to tape if their contents are to be saved. Most deterioration of sound recordings will occur during playback. When playback conditions are controlled, and good, properly maintained equipment is used, both disks and tape will incur little damage during playback. When conditions cannot be controlled, the use of dubbing or a backup acquisition plan is recommended. Damage fees, dissemination of proper handling information, and other techniques can be experimented with to encourage patron care of circulated recordings.

SUGGESTED READING

Cook, Warren ("Blob"). "Paper and Plastic," *Record Exchanger* 3:4, 4:1, 4 and 5 (n.d. [c1970s]).

> Excellent four-part article on record manufacture and preservation techniques, aimed at collectors of rock-and-roll 78s and 45s. Clear explanations and specific recommendations, most of which are backed up in other sources.

Hall, David. "Phonorecord Preservation: Notes of a Pragmatist," *Special Libraries* 62 (September 1971): 357–61.

> Practical measures for record preservation.

Hall, David. "The Rodgers and Hammerstein Archives of Recorded Sound — History and Current Operation," *Association for Recorded Sound Collections — Journal*, 6:2 (1974): 15–31.

> Good article with useful description of a major sound archives and some of its working policies.

McWilliams, Jerry. "Storage, Care and Preservation of Sound Recordings — A Bibliography," *Association for Recorded Sound Collections — Journal*, 9:2-3 (1977): 3–10.

> Extensive bibliography on the preservation of sound recordings.

McWilliams, Jerry. *The Preservation and Restoration of Sound Recordings*. Nashville: American Association for State and Local History, 1978. 138 pp.

A practical guide to the subject including a summary history of sound recording, annotated bibliography, directories of suppliers and major sound archives, and a discussion of restoration methods. Photographs.

Pickett, A. G., and M. M. Lemcoe. *Preservation and Storage of Sound Recordings.* Washington: Library of Congress, 1959. 74 pp.

The only major scientific study of the subject. The study does not include cylinder recordings. Essential reading.

U.S. Congress. *An.Act for the General Revision of the Copyright Law, Title 17 of the United States Code, and for Other Purposes, October 19, 1976.* Washington: U.S. Government Printing Office, 1976. 90 pp.

This law contains many important provisions affecting libraries and archives and bears careful study. Relevant sections include 106–108, 114, and 304.

Welch, Walter L. "Preservation and Restoration of Authenticity in Sound Recordings," *Library Trends* 21 (July 1972): 83–100.

A good article covering most phases of preservation and restoration of disk recordings and cylinders.

Wilson, Percy. "Care of Records," *Audio* 56 (December 1972): 30–32.

Description of various record-care techniques, including an anti-warp procedure. Discusses the problems inherent in washing disks.

Woodward, J. G. "The Scanning Electron Microscope — A New Tool in Disc-Recording Research," *Journal of the Audio Engineering Society* 16 (July 1968): 258–65.

A classic article, with excellent photographs of record wear caused by elliptical and spherical styluses.

10

Videodiscs

JUDITH PARIS AND RICHARD W. BOSS

One of the newest information technologies to be introduced into libraries is the videodisc, a technology for storing images or digital (machine-readable) information on discs similar in appearance to phonodiscs. The information can be displayed on a conventional television or display monitor when recalled from storage. The term *video* in videodisc is misleading because it suggests that the disc is strictly an audio-visual medium. The term was apparently coined by those who first developed it because their principal objective was to repackage old motion pictures. The importance and power of the medium lie in its present and future capacity to store digital as well as audio-visual information—either or both can be put on a single disc. As an audio-visual or image storage/transfer medium a videodisc can hold up to 108,000 frames of graphic or textual information (equal to an hour of motion picture film). The 54,000 frames stored on one side of a videodisc represent about 675 eighty-slide carousel trays, or 13,500 pages of text at one-quarter of a page per videodisc frame (about fifty four books of 250 pages each).

The optical disc which stores digital (machine-readable) information is expected to enter the marketplace within the next five years. When introduced this digital optical disc will have the capacity to store more than ten billion characters. In other terms, the contents of the Library of Congress in machine-readable form could be stored on one hundred optical digital videodiscs. One billion characters would be enough to store all of the telephone directories for the country's one hundred largest cities.

There are other factors that make videodisc technology so attractive. It has great potential as a low-cost distribution medium for audio-visual material. Since videodiscs are replicated much like LP records, thousands of copies can be "stamped out" for as little as $1.00 per copy. Another factor is the "radial" nature of the medium. Because of the compact storage area of a disc, any point on the disc can be accessed by a consumer model videodisc player in less than fifteen seconds. By contrast, film and video-tape—both of which are linear or ribbon media—require minutes to access a specific point. When used with a computer, the videodisc can provide interactive programming so that the individual user's program is presented based on selections and answers to questions. Unlike motion picture film, the videodisc image can be easily transmitted to a distant point.

Unlike other forms of digital data storage, videodisc-stored data can be rapidly duplicated to create numerous copies of the same data base. It is therefore possible to put bibliographic data bases or the full text of reference books on master videodiscs and produce inexpensive copies for individuals and libraries all over the nation.

How soon most libraries will have significant collections of videodiscs is uncertain. That will depend primarily on the rate at which software, or programming, of interest to libraries becomes available. There will be other factors which affect the demand, including available acquisition funds, public demand, perceptions about the medium's advantages vis-à-vis other media, etc. We are still relatively ignorant about the rate at which technologies are adopted and the factors which influence or constrain adoption. The communications technologies in common use today required from five to twenty years to "diffuse" throughout our society. The initial application of a technology may retard its adoption for other applications. For example, radio was originally applied as a communication system with ships since telegraph could not be used. The emphasis on this initial application was a significant factor in the delayed adoption of radio as an entertainment medium. The phonograph was first promoted as a system for recording wills and only later became a substitute for live musical and theatrical performances.

The initial applications of the videodisc have been for entertainment and for industrial education and training. Virtually all of the videodiscs acquired by libraries by early 1981 were entertainment programs. Most of the systems already in libraries were the laser optical systems sold by Magnavox and Pioneer, but in March, 1981, RCA placed a less expensive system on the market which uses a diamond-tipped stylus rather than a laser. The two systems are not compatible. RCA had nearly twice as many programs available in mid-1981 so it appears to have at least a temporary advantage in what may be a very competitive market. In the long term the laser optical videodisc may prove more successful in the marketplace because it is capable of both freeze-frame (holding a single frame on the screen), and random access of any frame. The laser optical system's discs also have a much greater life expectancy.

Whatever the applications and the relative success of the competing systems, it appears that there will be a significant enough number of videodiscs by the mid-1980s for us to be concerned about how the discs and the equipment should be maintained and preserved.

This chapter will discuss the history of videodisc technology, analyze the technology, describe the use of videodiscs in libraries, and make recommendations for the preservation of videodiscs and the maintenance of equipment.

HISTORY OF VIDEODISC TECHNOLOGY

The first successful experiments in recording video signals onto a phonograph record date back over fifty years. In 1927, a Scotsman named John L. Baird created Phonovision, a primitive television system that produced coarse but recognizable pictures. Using a gramophone disc, a cylinder, and a record-cutting machine, Baird reproduced video signals. Under the label "Major Radiovision," Baird sold his system in the London department store, Selfridges, in 1935 but was unsuccessful in gaining consumer acceptance.

Until the 1950s actual images were commonly recorded in the form of film and photographs using an intermediate film television system. Used for the first time at the 1936 Berlin Olympics, this system projected film into a television camera, exposed the television images onto film, and then projected the film onto a screen for viewing.

Attempts to record video signals directly using some form of optical image scanning were made during the 1940s. One example was the CBS Electronic Video Recording System which recorded the luminance (light) signal as a conventional photographic image and the chrominance (color) signal as a coded image adjacent to the luminance signal.

A major technological breakthrough occurred after World War II when German audiotape recording technology was introduced into the United States. The Electronics Division of Bing Crosby Enterprises in 1951 demonstrated the first working magnetic videotape recorder, sometimes referred to as the longitudinal video recorder. This machine consumed videotape at 100 inches per second and allowed quality recording of video information. Five years later Ampex introduced its quadruplex videotape recorder which consumed only 15 inches of videotape per second while increasing the rate of recording information to 1561 inches per second. This, of course, reduced the cost.

Within ten years of the introduction of the Ampex machine a magnetic disc system had been developed by ABC Television. In 1965 ABC-TV used a magnetic disc system for the first time to cover sports events. This system provided instant replay as well as stop action—two capabilities heretofore impossible to perform with videotape. Thus, within fifteen years of the introduction of audiotape equipment in the U.S., the technology was available for the creation of today's videodisc technology.

The breakthroughs of the 1950s and 1960s, however, did not fully resolve the major problems of expense in terms of machine cost, tape consumption, and uneven quality of video recordings. There was an additional and crucial problem concerning the tape duplication process: duplication of five one-hour videotapes took either five hours on one machine or one hour on five machines.

The entertainment industry, plagued by the aforementioned issues, also had problems with the pirating of videotapes. The unauthorized duplication of tapes was becoming increasingly more profitable and more difficult to control. The industry concluded during the 1960s that it needed a way to transfer motion picture films onto a medium that the consumer could afford for playback in the home or office, but which could not be easily replicated by any means other than the one owned by the studio/company itself.

The development of the videodisc available today resolves the problems of cost, time, and replication. Systems exist in the marketplace today that share the following common characteristics:

- low cost replication
- inexpensive storage medium
- playback ability only
- easily replicated programs
- rapid access to audio and video information
- consistently high recording quality
- quality control of the replication process
- imperviousness to dirt, scratches, fingerprint oils, and any other method of indiscriminant handling
- features including random access, freeze-frame, variable speeds, forward, and reverse
- two audio channels

In 1970, the first prototype mechanical system incorporating the majority of the aforementioned characteristics was introduced in West Germany. TelDec, a joint venture of Telefunken of Germany and Decca Records of Great Britain, demonstrated an initial black-and-white system that had a playing time of five minutes per nine-inch diameter disc. By 1977, TelDec had produced color discs with a playing time of ten minutes. The TelDec format closely resembled an audio phonograph with one principal exception: the pickup produced an electronic signal corresponding to the change between two levels of pressure between the stylus and the record groove. A simple analogy would be the rapid drawing of a stick (the stylus) across a picket fence, with the spacing of the pickets corresponding to the frequency modulation. Due to various technical and economic drawbacks, this system was not successfully received in Europe and is no longer available.

In the early 1970s inexpensive low-power lasers became available for commercial applications. These lasers permitted the design of optical systems capable of the high resolution necessary to scan densely packed recording tracks. Together, the availability of low-cost lasers and the ability to produce and record electronic video signals made it possible to create the consumer and industrial videodisc systems that have been offered in the U.S. and Europe since 1977.

CURRENT AND FUTURE APPLICATIONS

Videodisc systems are now being used for accurate and efficient information storage and retrieval for numerous training, instruction, and information display applications. The primary emphasis of the technology has been in two major areas: the commercial home entertainment marketplace, and the creation of prototype education/instruction/training videodiscs wedded to microcomputer technology. Applications can be divided into five major areas: (1) computer-based education and training (for example, medicine, basic skills, equipment maintenance); (2) instruction in private industry, government, and schools; (3) home entertainment; (4) publishing supplementary audiovisual teaching materials; and (5) data base management.

Examples of these applications include:

- basic skills education for army soldiers
- map learning and surrogate travel
- automobile point-of-purchase, maintenance, and repair
- low-cost portable simulators for skilled performance training
- experimental biology, college-level physics, and electronics
- medical case simulations for training in diagnoses
- operation of a computer without learning the language of the software developer

It is obvious that applications are as varied as are training, marketing, and communication needs. The videodisc is proving itself a powerful tool for all of these as well as for information management. As a stand-alone device, or as part of an instructional system, the disc is being tested and used as a means of bridging the gap between technology and human needs.

Videodisc sales competition for the home consumer market will bring to the library and other educational institutions an immense treasure house of low-cost, off-the-shelf programming of a wide variety of instructional, educational/training, and entertainment materials. It is likely that by 1990–1995, the videodisc will be a commonplace self-study home instruction device. Coupled to a home microcomputer and telephone, the video-disc will be used for teleconferencing (the use of computer networks for personal communications among widely dispersed people), electronic mail (the transmission of messages via electronic wave forms), the transmission of programming of a wide variety of instructional and test materials and the transmission of questions. Books that interact with the user will be available because of the coupling of videodisc and home computer technology.

A major approach to reaching a population with poor reading, reasoning, and reference skills is to take advantage of their basic visual literacy. During the 1970s, more and more training was packaged and distributed via the television medium. There was demonstrated success in both industry and education. This training capitalized on the medium's motivational powers. We believe this trend is likely to increase in speed, effectiveness, and efficiency during the 1980s. It is only a matter of time before the video-disc will begin to help bridge the gap between those who are only visually literate and those who also have command of the word, spoken and written.

ANALYSIS OF VIDEODISC TECHNOLOGY

Prior to a discussion of the various optical (noncontact) and capacitance (mechanical-electrical) technologies, a brief description of a videodisc system is in order. Simply put, it is a picture playback system which can be used to present a standard color or black-and-white picture on a conventional television set or display monitor. Prerecorded with television and video signals, the videodisc is played back on a compact player in a fashion similar to a phonograph record being played on a turntable. The following list illustrates the characteristics and capabilities of videodisc players.

Automatic frame stop: the disc will freeze on a frame that begins any formal sequence which requires a response from the user/viewer.

Frame numbers: each frame has a code number, or address allowing the user/viewer to branch rapidly to find specific information. When the player is connected to a microprocessor this address allows for automatic branching.

Dual audio tracks: listening can occur in one of three ways—in stereo; in any one of two languages on two separate tracks; in an elementary or advanced version in a single language.

Adjustable forward and reverse timing: provides motion continuity of sequences and can be adjusted to any desired pace; also allows for browsing.

Manual fast-forward and reverse search: provides browsing and allows scanning in variable speeds.

Still frame: allows the user/viewer to focus and dwell on discrete units, and makes possible a more careful look at detail and the addition of supplementary materials to motion sequences in graphic and textual formats.

Chapter stop: moves fast-forward or reverse to predesignated locations on the videodisc that may be considered as chapters.

Freeze-frame: provides viewing one frame at a time for as long as the user/viewer desires.

Slow: speed can be reduced to as slow as a single frame every five seconds.

Scanning: allows for high-speed search and review.

Fast × 3: normal playback can be speeded up three times in both forward and reverse modes.

There are two basic and incompatible videodisc systems: optical and capacitance. Optical videodisc technology, sometimes referred to as Video Laser Players (VLP) or as noncontact, uses one of two processes: (1) laser-based or physical replication, and (2) photographic replication technology. Capacitance videodisc systems are divided into two basic categories: grooved and grooveless technology. The key distinction between optical and capacitance videodisc systems is the method of reading the information on the videodisc. Optical systems use noncontact devices such as a low-power laser beam, whereas capacitance systems use a stylus.

OPTICAL VIDEODISC TECHNOLOGY

The optical videodisc looks very much like a iridescent, silver-colored phonograph record. This system uses high technology in the form of neon-helium lasers to both record (write) the information on the videodisc and read (playback) the information stored there.

Program information is stored in billions of micropits or microscopic identifications etched below and beneath the surface of the videodisc. Information is arranged in 54,000 circular tracks, each track constituting a separate video "frame" for continuous or individual display. Thus, there are 54,000 frames per single side of a videodisc.

A layer of acrylic (1.1 mm) is the protective coating of the videodisc. The micropits and the reflective surface of the disc produce a "rainbow" effect when the disc is viewed in ordinary light. When exposed to the highly focused light beam (0.001 mm in diameter) of the low-powered laser reading device, the disc reflects high-density audio/video signals for reproduction onto a television or display monitor. A radial tracking servo-mechanism electronically focuses and guides the laser so that it can accurately read the micropits of information despite distortions, wobble, waviness, or any other eccentricity on the disc.

The master optical videodisc is created by transferring the electronic video information, from either film or videotape, by a medium-powered laser beam. The disc is chemically treated, producing the string of micropits of varying lengths in the illuminated areas. This master disc is then electroplated to form a metal disc which is used for embossing and stamping out copies. Polished plate glass discs that are coated with a number of layers, one of which is photoresistant, are used by the optical master disc. Each copy takes only seconds to make since copying occurs simultaneously over the entire disc area.

There are two different types of laser-based videodisc systems: reflective and transmissive. Reflective discs may be read one side at a time providing access to 54,000 frames; transmissive discs allow the laser beam to read both sides of the disc (108,000 frames) without manually turning over the disc. The reflective system is produced by such companies as Sylvania, Universal, Pioneer, and Magnavox. The French electronics firm Thomson-CSF is currently the only producer of the transmissive laser videodisc system.

The other major optical system, formerly called ARDEV when a subsidiary of ARCO, is now produced by the Videodisc Division of the McDonnell Douglas Electronics Company, and relies on a photographic process. It uses a low-powered laser to master a videodisc but utilizes an incandescent light source—a light bulb—to read the information on a transmissive videodisc. This system is distinct from the laser-based systems because it uses a non-laser light source to read the disc, requires a relatively small amount of capital investment in equipment, and provides on-site mastering and replication, and rapid turnaround as well. This system remains in the research, development, testing, and evaluation stage. It is unknown when or if McDonnell Douglas Electronics will market a commercial videodisc system.

During the summer of 1981, a Chicago-based firm, Quixote Corporation, announced the creation of a new medium for videodisc production. This new medium permits local and rapid production turnaround time (less than thirty minutes from completion of recording to playback) and use with any commercially available reflective optical videodisc player (Pioneer, Sony, Magnavox). The company predicts that the product will be on the market at about the time this book is published.

The primary features of the optical laser video players include: freeze-frame, rapid and slow forward and reverse, scanning, two audio tracks, still/step frame, and optional remote control. Thus far, Magnavox is the only company offering a consumer optical player with a limited range of features. Table 1 is a comparison of the major optical videodisc systems and their capabilities including size of disc and weight of player.

CAPACITANCE VIDEODISC TECHNOLOGY

Capacitance technology is available in two formats: grooved and grooveless. Table 2 summarizes and compares the characteristics and capabilities of the various systems. Grooved capacitance systems, commonly called Capacitance Electronic Devices (CED), use a mechanical pickup technique similar to today's phonographic technology. A stylus is guided by the grooves in the disc surface and decodes information that is recorded as pits on the disc. This system does not rely on pressure changes; rather, hills and valleys of the vinyl grooves are covered with a thin metallic coating, forming continuous tracks of varying capacitance. The pickup is also partially metallic and acts as a probe to read out the capacitance, representing television information.

Since this system requires mechanical contact between the stylus and the disc, there can be no protective coating of the disc. The discs are produced in a manner similar to the manufacture of a master phonograph recording, and duplicates are made by a stamping process. The disc is encased in a thick protective plastic sleeve which deposits the disc on a turntable after insertion into the player. The sleeve is reinserted to remove the disc.

Offered by RCA solely as an entertainment medium, this system does not offer the same range of features available on the optical systems such as freeze-frame, random access, and variable forward and reverse speeds. It does, however, have a forward and reverse fast scan without variable speed and a "rapid access" feature that can locate the beginning of a particular program segment.

The grooveless capacitance system, commonly referred to as the Video High Density (VHD) system, is produced by Victor Company of Japan (JVC), an affiliate of Matsushita. This system is distinguished from the RCA system because of the absence of grooves. The VHD system uses a stylus about ten times larger than the RCA stylus. Separate tracking pits are laid between the main tracks to carry information used to position and guide the stylus. Since it is not necessary for the stylus to follow a groove, it is free to be directed laterally across the surface of the disc while it spins. This freedom allows random access, freeze-frame, and a variety of slow and fast speeds in reverse and forward.

Table 3 is a summary of the major videodisc system manufacturers, equipment vendors, and disc producers. It is apparent at this time that the three major systems are receiving virtually equal attention, interest, and involvement from the television and electronics industries worldwide. As yet, however, only the optical systems have been tested and applied in a wide variety of applications, as noted in the previous section.

VIDEODISCS IN LIBRARIES

The videodisc can be considered an audio-visual medium for entertainment or group instruction, an interactive tool for individualized instruction, or an information storage medium. As an audio-visual medium it is most closely comparable to the films and video cassettes which many libraries have been acquiring for a number of years; as an instructional tool it is most

Table 1
Capabilities of Optical Videodisc Systems, by Manufacturer

	Pioneer Industrial	U.S. Pioneer Consumer	SONY	Magnavox	Thomson-CSF
Remote control option	*	*	*	N/A	*
Freeze-frame	*	*	*	*	*
By-frame fwd/rev	*	*	*	*	N/A
Slow-mo fwd/rev	*	* (variable speed)	1/5 normal	* (variable speed)	* (variable speed)
Fast play fwd/rev	*	X 3	X 3	X 3 fwd	X 2
Random access	*	*	*	N/A	*
Scan/ search fwd/rev	*	* (30 sec.)	X 100 (20 sec.)	* (26 sec.)	*
Frame address	*	*	*	*	*
Dual audio tracks	*	*	*	*	*
Player weight	54 lbs.	38 lbs.	43 lbs.	35 lbs.	43 lbs.
Disc size	12″	12″	12″	12″	12″

* = capability available
N/A = capability not available on model
fwd = forward
rev = reverse

comparable to computer-assisted instruction (CAI) and programmed learning systems; as a storage medium it can be likened to computer discs and microform.

At this point it appears that most libraries have added videodiscs to their collections as a natural extension of their audio-visual services. They have

Table 2
Capabilities of Capacitance Videodisc Systems, by Manufacturer

	General Electric	U.S. JVC	RCA
Format	VHD	VHD	CED
Remote control option	N/A	N/A	N/A
Freeze-frame	*	*	*
By-frame fwd/rev	N/A	*	N/A
Slow-mo fwd/rev	*	* (1/16, 1/8, 1/4, 1/2)	N/A
Fast play fwd/rev	N/A	X2, X3, X4, X5	N/A
Random access (time)	* option 10-event	*	*
Scan/ search fwd/rev	*	*	X 16 (audio muted)
Time/ frame indicator	N/A	N/A	*
Dual audio tracks	*	*	only 1 track
Player weight	N/A	N/A	20 lbs.
Disc size	10.2″	10.2″	12″

* = capability available
N/A = capability not available on player
fwd = forward
rev = reverse
Note: General Electric discontinued production of capacitance videodisc systems in eary 1983.

made their selections using the same collection development criteria that they have used for films and video cassettes—in fact many of the videodisc titles selected have also been available in film or cassette. The libraries have

Table 3
Major Videodisc Systems Commercially Available by the End of 1982

Optical Reflective[a]	Optical Transmissive	Optical Photographic	Capacitance Electronic Disc	Video High Density[b]
* Gold Star (subsidiary of Lucky Group, So. Korean Co.)	* Thomson-CSF	Videodisc Division of McDonnell Douglas Electronics Co.	− CBS	NEC
			* Hitachi	Panasonic (subsidiary of Matsushita Electric Corp. of America)
			+ J. C. Penney	
* Magnavox (subsidiary of N. V. Philips)			+ Montgomery Ward	Quasar (subsidiary of Matsushita Electric Corp. of America)
Philco (subsidiary of N. V. Philips)			* RCA	
* Pioneer (U.S.)			Sanyo	Sansui
Quixote			+ Sears, Roebuck & Co.	Sharp
* Sanyo			* Toshiba	− Thorn EMI Ltd. of Great Britain
* SONY			* Elmo	Victor Co. of Japan Japan (JVC) (subsidiary of Matsushita Electric Corp. of America)
Sylvania (subsidiary of N. V. Philips)			− 3M	
− 3M				Yamaha
− N. V. Philips				

* = players available by the end of 1981
+ = retailers producing players under own brand label
− = disc plants

[a]Trademark name: Laservision Associates
[b]Not available in the United States

apparently relied on use statistics for film and video cassettes to determine which disc titles might be popular. A significant part of the collection, therefore, consists of entertainment and classics of literature. Libraries appear to have purchased videodiscs not to broaden the scope of their collections, but rather to try a new medium with the hope that it would prove to be less expensive and more durable than film and tape formats.

Economy appears to be a significant factor in several libraries' decisions to acquire videodiscs. Laser optical videodiscs were selling for $5.99 to $35.00 in late 1981 while films cost at least twelve times as much and video cassettes approximately three times as much for similar programming. A library can, therefore, add a much larger number of titles in the videodisc format than in either of the other two, providing that a choice of formats exists for the titles of interest. Equipment prices are also attractive. A laser optical videodisc system (player and monitor) costs less than $1,000. A high-quality film projector and a good screen cost at least $1,300 and are more difficult to use. A high-quality video cassette player with monitor costs $1,200 or more.

There are reasons other than initial purchase price of discs and players which make the new medium attractive to librarians, however. The discs are extremely durable. Laser optical discs have been used and tested in laboratories at Massachusetts Institute of Technology for several years with no apparent signs of wear. A year's use in libraries appears to have no effect on the fidelity of the program on a laser optical videodisc, while a year's use of a film or video cassette often results in obvious image and/or sound deterioration. Videodiscs are more compact than films and cassettes and can be stored vertically on conventional library shelving.

Patrons appear to like the new medium because the equipment is simple and the programs retain their fidelity even after a number of uses. Only a limited number of persons have equipment at home so the total number of users account for a large portion of the circulations.

One of the greatest concerns of public librarians is the prospective competiton among three incompatible videodisc systems at a time when the total number of available programs is limited. Most of those with whom the authors spoke insist that they cannot invest in more than one system. That system will probably be the one that has the most programs available, even if it is one that has fewer operational features or fewer costs for preservation and/or maintenance. In early 1981 many public librarians thought the RCA capacitance system might be the one they would acquire.

While many public libraries lend their discs in the same way they lend films and video cassettes, it is uncommon for equipment to be loaned. Equipment availability in the library also tends to be limited. Few public libraries have procured more than two videodisc players, even those with over one hundred videodisc titles. It is doubtful that many more would be acquired were the number of videodiscs in the collections to increase significantly, because most public libraries also own very few film projectors and videocassette players. Many public libraries with more than two thousand films and cassettes have less than five pieces of equipment. At the time of this writing, it appeared that by the mid-1980s many public libraries would have hundreds of discs, but as few as two videodisc players.

The pattern is different in academic libraries. While fewer of them have large audio-visual collections, they tend to encourage in-building use and own more equipment. Twelve or more viewing stations (or positions) is common. As of mid-1981 it appeared that only a few academic libraries were ready to make an early investment in videodiscs, but that those which did might purchase a number of machines.

The academic librarians with whom the authors spoke had a definite preference for the optical videodisc because the equipment has more features and the life expectancy of the disc is longer. Academic libraries expect to own fewer discs than public libraries and expect that many will come from specialized producers rather than from the motion picture studios.

While traditional school libraries rarely own equipment, the instructional departments almost always have equipment available to them. Materials in the library's collection are often loaned for classroom use and loans from the school district or other collections are common. In the last fifteen years a large number of media centers have been created which combine traditional library and audio-visual functions. Many have installed individual viewing positions. However, classroom use of media appears more popular and the educational videodiscs which are presently under development are all intended for classroom use. The discs in preparation for the school market are mostly optical videodiscs.

The school librarians with whom the authors spoke expect their schools to obtain some discs and equipment in the next few years. The expectation is that the optical videodisc will be chosen over the capacitance disc. Schools appear to be most likely to move equipment around and will probably incur greater maintenance costs than public or academic libraries.

The pattern in special libraries is uneven, with only medical libraries as a class making extensive use of audio-visual materials and equipment. Again, the number of units per library tends to be small because the number of users served is small. One of the major centers of research into videodisc is the Lister National Laboratory for Biomedical Communications of the National Library of Medicine, thus the level of awareness in the medical library community is high. Little videodisc equipment will be purchased until specialized software is available. Development is expected to be slow. The optical videodisc is expected to predominate. The corporate librarians contacted foresee little use of videodisc in the next five years. Law librarians think that development in their area will most likely follow the pattern set by the Pergamon PATSEARCH System, a large data base of information stored on a computer with patent drawings and other visual information on optical videodiscs accessed with a minicomputer. They anticipate that the early systems will be "turnkey" systems, with a single vendor providing hardware, software, installation, training, and maintenance.

PRESERVATION OF VIDEODISCS

The developers of optical discs claim that the discs are impervious to dirt, heat, scratching, and playing wear. The demonstrations given by North American Philips include a number of dramatic tests to confirm those representations. Grease is smeared on a disc; it is then held over a match, scratched with a key, and finally played without any evidence of damage. The most persuasive evidence to date, however, is a year's use in several libraries. The laser optical discs appear to be unaffected by either the use or the environment in libraries—even in those which experience dramatic changes in temperature and humidity. No systematic maintenance programs have been undertaken, nor has any appeared necessary. No inspection of returned discs is undertaken. Surface dirt is wiped off only when a library patron mentions that a disc is dirty.

There is no reason to believe that libraries will encounter any difficulty with optical videodiscs after the initial inspection at the time of receipt. Potentially, this is the most important benefit of the new medium. Inspection and replacement of worn films and video cassettes have been significant factors in the budgets of libraries with large audio-visual collections. It is nevertheless wise to follow good housekeeping procedures and shelve videodiscs after use, and to avoid extremes in environmental conditions. There may be hidden defects in the discs which may not be evident initially. Care in storage can help to minimize a latent problem. For example, Kalvar microfilm had some hidden defects when it first began to be produced, but some libraries had far fewer problems than others because they had superior conditions that retarded the breakdown of the emulsion.

The most suitable storage for capacitance videodiscs is regular bracket-type shelving, twelve inches deep, with slotted shelves to permit the insertion of vertical dividers every foot or so to keep the discs upright. This will keep the discs from toppling over when several have been removed and will make it easier to keep the discs in proper shelving sequence. Optical videodiscs should be stored flat, with no more than six on top of one another. The vertical dividers may be used to create convenient compartments.

The same environmental conditions recommended for books, microforms, and audio-visual materials should be provided for optical videodiscs. The temperature should be 65 °F–75 °F (18 °C–24 °C) and the humidity 40–55 percent. Dramatic changes in temperature or humidity should be avoided. The area should be kept clean.

While librarians have a high opinion about the apparent durability of optical videodiscs, they are most concerned that as many as 30 percent of the discs they have purchased had manufacturing imperfections. With such a high rate of defects it is imperative that every title be inspected in its entirety before being added to the collection. While that has been the intent of most libraries with regard to the films and cassettes they purchase, in practice libraries have done only spot-checking because the quality control of these media has been consistently good.

The general opinion of users after a year of experience with optical videodiscs was that economy and durability could be realized, but that if limited availability of titles were to continue, the value of the medium to libraries would be small. In early 1981 only 1 percent of the 3,000 titles available in video format were available in videodisc. Videodiscs, therefore, have remained a novelty rather than a basic component of a library's collection. A minimum of 1,000 titles will have to be available for the new medium to become a significant part of a library's collection development program.

The foregoing comments about durability and the maintenance-free character of laser optical discs do not apply to the new capacitance videodiscs. The capacitance disc is scanned with a stylus. Not only is it subject to wear because of the contact, but the disc itself cannot be provided with the same protective coating as the optical disc. Instead, the disc is inserted in a heavy plastic protective sleeve, similar in concept but larger and more substantial than the sleeve which protects the "floppy discs" which are common to most automated word processing systems.

The authors have had considerable difficulty with the capacitance discs which they purchased in June, 1981. During the playing of each program the normal speed is unexpectedly tripled at least once for a minute or more and the sound becomes distorted. The problem does not occur on the same place on the disc with each playing. The problem can be quickly corrected by putting the machine in fast reverse and replaying the last minute. Company representatives and dealers alternately blame the player, the discs, and the user.

Care should be taken in inserting and removing the capacitance videodisc. A staff member should demonstrate the technique to the first-time user. Even with proper use, there will be gradual wear in a capacitance disc because it is a "grooved system"; a needle rides in a groove. RCA dealers claim that the capacitance disc is capable of 200 plays without deterioration barring actual damage. This is superior to a film or videotape, but substantially less than the optical disc. Periodic inspection of returned capacitance discs will therefore be required. A library should seek to return damaged capacitance videodiscs for credit or replacement. Since the damage can be due to the equipment, poor disc manufacturing techniques, or patron abuse, there is no assurance that the request will be honored. A library should consider establishing a relationship with a single nearby firm for equipment purchase, disc purchase, and service to avoid finger-pointing among several suppliers.

Capacitance videodiscs should be stored under the same environmental conditions as optical videodiscs. Standards of cleanliness will be more critical, however. An accumulation of dirt or dust inside the sleeve which holds the disc or on the stylus can pose scanning problems and can accelerate wear of discs and equipment. The floor should, therefore, be vacuumed to remove dirt and dust on a regular basis and the shelves and disc jackets periodically dusted or vacuumed. Keeping a dust cover on equipment when the library is not open is highly recommended. The authors recommend against covering equipment during operating hours because that may discourage the use of the new technology.

VLP, Thomson-CSF, and McDonnell Douglas discs require no contact, and so they have, theoretically, an unlimited life. They should be stored and used in the same way as reflective laser videodiscs.

MAINTENANCE OF EQUIPMENT

All electronic equipment requires a regular maintenance program. Routine maintenance includes daily checks to see that each piece of equipment is functioning, periodic cleaning, and such minor adjustments as the staff may have learned to make. The library should have a maintenance agreement for periodic inspections/adjustments and for remedial maintenance, whether an annual plan or an agreement to provide services on call at prearranged rates and standards.

Equipment which is moved and handled by a large number of people will obviously require more maintenance than that which is stationary. No equipment loan program can be undertaken without back-up units and an equipment maintenance budget. While it is common for libraries to undertake only remedial maintenance on audio-visual equipment, a library with laser optical machines available for loan should have each unit inspected at least twice a year to keep the equipment properly adjusted. Even stationary equipment will require sound preventive maintenance and occasional repairs. The optical laser disc players may require more expert periodic service than the capacitance players because they are precision electronic devices. Identifying a nearby repair service which does good-quality work on laser optical players is imperative. A library in a small community can use United Parcel Service or one of the other small package express services to ship machines to a company in a larger city. An optical laser disc player should be moved or transported only when the locking screw and lens cap are in place. The unit should be carried horizontally, not vertically. These actions protect the laser mechanism.

The life expectancy and replacement cost of a laser are not yet known. It is claimed that the laser will last at least 10,000 hours. Replacement costs have been estimated at $100, but no one has yet placed an order for a laser alone. The stylus for the capacitance player is expected to wear out much more quickly, approximately every 200 hours. The replacement cost will be low, however, possibly $10. This suggests that a library with one or more optical disc players should not stock a spare laser, but that a library with one or more capacitance players should stock at least one spare stylus.

The capacitance players should be kept clean. The effect of unclean conditions is not yet known, but it is expected to be similar to the effect of unclean conditions on the "floppy diskettes" used in word processing systems: slow response and distorted information. Wiping the equipment and the counter or table on which it is kept should be a regular activity—at least once or twice a week.

The library may wish to consider fastening a metal plate with phillips head screws over the stylus access panel so that library patrons cannot reach in and remove the stylus. Despite the claimed seven year stylus life under normal conditions, it is not inconceivable that someone who has damaged his/her own stylus will remove one from a library machine.

Dealers that sell the RCA machine have reported a number of broken mode selector switches. The switch selects the load, play, or stop mode by simply moving it up and down. The library should ascertain that a local dealer stocks spare switches in case heavy use in the library results in similar wear of this switch.

SUMMARY

Videodiscs and videodisc playing equipment are still too new at this time to make unequivocal recommendations for their care and handling. It does appear likely that most of the early acquisitions by libraries will be for the audio-visual application of the new medium. Generally, the optical video-discs should be easier to preserve, while capacitance discs should require a higher level of care, but still less than most other audio-visual formats. The optical players, on the other hand, may require more expert maintenance than the capacitance systems. The standards of care which have in the past been prescribed for microform collections and equipment should be employed for the new medium until such time as libraries have more experience.

SUGGESTED READING

Barrett, R. *Developments in Optical Disc Technology and the Implications for In-formation Storage and Retrieval.* London: British Library, 1981 (British Library Research and Development Reports, June, 1981).

A summary of the author's investigations in 1980, the state-of-the-art assess-ment and evaluation of current developments in optical disc information stor-age memory. A section of this report is devoted to the controversy between microform and the optical disc for on-line remote accessing.

Broussaud, G., and C. Tinet. "The Videotape as a Means of Transferring a Video Picture onto Motion Picture Film," *Journal of the Society of Motion Picture and Television Engineers* 88:4 (1979): 247–52.

A discussion of the procedures for the transfer of video images to film, with the proposal that videodiscs be used for the purpose.

Goldstein, Charles. "Optical Disc Technology and Information," *Science* 215:4534 (February 12, 1982): 862–68.

The uses for information storage using videodisc technology, with some discussion of archival storage.

Heuston, Dustin H. *The Promise and Inevitability of the Videodisc in Education.* Washington, D.C., report for the National Institute for Education, 1977.

Description of technical applications of the videodisc and a discussion of the strengths and weaknesses of various educational technologies.

Long, Harvey S. "The Videodisc: A Picture Book in the Round," *T.H.E. Journal,* May 1981, pp. 38–42.

A review and comparison of the interactive videodisc to the book.

Rhodes, R. N. "The Videodisc Player," *RCA Review* 39:1 (1978): 198–221.

Describes the goals, functions, and requirements of a videodisc player.

Schneider, E., and J. L. Bennion. *Videodiscs.* New York: Educational Technology Publications, 1981 (Instructional Media Library Series, 16).

The first monograph published by experienced videodisc producers and designers. The book discusses basic concepts, types of educational applications, and economics, as well as more technical aspects of videodisc production.

Sigel, E., et al. *Videodiscs: The Technology, Applications, and the Future.* White Plains, N.Y.: Knowledge Industry Publications, 1981.

Discusses commercial and industrial videodisc systems; current applications in the educational, consumer, archival, and industrial arenas.

White, Robert M. "Disc Storage Technology," *Scientific American* 243:2 (August 1980): 138–48.

A clear description of optical disc technology, which enables data to be digitalized and stored, then retrieved and read by a laser scanner.

11

The Computer: When Tomorrow Becomes Yesterday

SUSAN B. WHITE AND ALLAN E. WHITE

The last quarter of the twentieth century has produced a quantum increase in the reliance on computers for the storage and retrieval of information, much of which formerly was not available at all or was stored in traditional paper format, that is, in books, on cards, or on sheets of paper in manila folders. The increasing reliance on machine-readable data files is commonly called the information revolution and has been termed the information explosion. Both are apt expressions given the speed with which the new technology is replacing the old. Equally apt is the "office of the future," or the "paperless office," where computer technology replaces paper, with remarkable benefits in cost, ease, and information newly available or available in quite new ways. In moving away from a reliance on paper for information storage and retrieval, the business community has become an information laboratory, providing both the technology and the rationale to lead those traditionally charged by the larger society to keep and make available the records of knowledge and progress of the civilization (the culture, the history, and the technology)—people called librarians in places called libraries.

The Library of the Future is called this because it relies on computer technology as well as traditional paper format. It contains not only books and print microfilm, but also machine-readable files, and computer-printed books, lists, and cards that people can read. It uses computer screens and printers which are interactive terminals where information can be retrieved and structured in a virtually infinite number of ways.

Librarians have literally millennia of experience with paper storage of information. It has been reliable so long as the enemies of the book have been kept at bay—fire, flood, insects, armies. Even the first blundering technology which made acid-based and therefore non-lasting paper the norm in the printing industry only came about in the mid-nineteenth century, and some books and other records from that time which have been given optimal storage conditions are still usable. However, a significant part of the record of Western civilization has been lost in the century since the 1870s, since bad paper became the printing norm. A new technology was embraced without consideration for the time when this bright future of publishing for the masses and for the increased profit of the printing industry had become the past—almost no one then gave any full measure of concern to the implications of the new paper and inks.

The one exception was newspapers. Librarians said and wrote much about how newspapers could be preserved. The library literature of the day gives much space to this concern, and at the time of the Centennial Library Conference in Philadelphia in 1876, one major report coming from this conference suggested to the newspaper printers that the beginning of each press run, a hundred copies or so, be on good paper, for *the future*. Newsprint was immediately perceived as not at all permanent or durable when made by the new technology. Alas, the suggestion was never heeded due to economic pressures, and the good paper battle was joined, at least on a small front. It, of course, spread over time but, at least to the present, has never been won.

When William J. Barrow began providing a rational explanation in the 1950s for why paper in books and journals as well as in newspapers was deteriorating, three-quarters of a century of exploiting a new technology for ease and profit had passed. A lesson of caution might be suggested to the community of record keepers, whether they are called librarians or information managers. Before relying on a new technology, we might well ask, what of those records we will surely want to have in the future? How archival will computers and their products be said to be when "tomorrow" becomes "yesterday?"

COMPUTERS IN THE LIBRARY ENVIRONMENT: THE COMING OF TOMORROW

Computer technology has a broad application in the library environment, and its use is growing. For housekeeping functions and for bibliographic access, libraries are increasingly relying on electronic data processing equipment, while full text storage is the next generation of computer application.

The "housekeeping" functions include ordering library materials, maintaining a control file, generating a bibliographic record for each item received, recording each circulation transaction, keeping use (and non-use) statistics, doing shelf inventories, and generating a "dead" file when the item is disposed of.

The Baker and Taylor Company, a major U.S. book distributor, has displayed a prototype of a system through which libraries can order books on-line, that is, in direct communication with Baker and Taylor's main computer. The Research Libraries Information Network (RLIN), the bibliographic utility of a consortium of American research libraries, is also developing an acquisitions system through which member libraries can order and control the order of materials. Both the private company and the library cooperative are representative of acquisition automation in that a system may be vendor supplied and, therefore, vendor specific, or may be one that originates in the ordering library or its bibliographic network and be used to order from a number of vendors.

Certainly, the creation of a bibliographic record is one of the well established areas of automation in library "housekeeping." Thus far, three-by-five inch paper catalogue cards have been the major product, with the on-line machine-readable record as a secondary product. Libraries envision a near future where the on-line record will become the primary record, rendering the card catalogue obsolete.

Keeping track of the circulation of books is also a long-established use of data processing equipment in libraries. The most advanced systems, at present, use a bar-code label on the book or other material, and one on the borrower's card as well. A bar-code reader, usually called a light pen, reads each label to create the circulation record. The transaction is stored, and various statistics can be generated for individual titles and parts of the collection to help make informed decisions on weeding at a later time. Also, circulation "accounts" with individual borrowers are easily and reliably maintained.

Beyond these control functions, bibliographic access is a second major job assigned to automation in libraries. The long-established subject data bases are national on-line indexes in which specific lists of materials can be easily generated in local library units. Interlibrary loan has been greatly facilitated through the capacity to look in an on-line cataloguing data base, such as RLIN or OCLC (the Online Computer Library Center, Inc.), for another library which holds the material. These national holdings lists are another by-product of the use of RLIN or OCLC to generate catalogue cards for individual libraries. Both systems now have, or are developing, an automated request system which allows one library to place a loan request on-line to another. These two data bases are, of course, much more up to date than any printed catalogue could be since their updating is done on a daily basis, while a paper catalogue takes several months, at best, to be updated. Speeding interlibrary requests makes viable the concept of "shared resources" in times of budget and space constraints.

In both of these applications, for housekeeping and for bibliographic access, computer technology is employed to facilitate the use of books and other traditional print media. What of storing the primary data, rather than information about the data, in machine-readable format?

In 1982, full text storage is still most often in traditional paper format, or, increasingly, in microformat—both of which are print media. Full text storage in machine-readable format, however, is rapidly approaching for files other than the U.S. Census tapes, which are the most visible intellectual and cultural property now consigned to machine-readable format. Indeed, there is a century's experience with using computer technology in the U.S. Census Office, since the 1880 Decennial Census employed punched-paper cards for data handling.

One area where computer technology is available as a full alternative to paper systems in libraries is in legal research. Since 1973, the LEXIS Data Base System of the Mead Data Central Company in New York City has provided both full text and historic runs of the records of court decisions, statutes, regulations, and other legal materials for the United States and the United Kingdom. Historic runs are full, going back as far as the early eighteen-hundreds where appropriate. Additional full text legal sources are joining LEXIS at the present time. They include JURIS, the system established and run for government attorneys by the U.S. Department of Justice, and WESTLAW from the West Publishing Company.

Comprehensive surveys of the current use of automation in libraries have been published by various elements of the library community. The April 1981 issue of *Special Libraries* is perhaps the most complete in one gathering. The April 1979 issue of *American Archivist* is devoted to machine-readable archives, and various articles in *American Libraries* and *Library Journal*, among others, cover computer use in public, academic, and school libraries. The *Journal of the American Society of Information Science* (JASIS), especially the *Conference Proceedings* each year, is always useful in understanding current applications.

A fourth computer application for libraries is the possibility that libraries will, themselves, become bibliographic utilities for their patrons, whether in a corporate, academic, school, or public library. The user could then dial up on a telephone line or use the local cable television channel assigned, and from a remote location (home, office, school) use a personal computer or a terminal to query a central computer system in the library for any request now made in person. In addition, there could be an additional broader base of personal, business, and community information. The OCLC Project 2000, which ran in the public library system of Franklin and Marshall counties near Columbus, Ohio, in 1980, placed 200 computer terminals in a random sample of user homes for a three-month trial period. Available were the library's "card" catalogue, story hours, hours of operation, a reference question service, book ordering (to be delivered to the home), as well as personal bank records, community bulletin boards, the Arete Encyclopedia online, and many other services, some obviously only available from the library in the bibliographic utility role. The experiment worked quite well in that information, traditional or innovative, was delivered, and patron response was very positive.

The Electronic Library Discussion Group holds spirited regular meetings at the American Library Association's twice-yearly conferences. Firmly resisting invitations to join one of the special interest divisions within the library association, this group is determined to remain an open forum for library automation, and is working toward repeating the Project 2000 experiment, not as a trial, but in three or more pilot areas that would be ongoing, and would serve as models for a library function genuinely of the Information Age.

OPERATING CONSIDERATIONS: THE ART OF THE COMPUTER

If so much in the future of the Information Society will depend on computer technology, how reliable will that technology continue to be over time? For how long will the computer and its products be usable? What conditions enable a computer to function well, and to continue to function well? What factors determine how well it will continue to work its art of reading and restructuring data *over time?* What are the enemies of the art of the computer, beyond the fire, flood, and armies that are universal enemies?

The machines themselves can be harmed through extremes of humidity, either excessive dryness or dampness, or through too high a temperature. And while the machine may not be damaged, performance can very likely be degraded through uncontrolled variations in the line voltage. Operating manuals will give maintenance schedules and environmental restrictions, but they may not discuss electrostatic discharge problems, which can cause erratic or odd behavior in the machines.

The machinery itself will not be harmed in usual operating ranges of 20-80 percent relative humidity noncondensing, although specific operating manuals will always address environmental tolerances and should be followed exactly. For example, the VAX system requires 40-60 percent relative humidity. It should be noted, however, that at high humidity, if cellulose input/output such as paper tape, punch cards, or printer paper is being used, the paper can absorb enough moisture to swell and jam or otherwise malfunction at operating speeds.

Excessive dryness in and of itself will not cause problems in the machinery, but at low humidity there is the tendency for static electricity to build up and cause problems, particularly if the computer or terminals are located in a carpeted area. A person who walks across a carpeted area can easily build up charges of several thousand volts on his or her body. The circuitry that is used in data processing equipment is easily and irreparably damaged by electrostatic discharges of a few hundred volts. A carpeted environment will require adequate humidification (about 50-60 percent), special treatment of the carpet, or the presence of an antistatic mat in the immediate vicinity of the terminal. Any of these will be sufficient, but some precaution must be taken. Adequate humidification is probably the most economical alternative and certainly the most reliable, since the other two rely on discharging. Humidification removes the source of the problem rather than correcting it once it exists. Antistatic mats are commercially available, but are relatively expensive, and carpet treatment may wear off in time and deteriorate below levels that would adequately protect the machine. Surface treatments can also be degraded through inappropriate cleaning of the carpet.

Checking the humidity frequently to be sure it stays within reasonable tolerances would be a worthwhile procedure, even for a small computer. A good quality hygrometer can be readily obtained for a fraction of the cost that can be incurred through damage to equipment associated with inappropriate humidity. Certainly, if a person walks across a room, touches something metallic, and experiences a shock, this indicates that a serious electrostatic hazard to computer equipment of any configuration exists.

A second environmental concern is temperature. In an area of elevated temperature, particularly if the computer lacks some active cooling mechanism such as a fan, heat build-up within the unit beyond the ambient (room) temperature can degrade performance. Also it will significantly contribute to the premature failure of the computer itself. Solid-state electronic devices, such as are used in a computer, do not function as well at higher temperatures as they do at lower ones. The physics of the components are such that prolonged exposure to elevated temperatures increases the likelihood that a component will malfunction. Lower temperatures, unlike low humidity, are not a problem for the machinery, but it is well to note that where human operators interact for long periods with a computer or remote terminal, a range of temperatures comfortable for the human operator will certainly be suitable for the computer.

Beyond humidity and temperature, a third area of concern in computer performance and longevity is the level of electric power. In the operating manual that comes with the equipment, there will be a statement of the power requirements for the computer device. The user should make sure that the service to which it is connected is capable of supplying that requirement. A power line is necessary, of course, for the operation of the machinery, but it can also be a source of problems. It is necessary to make sure that the computer is not overloading this service. Checking to be sure that the source of electrical power is sufficient will probably require the services of a building facilities engineer or an outside electrician. Although this is more of a concern in older buildings than in more modern ones, it is a necessary consideration.

Beyond the current capabilities, there are four sources of possible trouble in the power line. In most areas of the United States, the AC mains voltage will be between 105 and 125 volts. The facilities engineer or electrician should check not only current capability, but also voltage since that *can* vary outside the limits given in the operating manual for the equipment. The actual line voltage should be determined. If it is above or below the voltages specified in the operating manual, some sort of voltage conditioning equipment, such as a constant voltage transformer, will have to be used. This is a relatively inexpensive device.

Periods of subnormal voltage will probably not permanently damage the equipment, but could cause degraded performance, including slowdown and lost data. A brown-out or a sudden power failure due to extreme weather such as a thunder or ice storm, or damage or failure in the transmission equipment, may also cause lost data. A thunderstorm or other random power outage probably will not occur often enough to warrant installation of an uninterruptable power supply (UPS) or of a motor-generator set. These are expensive devices and, in general, are used only in critical applications where no amount of down time is acceptable, such as the central computer of a bank. If, on the other hand, absolute circulation records are essential to a library, a UPS device would be justified.

Periods of higher than normal voltage will probably not cause permanent damage to the equipment. However, through increased electrical stress or higher than normal heat build-up, they can contribute to premature failures in the computer equipment.

Transients are the final form that power problems can take. These can come from many different sources, such as nearby lightning strikes or large electrical devices in the vicinity such as arc-welding equipment or elevators, and they can cause permanent and irreversible damage to the computer. The higher power transients can cause permanent damage, while smaller ones can cause "noise" in the data stream and cause spurious data to be transmitted or received.

The facilities officer or a good electrician can determine which, if any, of these problems may be encountered with the "AC mains," and the computer equipment vendor should be able to suggest appropriate line-voltage conditioning equipment to prevent these conditions from causing trouble in the computer equipment. For most systems, power conditioning devices are available for roughly 10 percent of the purchase cost of the computer system itself.

A final area of concern in the preservation of computer equipment is that of abuse and neglect. If the potential for abuse exists in the library, put the equipment where a responsible staff member has visual control over it, because people, even staff—especially staff—like to play with terminals. In most cases, neglect will be a far more serious problem.

Follow the manufacturer's suggestions for routine maintenance procedures. For instance, printers and other devices moving paper accumulate chaff, which must be removed periodically. Ribbons should be changed and print-heads cleaned on a regular schedule. Certain problems are associated with certain categories of equipment. Determine what those problems are, and establish preventive maintenance procedures to take care of them early.

Cleanliness in the computer area is very important. The area around the computer should be clean and orderly, free of dust and clutter. Dust can cause problems with a terminal and clutter, such as paper clips, can end up in the equipment and cause mechanical or electrical damage. It is also necessary to periodically check all cable and plug connections to be sure they have not vibrated or brushed somewhat loose. This may seem an unnecessary precaution, but can easily save the cost (and down time) of a service call.

A far more sophisticated level of self-maintenance is described in Chorafas's book, *Computer Networks*, in Chapter 14, "Systems Maintenance." He advocates a careful program of understanding the system sufficiently well to be able to perform the kinds of maintenance that are, in general, only performed by a service company. His experience was in developing an understanding of the system while it was still under service contract, so that the in-house staff could achieve full competence in performing those tasks previously assigned to the technical representative of the service company. He describes in detail the methodology used to develop a self-maintenance system *more* reliable and far quicker than that of his particular service company. Obviously, the individual responsible for the computer system will have to determine *who* will do maintenance, but it must be done on a regular basis.

Certainly all of these areas will improve computer performance and insure a long working life. A computer's life, at best, is over when the virtual cost of down time and the real cost of maintenance and repair exceed the replacement cost of the equipment.

MACHINE-PRODUCED MEDIA: THE EFFECT OF THE COMPUTER

The output, the "effect," of the computer, comes in many different forms. Punched paper tape, punch cards, magnetic tapes, magnetic discs, all have had their day of being the primary technology. The media currently favored are magnetic tape for storage, and either tape or disc in working usage. Future technologies include optical disc, holographic storage, and magnetic bubble technology. In addition, "people-readable" printout and Computer Output Microform (COM) are widely used and have been over a long period of time, and the use of COM is certainly growing at the present time.

The early machine-readable formats of punched card and punched tape have been largely supplanted by magnetic tape and magnetic disc. Testing for permanence and durability of punched paper tape and punched cards, so far as we have been able to determine, has not been reported in the literature. Not could we find more than a passing mention of permanence and durability in conversations among computer professionals. The question seems not to have been addressed. Punched card and punched tape formats have been considered ephemeral storage media and the use of such files is declining. However, a testing program of the stability of these formats might be worthwhile. Punch cards must be stored under pressure or else they will warp and be unstable in a card reader. How much pressure, at what temperature and humidity, whether on edge or flat surface—these are questions that need to be addressed.

However, considerable work has been done on the storage and maintenance of magnetic computer tape. Edward F. Cuddihy, of the Jet Propulsion Laboratory, California Institute of Technology, published in the *IEEE Transactions on Magnetics*, July 1980, an article on "Aging of Magnetic Recording Tape" in which he reports that humidity is the principal consideration in the storage of computer tape:

> The primary mechanism of tape aging and degradation resulted from hydrolysis. . . . The chemical reaction is additionally reversible, a property which suggests a methodology for restoring and rejuvenating environmentally degraded tapes. . . . Being a reversible reaction, there exist environmental conditions of relative humidity and temperature which are ideal for long-term archival preservation. For the tape of this study, 24% relative humidity at room temperature was identified as its ideal storage humidity. (Page 558)

This article is extremely useful in understanding the technical basis of archival concerns for magnetic tape storage.

Tapes for archival use and service use benefit from different storage humidity. Long-term archival storage areas are best maintained at 20 percent relative humidity and 50 °F (10 °C), while tapes that are in use are best kept at 50 percent relative humidity and 50 °F (10 °C).

Humidity affects tape in that the tape absorbs water out of the atmosphere. The tape has a thin plastic backing and is covered with a binder and a magnetic oxide layer. In degradation, the binder absorbs water from the atmosphere and essentially loses its ability to adhere to the backing. This causes loss of the oxide which, of course, causes loss of the information. It is widely accepted practice to copy magnetic tapes at least once every six to ten years; six years is the safer number, and indeed is recommended by the Machine Readable Section in the U.S. National Archives. The copying does not alter the information content of the tape. A copy of a "first generation" tape is still a "first generation" tape in its information content, unlike copying of printed microformat, where each generation loses resolution. It is also essential that important data files have a back-up copy at another site.

Beyond humidity, a second area of concern in the storage of magnetic tape develops from the way that the information is put on the tape itself. By exposing the tape to an external magnetic field, the magnetic fields of the oxide particles on the tape become structured in patterns that correspond to the information stored on the tape—this *is* the information being stored on the tape. When a tape is wound on a spool, the magnetic fields of adjacent layers of the tape can, over a period of time, interact with one another in such a way as to alter the patterns originally on the tape and thus alter the information stored on the tape. It is accepted practice in the computer field to periodically rewind the tape in the opposite direction from which it was wound.

It is, of course, wise to avoid electromagnetic fields in areas where tapes are being stored. Common sources of such fields are transformers, large motors, certain types of technical and medical instrumentation such as nuclear-magnetic resonance equipment, X-ray machines, and color television sets.

Magnetic disc is not usually considered an archival storage medium, largely because its customary usage emphasizes the ability to be written and erased repeatedly. However, the same temperature, humidity, and protection from electromagnetic fields which are suitable for magnetic tape are also appropriate for the magnetic disc since both the magnetic disc and magnetic tape have basically the same structure. The developers and users of the relatively new Computer Output Microform/Computer Input Microform data storage media have well understood preservation requirements. These COM/CIM data are recorded on archival-quality microfilm at a 94 to 1 savings in space required for storage over magnetic tape. Magnetic discs should be stored under the same conditions as any microform.

While in general the same techniques and practices that are valid for the preservation of conventionally produced microformats are equally valid for the preservation of COM materials, it should be remembered that in standard COM generation, there *is* no master film; further, COM is commonly produced on diazo film, which cannot be copied readily and which is not itself considered to be archival. Obviously, the better the quality of the film, the better the quality of the COM/CIM product.

Much of the output of the computer is in paper format. The nature and use of paper printout are usually for the short-term presentation of current information. Therefore, the paper is not of archival quality. Further, the archival properties of thermo- and electro-sensitive printing have not been, to our knowledge, thoroughly explored; nor has the newer laser printing technology. While much paper printout is expendable after a brief period of time, some printouts serve as the documentation that enables a user to correctly set up computer equipment to run a machine-readable file. If the paper medium with this information is unstable, the operating "grammar" of a program could be lost, so that a file would not be usable, while the machine-readable record could well remain undegraded. We have examined ten-year-old printout that is clear and quite legible, and five-year-old printout that has developed a curious yellow staining spreading from the print areas so that it is barely legible. Both were produced on standard and well-maintained equipment and were given a clean and balanced storage situation. The permanence and durability of printout should be explored to determine if, and under what conditions, this is a feasible medium for long-term archival storage.

Future storage technology such as optical disc, holographic storage media, and magnetic bubble technology will undoubtedly present their own special problems of archival storage, which have not yet been documented. However, it is hoped that preservationists and archivists will make the technologists developing those media aware of the need to include archival storage considerations in the design of new data storage formats.

DEVICES, DATA, AND SOFTWARE: THE CRITICAL LINK IN PRESERVATION

Librarians and archivists are aware of the frustration of examining a well-preserved ancient artifact but not being able to read the record encoded there since the language is long lost and no Minoan B or Rosetta Stone has been found to provide the key. In the same way, it is important to stress here that in considering the problems of preserving records stored in computer format, we cannot restrict ourselves to those factors affecting the physical integrity of the artifact, whether data file or machines. Two additional and major areas of concern are the obsolescence of machines and the incompatibility of software (the machine instructions).

A machine may be perfectly preserved in terms of protection from shock, dust, and line surge, but may fall victim to a rapid technological change which makes the machine obsolete so that it is reconfigured or altogether replaced. While it is possible to make an audio recording on a given brand of cassette recorder and then successfully reproduce the sound on another arbitrarily chosen cassette recorder, this degree of standardization does not exist in the computer industry. Identical-looking computer tapes may have seven or nine data tracks with anywhere from 250 to over 6,000 bits (binary digits) per linear inch of tape. Additionally, there are twenty or so protocols that could govern the writing of the tape. Archivists, as of this writing, do not store old computers, so that data stored on older tape, even if optimally stored, may still not be usable.

The U.S. census tapes from the 1940, 1950, and 1960 censuses are still physically sound, but due to hardware and software changes, in a practical sense nothing produced earlier than 1970 in the U.S. Census still exists in machine-readable format. There is now at the University of Wisconsin a major project to recreate the 1940 and 1950 decennial censuses in machine-readable format for the "one in one hundred sample."

The earlier census tapes were "lost" because in a time of rapid innovation and major change, the "standards" for machines changed a great deal in a relatively few years. They were "standards" only of uniformity at a point in time, but not in the sense of giving continuity over a long time period. Until there are standards for machines in the preservation sense of lasting over time, it will be necessary to carry out a program of constant recopying if the machine one is using becomes obsolete.

Twenty years from now, an institution or area may well not have a main-frame computer, and if it does, the mainframe will be a very different one from that currently in place. Will data storage media now being produced be readable on the newer machines? If not, recopying onto a form that can continue to be read is essential for files with archival value.

For minicomputers, standardization does not exist between different brands, and over time, the problem will be exacerbated and files will become unreadable if the incompatibility is not recognized and recopying carried out.

Even if data files have been preserved from bit loss and spurious noise, and the machines are saved from shock and salvage auctions, they will be useless unless the machine instructions (the software) have been preserved. The software enables the machine (the hardware) to translate the binary code into charts and figures, words and ideas to be read by people, which, after all, should be the final effect of any effort to preserve the intellectual content.

It is a serious problem that software subsystems for computers rapidly change and become outdated. If the data file cannot have accompanying software instructions for the machine, the file has physical integrity, but the intellectual integrity is lost. In a software sense, if a system file has been produced, that is, if we have used some data base management program to produce a data file, then we *must* have documentation to enable a machine to read the data from the file. A short dictionary and a long poem frequently contain many of the same words, but the organization and presentation make a considerable difference between the two.

Software "standards" are almost nonexistent in an across-time sense. Because of this, it is imperative that software for a data file be documented, and that the documentation be available to the user of the file in ten or twenty years. At the present time, the operator (a person) must have access to the software documentation in order to select appropriate device manipulation of the data. To insure access to archival data stored in machine-readable form, it is necessary to store human-readable information on how the machine-readable media were written. Having the hardware but not the software for a data file makes it a virtual "write-only memory" where information is stored but cannot be retrieved, a standard nightmare among computer specialists. It is possible that COM/CIM technology will provide a way for the computer to transfer information stored in magnetic tapes to archival-quality microfilm, which can later be read directly back into a computer.

ARCHIVES AND THE FUTURE

The environment within which computer systems are developed is an extremely dynamic one. Often, information less than a year old is so outdated as to be technically useless. Therefore, it becomes necessary for archivists and preservationists to become sufficiently conversant with computer science and information technology to fulfill their roles as curators of the culture in this new environment of the "Electronic Age." They must do this by making the engineers and technologists aware of the necessity of standardization and permanence for that information which is, indeed, the heritage of civilization recorded in computer format, the importance of what we have termed the art and effect of the computer.

SUGGESTED READING

Abrams, Marshall D., and Philip G. Stein. *Computer Hardware and Software: An Interdisciplinary Introduction.* Reading, Mass.: Addison Wesley, 1973.

A general introduction to computers that does not assume that the reader has a background in computer science. Basic concepts are clearly and precisely explained.

Adams, J. Mack, and Douglas H. Hadew. *Social Effects of Computer Use and Misuse.* New York: John Wiley & Sons, 1976.

The first three chapters provide a good nontechnical introduction to computers. Each chapter has an extensive bibliography.

Brown, Arnold. "Equipping Ourselves for the Communications Age," *The Futurist* 15:4 (August 1981): 53–57.

Information as a basis of power. Also discusses some of the philosophy and mechanisms of communication.

Chorafas, Dimitras N. *Computer Networks for Distributed Information Systems.* New York: Petrocelli, 1980.

A technical but readable volume for those involved in managing information systems.

Cuddihy, Edward F. "Aging of Magnetic Recording Tape," *IEEE Transactions on Magnetics* MAG.-16:4 (July 1980): 558-68.

A discussion of the technical problems for magnetic tape storage.

Dollar, Charles M., and Carolyn L. Geda. "Archivists, Archives and Computers: A Starting Point," *American Archivist* 42:2 (April 1979).

An issue devoted to the topic of computers.

Freedman, Henry D. "Paper's Role in an Electronic World." *The Futurist* 15:5 (October 1981): 11-15.

Contrary to most popular thinking, computer technology will insure the continued usage of paper media.

Goldstine, Herman H. *The Computer from Pascal to Von Neumann*. Princeton: Princeton University Press, 1973.

A detailed account of the development of the computer until the beginning of "stored program" machines.

Kelly, Joseph F. *Computerized Management Information Systems*. New York: Macmillan, 1970.

Directed toward the reader with a management information system (MIS) background.

"A Library for 2000 A.D." *Computers and the World of the Future*, ed. Martin Greenberger. Cambridge, Mass.: MIT Press, 1962, pp. 134-78.

A view of the "Library of the Future" as seen before the appearance of the microcomputer.

Martin, James, and Adrian R. D. Wokman. *The Computerized Society*. Englewood Cliffs, N.J.: Prentice-Hall, 1970.

The possible problems and benefits of the widening use of computers in general society are discussed. A useful glossary is included.

Missimore, Phil. "Keeping Your Power in Condition," *Computer Merchandising* 1:9 (February 1982): 81-84.

Detailed discussion of power-line related problems in terminals and small computers, and what can be done to eliminate them. Very worthwhile if you are responsible for a terminal or small computer.

Neill, S. D. "Libraries in 2010," *The Futurist* 15:5 (October 1981): 47-51.

Interesting to compare with "A Library for 2000 A.D."

Orr, William D. *Conversational Computers*. New York: John Wiley & Sons, 1968.

A good but somewhat dated discussion of the development of interactive computer systems.

Parkhill, D. F. *The Challenge of the Computer Utility*. Reading, Mass.: Addison Wesley, 1966.

A readable discussion of the development of the concept of a "computer utility."

Von Neumann, John. *The Computer and the Brain*. New Haven: Yale University Press, 1958.

The view of the "Father of the Modern Computer" will be of interest to those involved with man-machine interaction.

RECOMMENDED JOURNALS

American Society for Information Science (ASIS). *Journal*. 1950–   . Bimonthly.

BYTE, The Small Systems Journal. 1975–   . Monthly.

Computers and People. 1975–   . (Formerly *Computers and Information*, 1951–1974.) Bimonthly.

Computerworld. 1967–   . Weekly.

Special Libraries. 1910–   . Eleven issues per year.

Suppliers and Supplies

Collected here is a list of suppliers that the contributors to this book have found to be reliable. With the increased concern for conservation, more and more manufacturers are marketing "preservation," "conservation," and "archival" supplies. However, there are no standards for what might be "archival" and what might not. We suggest that librarians collect a broad spectrum of catalogues and study them carefully in order to find the materials that will best serve the needs of the library at the best price.

Aiko's Art Materials Import, Inc.
714 North Wabash Avenue
Chicago, IL 60611
    binding supplies
    Japanese paper

Andrews/Nelson/Whitehead
31-10 48th Avenue
Long Island City, NY 11101
    binding supplies
    paper
    mat board

Art Handicrafts Company
3512 Flatlands Avenue
Brooklyn, NY 11234
    binding supplies

Basic Crafts
1201 Broadway
New York, NY 10001
    binding supplies
    paper

Bookmakers
2025 Eye Street, N.W.
Washington, DC 2006
    binding materials

Brodart, Inc.
1609 Memorial Avenue
Williamsport, PA 17701
    library supplies

Cadillac Plastics
134 Railroad Avenue Ext.
Albany, NY 12205
    UV filtering devices

Charles T. Bainbridge's Sons
40 Eisenhower Drive
Paramus, NJ 07652
    mat board

Charrette Corporation
31 Olympia Avenue
Woburn, MA 01801
    general art supplies

Chemplast, Inc.
150 Dey Road
Wayne, NJ 07470
    UV filtering devices

Cohasco, Inc.
CVP Division
P.O. Box 821
Yonkers, NY 10702
    archival storage materials

Cole-Palmer Instrument Company
7425 North Oak Park Avenue
Chicago, IL 60648
    environmental montioring devices

Conservation Materials, Ltd.
Box 2884
340 Freeport Blvd.
Sparks, NV
    polyester film
    mat board
    archival storage materials
    environmental monitoring
        equipment

Conservation Resources International,
    Inc.
1111 North Royal Street
Alexandria, VA 22314
    polyester film
    archival storage materials
    UV filtering material

Dennison Manufacturing Company
300 Howard Street
Framingham, MA 01701
    mending tape

E.I. DuPont de Nemours & Co.
Textile Fiber Department
Reemay Division
Central Road Building
Wilmington, DE 19898
    polyester film

Ernest Schafer, Inc.
731 Lehigh Avenue
Union, NJ 07083
    binding supplies

Fisher Scientific Company
711 Forbes Avenue
Pittsburgh, PA 15219
    environmental monitoring devices

Franklin Distributor's Corporation
Box 320
Denville, NJ 07834
    photographically inert plastics
    slide pages for storage

Gane Brothers & Lane, Inc.
1400 Greenleaf Avenue
Elk Grove Village, IL 60007
    binding material

Gaylord Brothers, Inc.
Box 4901
Syracuse, NY 13221
Box 8489
Stockton, CA 95208
    polyester film
    3M double-coated tape no. 415

The Hollinger Corporation
P.O. Box 6185
South Four Mile Drive
Arlington, VA 22206
    polyester film
    photographic storage sleeves
    3M double-coated tape no. 415
    mat board
    paper for interleaving
    archival storage boxes

ICI United States
Wilmington, DE 19897
    Melinex type O polyester film

JoAnna Western Mills Company
2141 South Jefferson Street
Chicago, IL 60610
    book cloths

The Kimac Company
478 Long Hill Road
Guilford, CT 06437
    photographically inert plastics
    slide sleeves

Light Impressions Corporation
Box 3012
Rochester, NY 14614
    polyester folders
    polyester film, rolls, and sheets
    mat board
    archival storage boxes

Matrix Division
Leedal, Inc.
1918 South Prairie Avenue
Chicago, IL 60616
    slide storage systems

New York Central Supply
62 Third Avenue
New York, NY 10003
    binding supplies
    Japanese tissue paper

Parix Distributors
P.O. Box 776
Champlain, NY 12919
    mending tape

Photofile
2000 Lewis Avenue
Zion, IL 60090
    photographically inert plastics

Pohlig Brothers, Inc.
P.O. Box 8069
Richmond, VA 23223
    archival storage materials

Process Materials Corporation
301 Veterans Blvd.
Rutherford, NJ 07070
    polyester film
    heat set tissue
    paper for interleaving
    mat board

Rising Paper Company
Housatonic, MA 01236
    mat board
    paper

Rohm & Haas
Independence Mall West
Philadelphia, PA 19105
    UV filtering devices

Rupaco Paper Corporation
62 Kent Street
Brooklyn, NY 11222
    mat board

S & W Framing Supplies, Inc.
120 Broadway
Garden City Park, NY 11040
    mat cutter
    Dexter bevel

Sanshar Crafts
P.O. Box 82, Homecrest Station
Brooklyn, NY 11229
    craft supplies

Science Associates, Inc.
Box 230
Princeton, NJ 08540
    environmental monitoring
        equipment

Solar-Screen
53-11 105th Street
Corona, NY 11368
    UV filtering devices

Sun-X International, Inc.
4125 Richmond Avenue
Houston, TX 77027
    UV filtering devices

TALAS
130 Fifth Avenue
New York, NY 10011
    polyester film
    binding supplies
    paper
    cleaning materials
    mending materials
    UV filtering devices
    archival storage materials
    archivist's pen
    pH strips

Thermoplastic Processes, Inc.
Valley Road
Stirling, NJ 07980
    UV filtering devices

3M Corporation
3M Center
St. Paul, MN 55101
    3M double-coated tape no. 415
    polyester film
    UV filtering devices

Transilwrap
2741 North Fourth Street
Philadelphia, PA 19133
    polyester film
    photographically inert plastics

University Products, Inc.
P.O. Box 101
South Canal Street
Holyoke, MA 01041
    polyester film
    Melinex film
    3M double-coated tape no. 415
    archivist's pen
    archival storage materials
    book and document stands
    mat board

Verd-a-Ray Corporation
615 Front Street
Toledo, OH 43605
    UV filtering devices

Washi No Mise
R.D. #2, Baltimore Pike
Kennett Square, PA 19348
    brushes
    Japanese paper
    wheat starch

APPENDIX 2

Sources of Advice and Assistance

American Association for State and
and Local History (AASLH)
708 Berry Road
Nashville, TN 37204
(615) 383-5991

American Institute for the
Conservation of Historic and Artistic
Works (AIC)
Klingle Mansion
3545 Williamsburg Lane
Washington, DC 20008
(202) 364-1036

American Library Association
Preservation for Library Materials
Section (PLMS)
Resources and Technical Services
Division
50 East Huron Street
Chicago, IL 60611
(312) 944-6780

American National Standards Institute
(ANSI)
1430 Broadway
New York, NY 10018
(212) 354-3300

Conservation Center for Art and
Historic Artifact (CCAHA)
260 South Broad Street
Philadelphia, PA 19102
(215) 545-0613

Foundation for the Preservation of
Recordings, Inc.
4317 Barrington Road
Baltimore, MD 21229
(301) 242-0514

Guild of Book Workers (GBW)
663 Fifth Avenue
New York, NY 10022
(212) 757-6454

Library Binding Institute (LBI)
P.O. Box 217
Accord, MA 02018
(617) 740-1592

Library of Congress
Preservation Office
Washington, DC 20540
(202) 287-5213

National Fire Protection Association
(NFPA)
470 Atlantic Avenue
Boston, MA 02210
(617) 482-8755

National Micrographics Association
(NMA)
8728 Colesville Road
Silver Spring, MD 20910
(301) 587-8444

Northeast Document Conservation
  Center (NEDCC)
Abbot Hall
24 School Street
Andover, MA 01810
(617) 470-1010

Society of American Archivists (SAA)
330 South Wells Street, Suite 510
Chicago, IL 60606.
(312) 922-0140

Index

ABC Television, 187
accelerated aging tests, 66
acidity, 34, 35, 37-38, 40, 46, 48, 49, 52, 60, 62, 63, 65, 74, 76, 89, 90-91, 96, 205
Adams, Randolph G., 13
adhesives, 45, 46, 47, 49, 65-67, 69, 71, 73, 87, 89, 94, 96, 115, 117, 134, 135, 146-47, 148, 181
air conditioning, 8, 18, 20-22, 36, 62, 117, 118, 145, 158, 166, 167
air filtration, 8, 18, 117, 137, 167
air pollution, 4, 6-7, 8, 13, 35, 62, 72, 89, 115, 142, 167
Albright, Gary, 5
alcalinity, 37-38, 48, 77
ambrotype, 81-83, 87, 88
American Association for State and Local History (AASLH), 14, 74, 123, 225
American Association of Museums (AAM), 18
American Film Institute, 150
American Institute for the Conservation of Historic and Artistic Works (AIC), 14, 74, 225
American Library Association: Electronic Discussion Group, 209; Preservation of Library Materials Section (PLMS), 6, 27, 74, 225; Resources and Technical Services Division, Bookbinding Committee, 6

American Museum of Natural History, 104
American National Standards Institute (ANSI), 225
American Society of Information Science (ASIS), 208
Ampex Corporation, 155, 187
Arago, François, 81
Archer, Frederick Scott, 85
archives, 31, 35, 37, 38, 39, 47, 49, 50, 108, 118-19, 121, 124, 131, 133, 142, 143, 145, 146, 149-51, 157, 159, 160-61, 163, 165, 167-68, 169, 173, 176, 178, 179, 182, 214-17, 218
archivist's pen, 38
ARDEV, 192
Association of Research Libraries, Office of Management Studies, 25
atmospheric conditions, 79, 80-81, 86, 89, 90. *See also* humidity; temperature

Baird, John L., 187
Baker and Taylor Company, 206
Banks, Paul, 5-6, 7
Barrow, William, 5, 77, 206
Barrow Laboratory, 5
Baynes-Cope, A. D., 6, 12
binding, 55-78, 130; adhesive, 58; case, 58, 65, 70-71, 72; conservation, 59, 70; edition, 58, 59, 60; hand, 59, 70; library, 5, 59; mechanical, 58, 70-72;

perfect, 58, 65; of slides, 107, 108, 114-17
Bing Crosby Enterprises, Electronics Division, 155, 187
Blades, William, 4, 8
bleaching, 33-34, 49, 91, 98
boards, 56, 64-65, 69-70, 73, 75
Bohem, Hilda, 23, 49
book cloth, 58, 63-64
books, 3, 5, 7, 11, 16, 17, 26, 31, 53, 55-78, 145, 163, 183, 199, 205-6, 207
Book Conservation Center, New York Botanical Garden, 6, 74
Book Manufacturer's Institute, 64
Booth, Larry, 123
Boston Athenaeum, 5
Bowser, Eileen, 160
British Museum, 6
brittleness. *See* acidity
broadsides, 31, 51
Buchberg, Karl, 5, 11, 26
budgeting, 4, 51, 72, 75, 125, 133, 196

Calhoun, J. M., 94
California Institute of Technology Jet Propulsion Laboratory, 213
calotype, 85, 90
Capacitance Electronic Devices (CED), 193. *See also* videodisc: capacitance
cartridges: disk, 170, 173, 176-78, 179; microfilm, 131
cassettes, 119; audio, 164-66, 167, 168, 170; demagnetizer, 182; microfilm, 131; video, 156, 157, 193, 195, 196, 197, 199
CBS Electronic Video Recording System, 187, 196
Centennial Library Conference, 206
Chorafas, Dimitras N., 212
Clapp, Anne F., 39, 45, 47
Clapp, Verner, 5
Clarkson, Christopher, 5
climate, 3, 142, 166
cloth. *See* fabric
cold-flow, 157, 158
College Art Association (CAA) and Art Libraries Society of North

America (ARLIS/NA) Visual Resources Groups, 113, 125
Columbia University School of Library Service, 6
computer-assisted instruction (CAI), 194
computers, 3, 17, 24, 26, 60, 117, 130, 186, 189, 190, 194, 205-19; mainframe, 216; micro-, 189, 190, 198, 216; personal, 208; printer, 205; software, 215-16
Computer Output Microform (COM), 130, 212, 214, 217
condensation, 11, 36, 45, 96, 114, 117
condition report, 50-51, 75
Conservation Center for Art and Historic Artifacts (CCAHA), 74, 76, 225
conservation planning, 49
conservators, 5-6, 7, 11, 13, 14-16, 24-25, 35, 47, 48, 49, 50-51, 52, 63, 66, 67, 73, 74, 75, 76, 88-89, 91, 94, 107, 124
construction, library buildings, 5, 13, 17-18, 20-21
Cooperstown Program, 5
copyrights, 108, 113, 121, 179
cords, 56, 68, 70
Cornell University, 104
Corporation for Public Broadcasting, 161
Council on Library Resources, 5
Cuddihy, Edward F., 213
Cunha, George Martin, 5, 20, 25
cyanotype, 81

Dagron, René, 129
Daguerre, Louis Jacques Mandé, 81
daguerreotype, 81-83, 87
Dancer, John Benjamin, 129
Darling, Pamela W., 6-7
data base. *See* machine-readable data files
deacidification, 46, 47, 74; mass, 26, 48, 76-77; of newspapers, 52; of photographs, 91
De Candido, Robert, 74

Decca Records, 188
De Laurier, Nancy, 104, 113
deterioration, 3
Dickenson, John, 34
digital information storing, 185, 186
Dinken, Bryan, 34
dirt, 4, 6, 7, 8, 45, 62, 71, 72, 87,
    88-89, 96, 97, 113, 114-15, 118, 122,
    125, 131, 133-35, 136-37, 146-47,
    148, 151, 158, 159, 167, 169, 170-72,
    173, 177, 180, 183, 188, 198-200,
    201-2, 212, 215
disasters, 5, 47; action team for, 23-24;
    planning for, 18-26, 49, 53, 108,
    123-24
distributors. See vendors
document. See manuscript
drawings, 41, 53; chalk, 31, 41; char-
    coal, 31, 41, 46, 48; pastel, 31, 41,
    46, 48; pencil, 31, 48
drop-out, tape, 158, 159, 167, 180, 181
dubbing, 168-70, 181, 183
duplication: film, 142, 149-51; magnetic
    tape, 213-14; videodisc, 188, 192,
    193; videotape, 159-60, 188
dust jackets: book, 59, 76; disk, 167, 179

earthquake, 20
Eastman Kodak, 86, 118, 123, 124,
    139-41, 143
edge decoration, 71
Edison Home Kinetoscope, 139
education, conservation, 5-6, 14, 74;
    of patrons and staff, 46, 50, 75,
    122-23, 125, 130, 151-52, 156-57,
    183, 212
electrical systems, 20-21, 210-11, 215
electromagnetic field, 157, 158, 168, 214
electronic data processing, 206
electronic mail, 190
electrostatic discharge, 41, 46, 53, 96,
    122, 135, 136, 159, 172-73, 209-10
encapsulation, 38, 46, 54; of news-
    papers, 52; of posters, 52
end papers, 62, 65, 70
environment. See air pollution; climate;
    dirt; humidity; temperature

Environmental Protection Agency
    (EPA), 64
ephemera, 31, 39, 52
erasure, tape, 168
Evrard, Blanquard, 84
exhibition, 16-17, 35, 36, 40, 97

Fabriano paper mill, 32
fabric, 16, 25, 63-64, 71, 83. See also
    book cloth
fading, photographic, 80-81, 84, 89, 95,
    96, 97, 98-100, 107, 109, 117, 118,
    121, 122, 123, 124, 131, 141, 142-43,
    145, 146, 147-48, 149
Federation Internationale des Archives
    du Film (FIAF), Preservation
    Commission of, 143
ferrotype. See tintype
ferrotyping, 89, 96, 120
film, 3, 7, 11, 17, 25, 26, 79, 86-87,
    94, 105, 107-8, 109-13, 114-22, 124,
    125, 133, 155, 158, 185, 186, 187,
    192; diazo, 130-31, 133, 214; motion
    picture, 26, 139-53, 157, 160, 185,
    188, 192, 193, 195, 196, 197, 199,
    200; inspection of, 147; nitrate-base,
    86, 94, 95, 134, 139-40, 141-42, 149;
    safety-base, 86-87, 94, 95, 134,
    139-40, 142-43; silver halide, 81,
    130-31, 133, 134; strips, 119;
    vesicular, 130-31, 133
Film Archives Advisory Committee, 150
fire, 18-25, 49, 86, 94, 95, 134, 137,
    139, 142, 158-59, 205, 209
Fitzgerald, Angela, 26
fixing, chemical, of film, 80, 83, 84, 130
flood, 20, 25, 72-73, 117, 120, 123, 137,
    167, 205, 209; Florence, Italy, 5, 25
"floppy discs," 200, 201. See also
    magnetic discs
Foundation for the Preservation of
    Recordings, 225
Fourdrinier machine, 34
foxing, 49
framing, 14, 41-45, 96
freeze drying, 25
French Academy of Science, 81

fumes, 48, 86-87, 89, 94, 97, 120, 130, 142
fumigation, 12-13, 45-46
fungi, 4, 8, 12, 13, 66, 108, 115, 117, 118, 124, 131, 135, 142, 166, 167
furniture, 3, 13, 15, 21

gases, 48, 76-77, 95, 131. *See also* fumes
gathering, 56, 68
generation, tape, 213-14
Glaser, Mary Todd, 5
glue, 13, 40, 54, 56, 58, 65-67, 70, 89, 170. *See also* adhesives
gluing-up, 69-71
Greenfield, Mary E. (Jane), 74
Guild of Book Workers (GBW), 74, 225
Gutenberg, Johannes, 26

hardware. *See* computers
Harvard University, 5, 104
heat. *See* temperature
heating, 20-32, 36, 117-18, 166-67
heat-set tissue, 47
hinging, 40-41, 54, 70, 99. *See also* joints
Hollander beater, 33
hollow back, 71
housekeeping, 6-8, 13, 20, 22, 72, 158, 199-200, 206, 212
humidity, 8-11, 12, 13, 16, 36-37, 45, 63, 65, 72, 89, 90-91, 94, 95, 97, 100, 107-8, 112, 114-15, 117-19, 120, 121, 122-23, 125, 131, 135, 136-37, 142, 143-45, 158, 160, 163, 166-67, 169, 180, 199-200, 209-10, 213-14
hurricane, 20
Hyltoft, John, 76

Indianapolis Museum of Art, 16
ink, 31, 33, 38, 47-48, 51, 52, 71, 206
insects, 6, 12-13, 18, 45, 63, 66-67, 108, 205
Institute of Electrical and Electronics Engineers (IEEE), 213
Institute of Fine Arts, New York University, 5-6
insurance, 17, 22

International Museum of Photography, 150
Irvine, Betty Jo, 104, 114, 119

Japanese paper, 35, 41, 47, 52
joints, 17, 62, 70-71, 79

Kathpalia, Yash Pal, 13
Keller, Friedrich Gottfried, 34
Keystone View Company, 103
Kuehn, Rosemary, 105

Langenheim Brothers, 103
lantern slides, 103, 104, 105, 107, 108, 113, 114, 120, 122, 124
laser technology, 26, 186, 189, 191-92, 196, 201
leather, 25, 45, 56, 57, 60-61, 68, 70-71, 74-75; oiling of, 62, 63, 71, 75
Lemcoe, M. M., 165
Lewis, Ralph H., 7
Library Binding Institute (LBI), 59, 64, 65, 225; Book Testing Laboratory of, 59
library buildings, 6, 7, 11, 17
Library of Congress, 5, 25, 40, 77, 150, 165, 184, 185; Preservation Office, 5, 24, 46, 76, 225
light, 11-12, 13, 17, 18, 21, 35-36, 53, 72, 80, 89, 95, 97, 98, 100, 107-8, 115, 117-18, 121, 123, 130, 131, 167, 192
Lister National Library for Biomedical Communications, 198
London Photographic Society, 89
Lumière Autochrome, 97, 105

McCrady, Ellen, 74
McDonnell Douglas Electronics Company, Videodisc Division of, 192, 201
machine-readable data files, 205, 207-8, 212, 215, 217
magic lantern. *See* lantern slides
Magnavox, 186, 192
magnetic bubble technology, 213, 215

magnetic discs, 187, 212, 215. *See also* "floppy discs"
magnetization, 182
Mailand, Harold F., 16
manuscript, 31, 32, 36, 39, 51, 52, 53, 56, 57, 65
Manutius, Aldus, 26
maps, 3, 16, 31, 40, 51, 52, 189
Massachusetts Institute of Technology, 104, 197
Matsushita Corporation, 156, 193, 196
matting, 36, 38, 40-41, 45, 46, 52-53, 54, 83, 87, 88, 94, 96
Maxell Corporation, 156
Mead Data Central Company, 208
measurement, environmental, 9-11, 210
melainotype. *See* tintype
Memorex Corporation, 156
mending: film, 148; paper, 46-47
Metcalf, Keyes, 18
Microcard, 132
microfiche, 131-32, 133
microfilm, 24, 26, 39, 52, 101, 120, 205, 214, 217; boxes, 97, 134, 137; Kalvar, 199; master, 131, 214
microform, 3, 17, 26, 118, 129-37, 194, 199, 202, 214; cleaning, 134-36; inspection, 133-34. *See also* Computer Output Microform
microformat, 207, 214
micro-opaque, 132
microphotography, 129
Microprint, 132
Mid-America College Art Association (MACAA), 104-5, 113, 114, 115
mildew, 63, 73
moisture. *See* humidity
mold, 6, 8, 12, 13, 25, 37, 45, 49, 63, 66-67, 89, 115, 125, 135, 136, 170
Museum of Broadcasting, 160
Museum of Modern Art, 150, 160
mutilation, 7, 15, 130

National Archives, U.S., 150; Machine Readable Section, 213
National Association of State Textbook Administrators (NASTA), 64

National Bureau of Standards (NBS), 18
National Endowment for the Humanities (NEH), 6
National Fire Protection Association (NFPA), 18, 20, 225
National Library, Florence, Italy, 5, 25
National Micrographics Association (NMA), 225
National Park Service, 7
National Preservation Program, 40
Newberry Library, 5, 6
newspapers, 31, 39, 52, 129, 130, 133, 206
Newton rings, 114
New York Public Library, 5
North American Philips. *See* Philips, N. V.
Northeast Document Conservation Center (NEDCC), 5, 12, 23, 24, 74, 76, 225

Ogden, Sherelyn, 5
Online Computer Library Center (OCLC), 207, 208
optical disc, 26, 184, 191-92, 193, 194, 196-201, 212, 215

packing and shipping, 28, 41
paintings, 13, 14-15
paper, 3, 11, 25-26, 28, 31-54, 56, 58, 60-62, 64, 65, 67, 70, 71, 72, 73, 75, 77, 79, 87, 95, 96, 100, 107, 121, 130, 167, 168-69, 180, 205-6, 209, 212-13, 214-15; photographic, 80-81, 83-85, 89-91, 107, 130, 132
papermaking, 31-35, 54
papyrus, 32, 55-56
parchment, 26, 31-32, 37, 56, 63, 65, 70
paste, 40-41, 47, 65-66, 96
Pathé Frères, 139
Pergamon PATSEARCH System, 198
pH, 37-38
phased conservation, 50, 75
Philips, N. V., 165, 198
phonodisc. *See* sound recordings
Phonovision, 187
photocopies, 39, 72, 101

photography and photographic prints, 3, 7, 16, 39, 79-102, 103, 125, 130, 187, 192; albumen, 84, 89, 90, 91; black-and-white, 80, 85, 100; color, 80, 97, 98, 100, 125; copying, 94, 100-101, 104, 108, 113; negative, 80, 81, 83, 85-86, 91-94; positive, 80, 81, 83. *See also* plates, photographic
Pickett, A. G., 165
pigment, 47-48, 81
Pioneer, 186, 192
pitting, 166
plates, photographic, 85-86, 94, 95, 97, 103, 105, 107, 124
playback, 156, 163-64, 167, 168, 170-82, 183, 188, 190, 191, 192
plumbing, 20-21
Pollack, Peter, 81
Poole, Frazer, 5
posters, 31, 52
Princeton University, 104
printed sheets, 31, 51
printing, 26, 33, 55, 56-57, 68, 214
prints, graphic art, 3, 7, 16, 41, 53
print-through, 157, 169-70, 180, 214
processing, photographic, 39
projection, 97, 108, 112, 114-15, 118, 121-22, 123, 125, 141, 143, 145-48, 149, 151
Project 2000, 208-9
Public Archives of Canada, 76

Quixote Corporation, 192

RCA, 164, 186, 193, 197, 200, 202
reading machines, 129-30, 131, 132, 133, 134, 135-37
reduction ratio, 132
replication. *See* duplication
Research Libraries Group (RLG), 6
Research Libraries Information Network (RLIN), 206-7
Richardson, Arlene Zelda, 105
Rittenhouse, William, 32
Robert, Nicholas-Louis, 34
rodents, 12-13, 18, 66
rounding and backing, 69-70
Rutgers University, 8

salvage operation, 24, 25
Sargent, Ralph N., 158, 159
scanning, 191
Scheele, Karl Wilhelm, 33
scientific investigation and research, 5, 66
Scott, Gillian, 105, 127
sculpture, 3, 15-16
security, 7, 17, 129, 130, 131, 168
sewn bindings, 56, 57, 58, 65, 68-69, 73; oversewing, 68-69
shelving, 72-73, 158, 163, 165-67, 197-99
signature. *See* gathering
silica gel, 118
size/sizing, 13, 33-34, 38, 64
slides, 3, 17, 103-28, 157. *See also* lantern slides
Smith, Richard, 76-77
Smithsonian Institution, 76
Society of American Archivists (SAA), 74, 225
Society of Motion Picture and Television Engineers, 139
Sony Corporation, 155, 156, 192
sound, 141, 146-48, 149, 200
sound recordings, 3, 17, 26, 163-84, 186, 187, 188, 193; cylinder, 164, 168, 169, 187; digital, 26, 165, 183; Edison Blue Amberol, 169; 45 RPM, 163; instantaneous, 164; long-playing, 163; shellac, 163-64, 165, 169, 170, 172; tape, 164, 169-70, 179-82, 215; videodisc, 190
Spawn, Willman, 24-25
spines, 56, 69, 71, 73, 88
splices, 134, 135, 146, 147, 148, 159, 166, 180-81
stamps, postage, 31, 52
starch, 13, 63, 66
static electricity. *See* electrostatic discharge
stereograph, 103
storage, 7, 14, 35-36, 37-38, 39, 40, 45, 49-50, 51-53, 62, 72-73, 79, 87, 88, 90, 94-97, 98, 100, 107-8, 112, 113, 117-21, 124, 125, 133, 134, 137, 143-45, 149, 156-60, 163, 165-69, 188, 193, 197, 199, 215; cold, 100,

101, 108, 118, 143, 149, 160; data, 216; disc, 214; full text, 206, 207-8; holographic, 212, 215; magnetic tape, 213
storms, 211
styluses, 170, 172, 173, 176-78, 186, 188, 191, 193, 200, 201-2
sulfuric acid, 34
Sundt, Christine L., 114
supplies, conservation, 24, 221, 224
survey, conservation, 7, 20, 39, 51, 75
Sylvania, 192
sync signal, 159

Talbott, Henry Fox, 83, 85
Talbotype. *See* calotype
tape, magnetic, 26, 130, 155-61, 163, 166, 188, 212-15, 217
Tate, John, 32
TDK Corporation, 156
Technicolor, 140
TelDec, 188
Telefunken, 188
telephone, 190, 208
television, 153, 155, 157, 187, 190, 191, 208
temperature, 8-11, 12, 16, 36-37, 45, 66, 72, 88, 90-91, 95, 100, 107-8, 114, 117, 122, 123, 131, 135, 136-37, 142, 143-45, 157, 158, 159, 163, 165, 166-67, 170, 172, 180, 198-200, 201, 209-10, 211, 213
terminals, computer, 205
text block, 17, 56, 69-70, 71, 73
theft. *See* security
Thompson-CSF, 192, 201
Thorn EMI, 196
3M Corporation, 145, 156
tintype, 81, 83, 87-88
tone arm, 176, 178-79
tornado, 20
Toshiba Corporation, 155
transients, power, 211
transparencies. *See* slides
treatment report, 51, 75
Ts'ai Lun, 31
Tull, A. G., 114

ultrafiche. *See* microfiche
UNESCO, 13
Universal, 192
University of California library system, 23
University of California-Los Angeles Film Archives, 150
University of Wisconsin-Madison, 114, 216
U.S. Census, 208, 216; Office, 208

Vacudyne Company, 12
Vanderbilt Television News Archive, 160
VAX system, 209
vellum, 26, 31-32, 55-56, 57, 63, 65, 70, 71
vendors, 57, 113, 132-33, 145, 156, 159-60, 198, 200, 206-7, 211
ventilation, 12, 45, 48, 94, 95, 117, 134, 136, 148, 166, 169
Victor, Alexander F., 139
Victor Company of Japan (JVC), 193
videodisc, 3, 17, 26, 185-203; capacitance, 190, 191, 192-93, 195, 196, 197, 198, 199, 200-201, 202; optical, 185-86, 191-92, 196, 197-98, 201, 202; major available systems for, 196; reflective, 192; transmissive, 192
videodisc players, 185-86, 190-91, 197, 201-2
Video High Density (VHD) system, 193
videotape, 17, 26, 141, 150-51, 155-61, 186, 187-88, 192, 196, 197, 200. *See also* tape, magnetic
Virginia Historical Society, 5
voltage, 209, 210-11

Walker, R. Gay, 12
warping, 145, 166, 167, 178, 182, 184, 213
washing: motion picture film, 143; paper, 47-49; photographs, 80, 83, 84, 88, 89, 91; sound recordings, 183
water and water damage, 5, 18-25, 37, 45, 47-48, 49, 63, 67, 72, 91, 120, 123-24, 131, 135, 142, 159, 169
watercolors, 31, 33, 48, 53
Waters, Peter, 5, 25, 49
weeding, 207

Weinstein, Robert A., 123
Western Conservation Congress, 6
West Publishing Company, 208
Winterthur Program, 5
Woodward, J. G., 176

word processing systems, 200, 201
wrappers, book, 57, 74, 75-76

Yale University Library, 5, 8; Book
    Conservation Laboratory at, 74